ally important people were the linguists, analysts, and reporters—he needed groups of each to be working around the clock.

Soon thereafter, the director of the NSA, General Michael Hayden, directly asked Bill. "What do you want to do with your people? You're the core. Do you want to go to some underground facility?"

"No," said Bill. "We'll stay here."

At midnight, Bill and his deputy stepped out into the cool nighttime air. A nearly full moon floated alone in the sky. The NSA was near the flight path for Baltimore/Washington International airport, but tonight there was no noise and no contrails. The flashing red lights that warned approaching planes of the Fort's presence had been turned off. The normally busy Baltimore-Washington Parkway was silent. But when Bill turned around he was nearly blinded by the row of lights shining on the sixth floor of the otherwise blackened building.

"We've got to turn those lights off," said Bill. Less than twenty-four hours after the completely unforeseen attacks on both the iconic buildings that had towered over Manhattan as well as the smoldering Pentagon, who knew what was next? Someone could be sitting in the woods surrounding the building, taking potshots at its windows. The next day, the NSA's logistics team came in and covered the windows with a heavy black material that kept the counterterrorism floor's lights completely hidden. It didn't come down until Christmas.

IN THE YEARS FOLLOWING 9/11, AMERICA WAS CONSUMED WITH WHAT went wrong and how the nation could have left itself so open to this horror. But in the immediate aftermath, there was also an unprecedented sense of unity and a surge of energy as the whole country dusted itself off—and resolved to never again be subject to a day like that.

This is the story of the people who took up that challenge, the task of reimagining our aviation and transportation security. On the day of the attacks, some of these people were already deeply involved in America's security and government network. Others were retired, working for private industry, even attending college or playing in bands. But over the next eight years, their individual contributions, sense of purpose, and commitment would be irreplaceable. In a breathtakingly short period of time, they created from scratch an agency that was simultaneously ambitious, flawed, inspired, ridiculed, innovative, and entirely unique within the federal government: the Transportation Security Administration.

TWO

FIND SOMETHING AND DO IT

THE COLD BLUE WATER CRASHED AGAINST THE ROCKS, LEAV-
ing a wash of foam as it melted back into the ocean. A steep yellow cliff
covered in scrubby green bushes and yellow flowers rose above the coastline.
And along the highway at the top of that wall, I was piloting my black Audi
with its newly affixed American flag decal on the back window, staring out
at the Pacific's limitless blue expanse. It was a few days after the attacks, and
I was on my way back from work in Silicon Valley to Pebble Beach, a haven
tucked into the California coast that is also home to a famous golf tournament or two.

My windows were down and a vintage Rolling Stones album was in the
CD player. Forty minutes before, I'd walked out of my office at Arzoon, an
innovative supply chain software company south of San Francisco. It was a
stunning Friday, and the West Coast never looked better.

I had spent my first 39 years on the other coast—from my childhood in
Boston to college in Providence, Rhode Island, on to a law degree in Char-
lottesville, Virginia, followed by a stint at the Department of Transportation
and the Reagan White House—before beginning my journey westward. And
I had no desire to go back East. Why would I? Here in California, people
pushed the boundaries of what was possible and worked with a purpose.
Nobody wore suits. I could walk out of my house and, in minutes, be jogging along craggy coastline, past lush groves of Monterey pine and banks

of purple ice plant. Both of my sons were more or less happily enrolled in Robert Louis Stevenson High School, a half mile down our street. My wife, Janet, was enjoying leadership positions with the school's parent organization and was a core presence in the area's Juvenile Diabetes Research Foundation fund-raising effort. And, in an underappreciated perk, when the Green Bay Packers (the football team I adopted as a kid during the 1960s) played on Monday Night Football, the game was over by nine. There was no reason to rock the boat.

But that Friday, as I gazed at the translucent fog bank hovering above the ocean, an uneasy feeling continued to flare, the same one that had plagued me for days whenever I was alone. Like everyone else, I was haunted by the attacks deeply and personally. Yes, I had been stunned, horrified, outraged, and saddened, but I was also discomfited by the possibility that the most monumental event in a generation hadn't really affected my daily life that profoundly. It was a national trauma with thousands of lives ended and millions more upended, but here I was rolling down California's Highway 1, pretty much on schedule.

A few days earlier, my family had gone out to dinner, in part to get the boys away from the television, when my cell phone rang. It was my friend Michael Jackson. We had first met while his wife Caron and I worked in the Reagan White House and our families became close. Now he was calling from his office at the Department of Transportation. I excused myself and walked out to the parking lot. After the planes went down, I had called Michael and left a message offering my support. I figured he would be up to his neck sorting out what had happened, stopping any follow-up attacks, getting the aviation system back up, and figuring out a long-term game plan, so I was shocked he'd found the time to return my call. I again offered my support and "any help he needed" before he ran off to a meeting.

I paused before walking back inside, looking up at the clear, darkened sky. Despite the glare from the California Pizza Kitchen sign, I could see a few flashing blips headed north, toward San Francisco or Seattle. Air travel had resumed a few days earlier.

Now I felt embarrassed. Michael was gracious to tell me how much my words of support were appreciated, but what did my offer really mean? Nothing. And I did, in fact, really want to contribute beyond the grieving, the candles, and the flags. But how?

Twenty years before, while working on the Intergovernmental staff at the White House, I'd gotten to know both Michael, who became one of my best friends, and Norm Mineta, whom I also respected and liked. They were now the people charged with salvaging and securing American aviation. I wondered if I could help them. In the two decades following my stint at the White House I had worked in the transportation industry, mostly with the Union Pacific railroad. I thought I might be able to help triage the incoming demands of their regular DOT work while they handled the 9/11 recovery.

I had absolutely no desire to move to DC permanently. My life, family, and job were in California. But that might even be an advantage. There was some unique value in my *not* wanting a regular federal paycheck. I could focus on the necessary tasks and then go home. And I could at least offer something tangible to Michael, if he wanted it. That was the answer. I'd move to Washington for a month or two and put my transportation and organizational expertise to good use.

I ARRIVED IN WASHINGTON IN MID-OCTOBER 2001 AND MADE MY WAY TO the DOT, which then sat in a ten-story white building that took up a whole block just south of the Smithsonian buildings up on the National Mall. (Not inappropriately, it was called the Nassif Building, which rhymes with massive.) Over the years, the DOT has grown to envelop a mishmash of different agencies with regulatory power over highways, waterways, pipelines, railroads, Hazmat transport, and the merchant marine, as well as the mysterious and magical task of determining when daylight savings starts. But it was DOT's authority over the Federal Aviation Administration and the process of remaking airport security that was now keeping the leadership there for twelve to fourteen hours every day.

I went up to the tenth floor and waited in the reception area for Michael, who, at six feet tall had a few inches on me, though his hair was gray by the time he was thirty. As he led me into his executive office, steeped in that signature Washington air of solemn formality and replete with large windows overlooking Ronald Reagan Washington National Airport, Michael somehow managed to look both exhausted and energized.

Michael launched into the problems he'd faced and pressures the department had been under. One story in particular painted a striking picture of post-9/11 life on the tenth floor of the DOT. A few days after the attacks,

Michael had watched President George W. Bush go on television and tell the American public that he was switching the airport system back on.

"It was a good speech. We helped him write it," said Michael as he flopped down into his chair. Of course, restarting flights was no easy matter. Planes from Europe had been forced to land over Canada's northeast coast, cramming the small airports. Jets sat checkerboarded nose to tail on the runways. On the day flying resumed, hundreds of planes flew empty but for their flight crews and pilots to get back in place for their normal schedule.

During his speech, the president also promised that his cabinet members would take to the air the next day as a show of confidence. As soon as the president had uttered the words, Michael thought about his next problem: If you wanted to take out the government, that would be a pretty good place to start. He dialed the ex-general in charge of the Federal Air Marshals, or FAMs, the specialized group of law enforcement officers who are authorized to carry guns on aircraft, and told him to make sure there was a team on every flight with a cabinet member.

Michael leaned forward. "But this general took umbrage that some political hack was telling him what to do, and I get a text from Jane Garvey telling me that the general has decamped." Garvey was the head of the Federal Aviation Administration and the general's direct superior. "So," continued Michael, "I said to Jane, 'Fine, good. If he doesn't realize that we are in a shooting war and we're the target, fire him.'" Michael grimaced. "The general tried to apologize, but it was too late, he was gone."

I studied Michael's face while he recounted the story. His mustache and hair hadn't gotten any grayer, but my friend, already thin, seemed to have lost some weight and gained enormous black circles under his eyes.

Next he walked me through his office's back door to see Secretary Mineta. If Michael looked both exhausted yet energized, Norm Mineta looked vigorous. He was seventy years old, looked fifty, and acted forty.

We sat on a couch while Norm diagrammed the task of rebuilding security on a yellow legal pad with a green felt-tipped pen. He talked a mile a minute, firing off innumerable deadlines and tasks that had to be lined up and prioritized. Marshaling the resources would be an endless search. The government had never attempted such intense aviation security. There was no existing playbook in the government and no ready market in the private sector to meet America's radically expanded security needs.

Norm flipped the page and drew a horizontal line across the top, jabbing at points along it and leaving a trail of dots leading up to a vertical slash at the end. As he was running out of room on the right side of the page, Norm circled the vertical line and circled it again. Then he underscored it, and for good measure thickened it with a few intense strokes. "We have to. We have to meet the deadlines. We *have* to meet the deadlines." He paused. "Do you think you can help us do that?"

Suddenly, I realized what I was actually there for. These guys wanted me to construct and drive the new security process, not manage someone's inbox.

Michael led me over to his windowless hideaway office complete with a desk and a small washroom about fifty feet away—a room that was jokingly referred to as "Michael's Bathroom." Putting me to work next door to him was meant to show my job's importance, but Michael did have to walk through my new office to get to his executive washroom. "Grab a seat!" he said with a smile, gesturing to the desk, which was covered with two-foot-tall stacks of multicolored folders. A large gray safe sat adjacent to the desk, its fortified drawers pulled out and crammed with more folders. Helpfully stuck in the drawer's front handle was a large sign marked "Open." Welcome back to government, I thought. The stay ended up being seven months, six of them as a guest of the Jackson household, living in the guest bedroom off their family den.

ON NOVEMBER 19, MICHAEL, NORM, AND THE REST OF THE DOT LEADERship went out to Reagan National for a media event in which the president signed Aviation and Transportation Security Act into effect. The ATSA gave shape, mandates, and some legal authority to the Transportation Security Administration, the new entity I was suddenly tasked with building. Most germane to me were the thirty-six dates engraved in the statute. ATSA dictated that each security mandate, from the government taking over airport security screening to massive technology purchases be knocked off over the next year, over a rolling series of three dozen deadlines. The first one was sixty days away.

A few weeks earlier, Secretary Mineta, his chief of staff, John Flaherty, Michael, and I had talked about those deadlines. If we were going to do anything other than just implement ATSA's particulars—good, bad, and ugly—there was no possibility of making the big deadlines later in the year. For instance, a credible case could be made that rushing to hire 50,000 new employees into an agency that didn't previously exist might result in excessive cost and uncertain hiring quality. Also, since the physical act of buying and installing brand new screening equipment across the country would use up virtually all of the time allotted, there was precious little time to consider the full range of technology options. Meeting the ATSA deadlines would require skipping over any independent review of the staff recommendations for more than a billion dollars of spending. If the DOT was going to push back on the fine print contained in ATSA, it would have do so now and take the public flak for not being able to achieve the urgently needed security improvements. "The choice is to debate the best way to move forward or simply implement, one or the other," I said. Secretary Mineta did not hesitate, fiddle, or flinch when he told me, "You are going to make every one of those deadlines."

Now, sitting alone at my desk at the same time my bosses conducted the ceremonial creation of the TSA across the Potomac, I puzzled over how to actually jump-start the organization. A rollout of this size had never been attempted before, anywhere. Securing the aviation system alone meant going into 450 airports across the country to guard the lives of two million passengers a day. There were a billion details and no precedent. The walls started to close in. *I have one hour,* I thought, staring at a blank sheet of paper, *before they come back and ask me, "Well, where do we start?"* I started sketching process maps.

A FEW DAYS LATER, MICHAEL USHERED A SHORT MAN WITH BROWN skin, dark-framed glasses, and a pleasantly disheveled, professorial air into our newly established world headquarters, a hastily cleared-out conference room on the tenth floor. It held about twelve gray metal desks lined up in rows of three. I sat at a desk more or less in the middle. Ashley Cannatti, a tall, dark-haired volunteer from the White House, had a desk just behind me. She had her phone wedged into one ear and mine in the other as she organized a collection of folders labeled with yellow stickies. A stack of unopened BlackBerry boxes threatened to cascade off the edge of her desk.

"This is Kip Hawley," said Michael, gesturing at me. "And this is George Zarur. I'll leave you to it." George and I shook hands and stood there briefly before he said, "OK, what do I do?"

"We've got an agency to set up," I replied. "Find something and do it."

George selected a desk down front on the left wall and sat down, somewhat confounded. He later told me he wondered when the firing squad was going to come in. But soon he was considering the logistics of hiring and vetting the agency's huge numbers of new employees—at that point, a force intended to include 30,000 airport screeners. George had just finished a stint with the US Marshal Service, helping it become the first federal agency to electronically integrate with the Federal Bureau of Investigation's fingerprint database. Before that, checking suspects against the database meant inking out fingerprints and mailing them to the FBI. It took two weeks for a report to come back—unless the prints were one of the 10 percent rejected because of smudging. For law enforcement, two weeks was a long time to detain otherwise innocent people. George sorted out a way to use digital fingerprinting machines and then FedEx discs of prints to Washington. The FBI could then return the rap sheets electronically. With the TSA looking to process up to a million background checks before we could put our new security force on the ground, that technology would be extremely useful.

"Well," thought George, "that's something I could do."

George had first come to Washington, DC, from Bethlehem, Palestine, where he grew up part of the then-majority Catholic community. He arrived at Georgetown University in the 1960s where, through mutual friends, he met Michael Jackson. During his time at Georgetown he also became a passionate fan of Big East basketball. After finishing his undergraduate work, George went on to earn simultaneous PhD degrees in chemistry and physics at the Catholic University of America before heading off to Princeton for post-doctoral research in liquid physics. He somehow also found time to tack on stretches at the Military Defense University and Stanford's Graduate School of Business.

All the while, George remained close with Michael. In 2001, George returned to Washington after a start-up venture using his scientific background in Florida fell apart in the wake of the dot-com bubble's collapse. A few weeks after the attacks, George got a call from Michael, saying, "We're setting up an agency. I need your help."

"OK," said George. He hopped on the Metro and came straight over to the Department of Transportation. (George was also a big fan of DC's Metro system.)

GEORGE WAS THE FIRST OF A STEADY STREAM OF PEOPLE, FROM BOTH private industry and federal agencies, who began arriving at the TSA's make-shift headquarters. In the aftermath of the attacks, there was tremendous energy and drive to make the country safe. The same impulse that drove thousands of young Americans to volunteer for the armed services also brought people to the TSA. Others came on board excited about the possibility of creating a new government agency from scratch, without all the inefficiencies and institutional inertia endemic to most of the federal government. It was an exciting time—and totally chaotic.

As our first office filled up, the converted conference room began to resemble an overcrowded call center. To cross the room, people crawled over desks. Meetings—new-employee interviews or negotiations over hundreds of millions of dollars in requisitions alike—took place in hallways, closets, or any other room we could wrest from the DOT. We looted pens and notebooks from unattended offices. The concept of "office" was reduced to essentials: a space to stand and a BlackBerry.

Outstanding people continued to flock to the TSA, and in about a month we finally outgrew all the space we could beg, borrow, or steal from the DOT. So we relocated to the nearest available government building, the bottom of the General Services Administration.

The GSA basement was a windowless pit, a dirty, unfinished space with no desks or chairs. When we moved in, there was crumpled paper, garbage, dust, and mold on the floor. Our teams worked in a series of musty open rooms, which was good for a collaborative, open effort but not as useful for more focused conferences or meetings.

One of our private-industry contractors, Stephanie Rowe, still has a picture of her suit-clad colleague sitting on a trash-strewn floor in front of a computer that rested on an upside-down cardboard box. A few weeks after she snapped that picture, Stephanie came in to find her former office space sealed off with plastic and signs warning, "Do Not Enter—Asbestos." But it didn't matter. The start-up team wasn't driven by comfort, status or riches, but the need to "do something" after 9/11. They would have worked in the DOT's parking lot if we asked them to.

By the time John Magaw, a no-nonsense former director of the Secret Service, was confirmed as the first head of the TSA in January 2002, our team had become an eclectic mix. The first people on board other than myself, Ashley, George, and Michael's donated policy assistant Justin Oberman were FAA volunteers sent over by Jane Garvey and a few consultants donated by companies such as AT Kearney and McKinsey. For these and other private sector volunteers, DOT lawyers devised a stringent but workable way to manage ethics recusals and other conflicts of interest. I dragged in my friend Ben Smith from Kearney's Silicon Valley office. When Ben griped, I replied: "You'll feel better once you drag a few other people away from their families and give them unpaid work. Give it a shot."

I was joking, but the response from private industry really was outstanding and the TSA received an injection of top corporate talent who were known as Senior Advisers. Their skills, and those needed to start-up a new federal agency, did not reside in the government, nor were they likely to be needed after the agency started full operations, but for most of 2002, the Senior Advisers were indispensable to the national response to 9/11. A Disney engineer helped design our queuing systems; Intel sent an expert in technology procurement; Marriott assigned us one of their vice presidents of customer service; the electronics firm Solectron loaned us an executive who had twice won the presidentially-awarded Malcolm Baldrige Quality Award. Each Senior Adviser served on several of the more than fifty "Go Teams" that sequenced out the steps needed to make all the puzzle pieces come together to meet ATSA's deadlines and also build the TSA into a functioning federal agency. Most of the Senior Advisers went quietly and uncelebrated back to the private sector after their six to twelve month commitments. They were business process experts who shared with each other the common reference points of metrics, customers, and bottom-line accountability but a cultural disconnect soon became clear between these private sector executives with their own vocabulary and the cadre of law enforcement veterans who came in with Magaw to dig in and run the TSA. Of course, we had aviation experts from the FAA. But since this was the Transportation *Security* Administration, we also needed to bring in some security people. Again, we got great talent and enthusiasm, if not a lot of experience in the transportation arena.

One of the first security-and-operations recruits was Mike Restovich, a tanned, athletic man who wore a large silver Secret Service retirement ring on his right hand. Mike had paid his own way from Dallas up to DC—and his accommodation at the Holiday Inn across the street. Early on, he and his boss, a ruddy-faced former Marine and Secret Service executive named Kevin Houlihan, received an immediate request from several airport CEOs for 300 explosive detection system (EDS) machines. Naturally intense, direct and hands-on, Kevin turned to Mike, grabbing him by the shoulders.

"What the hell's an EDS?"

Mike stared back for a second. "Ah don' know," he replied in his understated Louisiana drawl, before turning to look up the answer.

Every afternoon at five we'd have a meeting to discuss what everyone had done, what their problems were, and what they needed, be it more expertise, more people, or more money. Aside from acting as architect of the new agency, one of my primary jobs was to figure out what all the teams needed and then, utilizing the most enlightened management techniques, go and figuratively whack someone on the head to keep things moving forward.

The TSA would have had more initial expertise if it had been staffed entirely with experienced FAA veterans, but it almost certainly wouldn't have had the same dynamism. The people drawn to the TSA were constantly trying to circumvent the lengthy, process-driven dynamic of normal government business; creative thinking was only way to meet our deadlines. The early TSA was results-oriented in a necessarily urgent, seat-of-the-pants fashion. In its first year, the agency was practically homeless, with few supplies and basically no infrastructure. But the team learned quickly and worked tremendous hours; they were energized and, ultimately, very productive. It was out of this chaotic and bracing environment that the fundamentals of our current aviation security system emerged.

MEANWHILE, HALFWAY AROUND THE WORLD, ANOTHER TALENTED, driven person was also inspired to action in the wake of 9/11. Abdulrahman Hilal Hussein, a nineteen-year-old Austrian then in his second year of university in Cairo, was studying under the auspices of Salafist religious scholars. A top student with a natural aptitude in science, strong soccer skills, and an easy charm that made him popular with his teachers and fellow students, Abdulrahman had been blessed with many talents. After 9/11, he knew how he wanted to apply them. The attacks had proved that his mentors were more than pious men of words, and that actions—serious, calculated plans—could succeed even against the mightiest powers on earth.

The eldest of five children, Abdulrahman was born on January 15, 1983, in the small town of Mödling, months after his parents arrived from Cairo. Just fifteen miles south of Vienna, in rolling green countryside, Mödling is a kind of metaphor for Europe's bifurcation: a quaint old city where Beethoven died with a megamall just outside the town that attracts shoppers from all over central Europe. By the early 1980s Mödling also had a smattering of immigrant families from Turkey, Egypt, and elsewhere in the Muslim world.

Abdulrahman's mother stayed home while his father, a religious scholar and preacher, worked the circuit of mosques in the area. The elder Hussein, from the same fundamentalist Islamic community as al-Qaeda's Ayman Zawahiri, soon became a prominent and in-demand speaker throughout Europe.

When Abdulrahman's mother became pregnant again the next year, the family moved to Wiener Neustadt, a larger town further southwest of Vienna where the second boy, Ahmad, was born in the spring of 1984. Three sisters followed, but Abdulrahman remained the focus of his mother's attention. Because of his dad's travel schedule, Abdulrahman wasn't especially close to his father, but he did inherit his charisma. With his trim muscular build and light brown hair, Abdulrahman looked, talked, and acted like the other Austrian schoolchildren in the Vienna suburbs. By the time he left for school in Cairo at age 16, his intelligence and charm had made him popular with his middle-school peers.

But after 9/11, Abdulrahman was determined to join the bloody fight against the same Western culture in which he had been raised and, to all appearances, still belonged. By the time this bright teenager, one who had grown up both European and in a devout Muslim household, decided to join this battle, his path to jihad was wide open. In addition to being skilled and ambitious, because of his father's prominent religious role, people with connections took notice of him. Another two years in Cairo studying was required, but when he was told that he would get to go to Pakistan for specialized training, Abdulrahman was feverish with anticipation.

THREE

SPRINTING THROUGH
THE AIRPORT

WHEN MOST PASSENGERS DROP OFF THEIR LUGGAGE AT AN airport, they assume that their bags will be scanned for dangerous items. But before 9/11, almost all baggage went straight from the check-in counter to the hold of an aircraft without any assurance that there were no bombs or biological weapons inside.

Then, just before Christmas 1988, a forty-nine-year-old man with curly black hair and a long nose arrived at the airport in Luqa, Malta, carrying a suitcase. Abdel Basset al-Megrahi, the head of security for Libya Arab Airlines, headed to the departures counter and checked his bag through London's Heathrow Airport and on to New York's Kennedy. He then hopped on a short flight back across the Mediterranean to Libya.

At Heathrow, his unaccompanied luggage was transferred onto Pan Am's Flight 103. Just a half hour into the flight to New York, a timing device hidden inside a cassette player in al-Megrahi's suitcase set off a military-grade plastic explosive called Semtex and blew a gaping hole in the aircraft's wall. Oxygen levels are much lower at cruising altitudes than they are on the ground, so aircraft interiors are pressurized, allowing passengers to breathe normally and stewards to recite their immortal preflight mantra: "In case of sudden lost of cabin pressure, oxygen masks will fall from the ceiling . . ."

But this pressure differential also creates a massive force pushing outward on the walls of a plane. As a result, bombs that puncture an aircraft's skin at high altitudes are far more destructive than they would be on the ground. In the wake of the bomb blast and the pursuant outward rushing force, the airplane quickly disintegrated, killing all 243 passengers, sixteen crew members, and even eleven people hit by debris on the ground. The event became known as the Lockerbie bombing, after the Scottish village unfortunate enough to be directly underneath the devastated aircraft's path when the bomb hit.

The event was the worst terrorist disaster in the history of American air travel. The Federal Aviation Administration issued regulations to prevent a repeat of such a tragedy, most notably a requirement that US carriers ensure that passengers on international flights travel with their luggage. Taken by themselves, the regulations made sense but, in a classic example of the pre-9/11 regulatory logic, the precautions only eliminated a narrow sliver of possible attacks. For example, the new laws would do little to prevent an attacker willing to die in the explosion from checking bombs onto domestic flights. Most Americans did not envision this scenario.

But the Lockerbie bombing did nudge scanning technology forward. On the few flights where luggage *was* screened before going into an aircraft's hold—primarily international flights—x-rays had been the industry standard for decades, using dated machines that were only effective at identifying the outlines of metallic weapons like guns, knives, or metal bomb components. But after Flight 103 went down, some companies looked into developing the technology used in medical CT imaging to scan baggage for explosives.

CT (computed tomography) machines are essentially densitometers. When a hospital patient is rolled into one of the giant white machines, the devices within are able to identify the different densities between, say, a tumor and normal brain tissue. Explosives also have specific densities, and by adapting the CT's algorithm for airports, screeners could easily detect the difference in density between peanut butter, clothing, and explosives—or anything else that might be packed away in luggage. Following Lockerbie, a small market developed for a state-of-the-art explosives detection system (EDS) that could replace the decades-old x-ray machines and their blurry images.

But while these EDS machines had exquisite imaging capability that had the potential to be an important bulwark against terrorism, in practice they were riddled with mechanical problems. They cost around a million dollars a pop, measured about seven by eight feet, weighed in at eight tons, and had massive external power requirements. The floors at some airports had to be reengineered to support their weight.

There was also another problem typical of government contracting. Because of a congressional earmark, the FAA had to buy an equal number of machines from two different manufacturers, Invision and L3. Having two suppliers can have advantages, but it certainly didn't in the case of the EDS machines. The machines' massive price tag meant that the FAA could only afford to buy three or four a year. Worse, one vendor's machines consistently broke down when the belt conveyer system fed suitcases. But the FAA had to buy them anyway, or Congress wouldn't approve the purchase in its appropriations legislation. As a result, on the morning of 9/11, there were several million dollars' worth of these huge boxes parked in a warehouse somewhere.

In the aftermath of that day, however, these practical limitations did not deter Congress from mandating that the TSA deploy them throughout the 450 airports in the United States. The devices were far from perfect and not even the only option for explosive detection—sophisticated detectors that could pick up trace explosives' residue and manual bag checks were among other possibilities in the mix, but what mattered to the powers that be was that they were a known step up in security capability. After this Congressional mandate, George Zarur and the legacy FAA explosives team along with DOT officials and their Senior Advisers were tasked with fixing the imperfect technical legacy of Lockerbie.

Originally, CT machines were designed to sit in an antiseptic room at a hospital and process patients ushered into the dedicated imaging room, maybe one or two an hour. But George needed machines that were consistently capable of checking 300 to 400 bags in an hour in a much more stressful environment. This wasn't just a matter of speeding up the conveyor belt, but figuring out how these massive but surprisingly delicate machines could operate within the bowels of an airport loading area during, say, the brutal humidity of a Florida summer. When George started on the project, one of the models certified for its brilliant imagery would run for five minutes and then keel over, even in good conditions. Both L3 and Invision's machines would have to be significantly toughened up. Baggage backups meant delayed or even canceled flights.

One of the reasons that these boxes weigh so much, use so much energy, and are prone to breakdowns is that at the heart of a CT machine sits a massive mechanism that seems like a relic of the factory-driven industry of yesteryear. The whirring sound patients hear after being sucked into the CT machine's tunnel is a half-ton steel gantry spinning around them at speeds of up to 120 RPM. George described them as looking like airplane engines. This spinning motion allowed the CT to "see" the object or body from all angles, but also made the machine especially vulnerable to wide variation in heat, dust, humidity, and overuse.

First Michael put the manufacturers' feet to the fire with an ultimatum: Give us the intellectual property rights to your machines, or no deal. That way, if the vendors didn't adequately ramp up their production, the TSA would bring in a different manufacturer who could. It worked. Facing the possibility of missing out on contracts worth hundreds of millions of dollars, both L3 and Invision retooled, leaned on their suppliers for better parts, and began working feverishly to roll out more effective machines—an effort reminiscent of the massive manufacturing expansion that accompanied America's entry into World War II.

The machines' final test before being sent to the field took place at the FAA labs in Atlantic City, New Jersey. Technicians ran the machines for hours, continuously feeding baggage through them, and then reported to the vendor's representatives when and how the devices failed. As soon as a new kink was detected, engineers sleeping in nearby hotels hopped onto their computers and began working on fixes, improving or developing new software. For six adrenaline-fed weeks, the East Coast's gambling hub became an unlikely center for software innovation. By June 2002, the machines were field-tested, certified, and on their way to airports across the country. They still scan 90 percent of checked baggage today.

AIRPORT CHECKPOINTS, TOO, HAVE UNDERGONE CHANGES SINCE 2001. Before then, checkpoints were generally staffed by poorly trained screeners working for whichever giant security corporation had gotten the contract. The FAA mandated the security requirements, but the contractors were paid by the airlines, and because of the relatively low threat of hijackings, these security firms mainly competed on price, leaving their underpaid screeners to get by with bare-bones training and outdated x-ray machines and metal detectors. Their main objective was narrowly focused on stopping guns and knives from being carried on board planes.

Immediately after 9/11, private screeners continued to run the enhanced checkpoint operations, but they were now backed up by the National Guard.

For many passengers, the sight of armed soldiers positioned around the airport was disorienting and disquieting; other passengers found their presence comforting. Either way, the new demands on the system, like seizing small scissors after an exhaustive manual bag check, left checkpoints overwhelmed by long lines and backlogs.

Since then, wait times have generally decreased, even as the checkpoints attempt to manage a rapidly expanding array of threats, including remarkable advances in explosives technology. But the lines are still more invasive and time-consuming than that bygone era that travelers over the age of thirty might remember as "the good old days." Now, instead of simply emptying their pockets of change and keys before walking through a metal detector, most passengers must present their boarding pass and ID, take off their shoes and jackets, place regulated-capacity liquids in a quart-size plastic bag on the conveyor belt, segregate their laptop computer, and walk through a metal detector or body scanner. Sometimes there are pat downs. The transition between airport security protocols of the '70s, '80s, and '90s and today primarily can be traced to the spring of 2002 at Baltimore/Washington International airport where, over a month and a half, the checkpoint was reinvented.

Stephanie Rowe, a brown-haired, long-limbed burst of energy, was one of a handful of the private-industry contractors who worked to redesign the checkpoint alongside FAA and TSA personnel. An employee of Accenture, the global management consulting giant, Stephanie had no previous aviation or security experience before she joined the TSA—aside from having flown almost continuously for ten years—but she was equipped with valuable process management skills. *Everyone wants to enhance security,* she thought, *but what are the specific mechanics at the checkpoint that generate additional security value without creating unsustainable delays?*

To find out, Stephanie and her team did what consultants call a workflow analysis delving into the minutiae of checkpoint activity at BWI. How long did it take to pass from one point to another? How did travelers' behavior affect the line speed? How were people interacting with the equipment, screener requests, and other passengers around them? Stephanie became completely immersed in the checkpoint. She learned how to pat people down, how to test people's bags for explosive residue, how to inspect shoes for hidden bombs, and every other aspect of a screener's job.

One time-consuming procedure is the explosive tracing on baggage. In 2002, screeners swiped books, shoes, and electronics in selected bags and around the luggage interior and exterior before placing the fabric into an explosives detector. Watching from the sidelines, Stephanie put a question to FAA personnel: "Is it really necessary to trace everything inside a single bag?" She saw an opportunity to strike a better balance between security and time. Soon thereafter, the procedure was altered to trace fewer items and more bags, a direction the TSA has continued. Today, such screening is only required for objects that, based on scientific study, may contain a threat including explosives.

After repeatedly inspecting every nook and cranny of the checkpoint (Stephanie walked through the metal detector so many times she wore holes in her socks), the team was ready to make some decisions. But improvements like these always open up the possibility of political pushback based on complaints from passengers, airlines or airports, and the TSA's mission at the checkpoint varied according to each.

Within the agency's first few months, Secretary Mineta sparked a mania after mentioning in a congressional hearing that the wait times in security lines would be ten minutes. In fact, ten minutes was a target Michael and I had created—somewhat unscientifically, as there had never been a set wait time before—as a basis for design, not a maximum limit. Theoretically, we could have set any amount for the wait times, but each had its own consequences. A two-minute standard would delight travelers but cost billions more in extra staffing; conversely, ignoring wait times would have choked the system. Ten minutes was a variable around which to extrapolate personnel and equipment needs. But after Mineta's comment, members of Congress, who often fly home to their districts for the weekend, began demanding that no line be longer than ten minutes The media, smelling a "gotcha" moment, seized on the issue. Less than six months after the 9/11 attacks, America's sense of common purpose was fraying. Increasingly, the focus moved from "How do we fix this?" to scoring political points by sniping our evolving and far-from-perfect transportation security.

Stephanie's BWI team members, including the eighty-six private screeners working on Pier C, however, saw their primary job not as making things faster, but making security better without slowing down the lines. In a back room at the airport, several of them mocked up a checkpoint with tape on the floor. They had a million ideas, but with no infrastructure, acquiring even the most ordinary items became a quest. For example, when people first arrive at checkpoints and have to remove some items of clothing—"divestiture," in TSA parlance—they need a surface on which to place other items. But there were no tables to spare at the airport, and ordering them meant going through a lengthy government requisition process. Instead, a team member went to Costco to buy extra tables.

Next, passengers would place their keys, jewelry, and change into a container before walking through the metal detector. The long, skinny plastic dishes in use at the time were actually designed to hold an airline mechanic's screws and bolts. But these receptacles fell over frequently, slowing down the process. So another team member went to PetSmart, bought a bunch of different dog bowls, and tested each. The result was the white bowls with rubber bottoms that are still in use at many airports.

Then, after depositing their metal objects in a dog bowl, people walked through the magnetometer. Those who set off an alarm would be scanned with a wand to determine why. When observing passenger behavior, Stephanie noticed a way to shave a few seconds off that process. If the outlines of two footprints were drawn on a mat in the wanding station, most people automatically stepped on top of the feet with no prompting and spread their legs into the most efficient stance. When screening thousands of passengers a day, every second counts. The new wanding station mats were also positioned so passengers could see their bags at all times, because although the search normally takes thirty seconds or less, many travelers experience almost immediate separation anxiety from their belongings.

Finally, in March 2002, the newly designed checkpoint went live at BWI. Most airports open around four o'clock, so screeners were bused in from local Baltimore airport hotels at three that morning. At that hour the checkpoint sat hidden on the other side of a huge steel curtain, behind which it felt like opening night of a high-school play. People were running around asking for directions and shouting things like, "We need a table over here!" Meanwhile, industrial engineers stood on the sidelines with stopwatches to track the workflow. Then, at exactly 4:00 A.M., the airport rolled back the heavy curtain and everyone was suddenly in their places. Soon thereafter, the first passengers began filtering through the redesigned checkpoint.

After a half hour or so, the smooth moving lines underscored that a bunch of smart people had done their jobs and largely succeeded in using modern technology, process design, and sophisticated security thinking to quickly overhaul the most prominent defense against onboard terrorism. But their job wasn't done: Anytime elements in a system are dramatically changed, unforeseen consequences—say, a change in passenger behavior—can wreak unpredictable havoc. Sure enough, as the morning rush picked up, the lines started to lengthen.

Stephanie was fascinated by the unexpected intricacies in the checkpoint's ecosystem. If a station was short one person—or even if one person wasn't working on the right task at that moment—lines would start backing up within seconds. There was an art and a science to all of it. But there was also a bottom line, and soon the engineers were glaring up from their stopwatches and issuing warnings: "If you don't get a second person to run shoes here, you're going to back that line up and the whole thing will crash," or "You need somebody else down here, tracing these bags." They would also yell out if they saw any piece of machinery momentarily sitting idle: "No one's using that electronic trace detector. Someone should be on it!" On one hand, the engineers were right, but their wait-time expectations were also tighter than the staffing model Stephanie and her team had developed. Security is always about tradeoffs; for the TSA team, the goal was creating a checkpoint worthy of their "never again" mantra.

Nonetheless, as the debut morning grew more hectic, Stephanie saw her TSA client, the head of the whole BWI design operation, Hans Miller, a tall, slender, brilliant, and hyperactive man, begin to freak out. "This isn't working!" he yelled, gesturing at the stalling operations. As he threatened to rip apart the process midstream, Stephanie tried to talk him down. "It will level out," she said. "You have to give it a second."

And it did. After a few more tweaks, the checkpoints were fully operational. Stephanie's work was done, and she left BWI later that month and returned to TSA headquarters to work on the national rollout. During the forty-five days she spent redesigning the checkpoint, she had barely slept and lost five pounds off her already slender frame. But she still claims it was "painful fun."

MEANWHILE, THE REMAKING OF ANOTHER SECURITY MEASURE WAS driving Michael crazy. After firing the insubordinate ex-general in charge of the Federal Air Marshals (FAMs) in September 2001, Michael asked around for a replacement and got rave reviews about a former senior DoD official named Walter Pankow. Michael had been impressed by the officers he'd met during his time in Washington, and he gladly asked Pankow to come on board.

Once he arrived at the Department of Transportation, Michael briefed Pankow on his mission. Putting armed FAMs on flights had long been an attractive option. President Richard Nixon had ordered the creation of the force three decades earlier (oddly, on September 11, 1969). Confronted with a decade-long spike in global hijackings, including the first American casualty in such an incident, Nixon requested a small force of officers to help keep the air safe for aviation. But the relatively low profile of hijacking over the following decades meant that the FAMs' numbers did not grow in step with air travel. As a result, on 9/11, 32 FAMs were assigned to cover thousands of flights a day, the same size as the force Nixon had created 32 years earlier.

But after the attacks, President George W. Bush envisioned a different role for the FAMs. Rather than populating the force with FAA inspectors rotating through tours as air marshals, the president wanted a commando squad of many thousands. Immediately. For Michael, simply finding that many qualified applicants was hard enough; never mind endowing them with the training necessary to create a law-enforcement team with the fitness, defenses, and offensive prowess of other specialized forces, such as the Navy SEALs.

Despite their limited numbers, the FAMs played an almost immediate role in reopening American aviation. After 9/11, the Secret Service recommended permanently shuttering the airport closest to downtown, Reagan National. As anyone who has flown into that airport can attest, its runways sit fewer than five miles from most of Washington's major landmarks, including the White House. This proximity makes for a beautiful approach: the city's Enlightenment-era design of green spaces and broad avenues intersecting at the seat of government are laid out as if on an architect's table. But that lovely view also means a plane could hit the White House in fewer than sixty seconds after deviating from its flight plan. President Bush, ignoring the danger and the Secret Service's advice, had the guts to reopen National a few weeks after the nation's other airports in early October. His decision rested on the promises that Michael and Secretary Mineta had made to him about the additional measures they would take to secure the airport. Michael knew that he had to make sure that changes in flight numbers would work for the FAMs.

As Michael finished his recommendations, a wry smile came across his face. Prior to the 1980s, when the industry was deregulated, the now-extinct Civil Aviation Board (CAB) had exercised control over a much broader scope of airlines' activity, including where they could fly and the maximum they could charge for flights. But during the first Reagan administration, in which Michael had served, the authority was dismantled with the fervent support of a young Democratic member of Congress, Norman Mineta. Michael walked to the phone and called his boss.

"Hello, Michael," said Mineta, now used to these weekend calls from his deputy.

"Hi, Norm. I've just been working on the spreadsheets, and I was thinking how weird it is that the guy who ended government route-making is going to bring it back," joked Michael. "Are you ready to gavel the son of CAB back into existence?"

Mineta assented. Michael's initial schedule was approved and Reagan National inched back up toward full capacity.

Even a few months after the attacks, there was a lot to catch up with regarding the FAMs. As Michael briefed their new leader, Pankow, he emphasized how much political capital and importance had already been invested in the team. The FAMs were immediately in demand by travelers throughout the government. A short while after 9/11, a West Coast member of Congress called up the FAA ops center to put in a request that was eventually passed up to Michael: "She wants to know if there's a FAM team on this United flight Friday night and on this Sunday flight coming back to DC, and if not, would we put one on there?" She certainly wasn't the only one making personal security demands in the period after the attacks, but Michael told her that we weren't going politicize these types of decisions. It was the right thing to do, but it did not sit well. He never heard another word.

Pankow was also privy to how the immediate need for FAMs—with the backing of the White House—had helped Michael quickly enlarge the team's numbers by raiding other government agencies, and not just the usual suspects, like the Bureau of Alcohol, Tobacco, and Firearms (or ATF); the FBI; or the US Marshals. There are armed federal law-enforcement officers spread throughout the government; for example, the Department of Housing and Urban Development has a handful. Badgering other agencies, the TSA grabbed 600 people, put them through a crash course, and got them in the air.

But the permanent expansion of the FAMs to a sustainable force of thousands would not be so easy. Soon after arriving, Pankow met with Michael and launched into the sort of PowerPoint presentation typical of the military—no questions, no interactions, and with Pankow hewing closely to an accompanying three-ring binder "script," which he would flip through as he decided he was ready for Michael to see the next slide.

The presentation style initially irked Michael, but then it dawned on him: *This guy,* thought Michael, *is telling me—in as nice a way as he can—that I'm crazy.* Slowly and resolutely, Pankow outlined the history of federal agencies that had had to hire large numbers of law-enforcement officers, detailed how hard it was, how it would be very expensive, and that there weren't existing facilities able to handle more than a fraction of the necessary personnel.

After a while Michael interrupted the wooden presentation. "Pardon me, but all this stuff is total BS. First of all, don't ever bring one of these PowerPoint things in here again. I don't do PowerPoint. If you have something to say, look me in the eye and say it. If you have something you want me to read, send it to me and I'll read it in advance—and then I'll ask you questions about what I don't understand."

Warming up, Michael continued, "I don't need to be spoon-fed these points. And the punch line is that obviously you don't think we can do this. You're wrong. You tell me your problems; let me try to find solutions. "

"Well," began Pankow, "when we do the shooting stage of the training in Arizona, we don't have facilities to house that many people."

"Let me call the deputy secretary of defense and see if there's a military facility we can use, like an abandoned Air Force base. Or, if that doesn't work, we'll just buy a hotel."

"Sir, buy a hotel?"

"Yeah. Either buy it lock, stock, and barrel, or we'll do a wet lease—lease it with services intact," replied Michael.

The meeting continued like that, with Michael proposing solutions to the problems of training, gathering security clearances, and dealing with ethics problems that might arise in unconventional relationships between different agencies or with the private sector. Normally the government needs to color inside the lines, avoid risk or controversy, and operate at a sane pace with everybody on board. Pankow had been a star in that world, well practiced in the art of identifying problems over the horizon and mitigating them in an orderly way. Like everybody else, he knew the mantra that "everything changed after 9/11." But, like many others reciting that line, it did not change the way he did his job, even now, as he found himself at the center of an effort expressly created to stop terrorism.

His allegiance to established protocol would crop up again and again. At a later meeting I attended, Pankow explained to Michael that he reported to the head of the FAA, Jane Garvey, and was going to have to check with her before he agreed to do anything that Michael had asked him to do. Michael snapped. "The FAA administrator and I are in lockstep, and neither of us wants to wait around for you to cover yourself, " he shouted. "Now get on board or get your ass out of my sight!"

After Pankow left the room, Michael turned to me. "Sorry to be so heavy," he said, with palpable frustration. "I respect the chain of command and Jane's prerogatives to manage her people, but with this, I don't have the time." The TSA really was different; it had to be. There couldn't be people hiding out in bureaucratic fiefdoms or scrapping over territory or kicking the can up and down the org charts. We were supposed to be salvaging national security.

IN DECEMBER, SECRETARY MINETA AND MICHAEL WENT OVER TO THE Situation Room, in the basement of the West Wing of the White House, to brief the president on how the TSA was going to be built and meet the congressional deadlines. Sitting at the conference table, with Bush at the head, flanked by a varsity team of cabinet-level National Security Council officials, Mineta promised him that we would get the FAMs in the air by July 1, the exact midpoint of 2002.

It was a bold promise, but after their early battles, Pankow had stopped objecting to Michael, and we were counting on him to move mountains to make the FAM team a reality. That winter, though, it became clear that Pankow was instead relying on a time-tested process of governmental intransigence. He'd go quietly about business as usual, miss the target, and then claim we were "crazy for trying to get things done that quickly. There are normal processes in the federal government that you don't understand," or some other excuse.

This house of cards collapsed at a meeting late on a particularly frosty January night. Suddenly realizing he hadn't received any updates from Pankow for a while, Michael called a short-notice meeting to review the status of the FAM program. About eight of us met over in the newly appointed TSA conference room, on the opposite side of the DOT's tenth floor from our original war room. Pankow was not available, so his deputy, a career Secret Service agent named Tom Quinn, got up to talk about their progress, this time without the aid of PowerPoint.

Eliminating such crutches was part of Michael's attempt to create a more interactive environment in meetings where everyone talked, everyone could ask questions—even interrupting others to do so—and everyone could disagree. And, sure enough, in the middle of Quinn's pitch, Michael interrupted, "Tom, can I ask you a question?

"Yes, sir." Tom is a powerful man, given to buttoned, unwrinkled suits, who bears more than a passing resemblance to Clint Eastwood.

"Correct me if I'm wrong," said Michael pointedly, "But in ten minutes aren't you somewhat reluctantly going tell me that we're behind schedule on the promise we made to the president? True or false?"

There was silence for a moment as Tom considered the question and how to answer. The rest of us checked the status of the carpet beneath our chairs. Then, after calculating his fate, Tom looked back at Michael and assumed the classic Secret Service stance, feet apart, arms at sides with hands crossed. "Well, sir, to be honest, sir . . . that's right."

"This is unacceptable," Michael shot back. "How come you didn't come tell me that we had a problem earlier than now? This is what we'd agreed on."

Michael then turned to Ralph Basham, another former Secret Service agent now serving as the TSA's chief of staff. "Ralph, Pankow is fired. I don't care who tells him. I don't care if I ever see him again. He should not show up for any other meeting at the department headquarters. He said he'd get it done. He didn't bring his problems to me. He played me. I personally promised the president we were going to do this."

Swinging back to face Tom, who had been left standing while his superior was being dismissed, Michael pressed forward. "Tom, you're next in the chain of command. Do you want the job of being in charge of this office? Only say 'yes' if you can promise me dead cold that you are going to get this done by July 1 and exactly as planned." Michael paused for a beat. "You're about half a month behind now."

Tom stood there for a moment and then, in one of the ballsier displays I've seen during a cross-examination, said, "Can I ask some questions?"

"Tom, you can ask questions all night long until you are sure we are going to get this thing done as promised. The American people need these FAMs because we don't know when those bastards are coming back."

After a discussion about budget and what Tom would need from upper management, he made his decision. "I would love to have the job," he answered.

"Great, you've got it," said Michael. He turned back to Ralph and told him to draw up the paperwork.

ONCE AGAIN, THE TSA'S CONCEPTION IN A CRUCIBLE WAS EXPRESSLY results-oriented. But because of the strong emotions surrounding 9/11, there seemed to be a higher ethical standard for how we did the work. We had to live up to the country's expectations as well as those of the Government Accountability Office, whose investigators were already on site, reviewing everything we did. They evaluated not only what we had done but also what we were working on for the future. We didn't do anything immoral or illegal, but we broke plenty of glass to get the job done quickly. Our actions may also have nudged against the expected norms of government behavior—a brand new agency contemplating taking over a huge retired Army base—but were always true to its larger spirit and the necessary urgency. I am certain, at least, that no other agency could fire and replace one of its leaders in the two minutes that Michael took to rid himself of Pankow. Fortunately, Tom Quinn was smart, systematic, and full of conviction. On the night of June 30, 2002, Tom phoned Michael.

"Sir, I wanted to tell you that I've just given the graduation address to the last class of FAMs necessary to meet the number that we promised the president." (The actual number of FAMs was and still is sensitive. The President had initially asked for a higher number but the force today numbers somewhere in the thousands.) "And I promise, sir, that every single one of them will be in the air tomorrow," continued Tom. "So you call the president, the secretary, or the Congress or whomever you have to call and tell them it's done."

Today, there are air marshals on thousands of flights a day, some selected for their city pairings—maybe Washington to Boston—and some selected at random to make sure terrorists don't get comfortable with the idea of taking over a flight from, say, Denver to Cheyenne.

THE BIRTH OF ANOTHER, LESS VISIBLE SECURITY CAPACITY ALSO BEGAN soon after the attacks, when FAA administrator Jane Garvey wrote a letter dated September 24, 2001 to defense secretary Donald Rumsfeld asking for his department to provide counterterrorism personnel. Rumsfeld concurred and sent over one: Captain Joe Salvator, a solidly built man in his thirties with olive skin, close-cropped black hair, and a straightforward but somewhat wry manner.

Joe had been an MP when the Marine Corps founded its training course in counterterrorism. After a while, Joe decided that counterterrorism held little promise—he'd never use those skills defending US soil—and, after six years, left the service for a corporate security management job in private industry back home in Rhode Island. Then, in late September 2001, Joe received a letter telling him he'd been involuntarily reactivated. He was set to deploy to Afghanistan, but a few weeks later on October 27, 2001 he found himself reporting to Washington, DC, in his Marine uniform.

Joe quickly became enmeshed in the complicated dynamics of the TSA's start-up. Officially he was on loan to the FAA from the Department of Defense, but the existing intelligence officers at the FAA weren't about to stop what they were doing to train a new guy, so Joe was sent over to brief TSA.

On the morning of September 11, 2001, the DOT had practically no experience in counterterrorism. The FAA had thirty to forty analysts, but the agencies that could have fed them good information—the Central Intelligence Agency and the National Security Agency—had no idea that the FAA's intel shop even existed. Of course, on September 12, they turned on the intel spigot, and now the FAA faced the opposite problem as it struggled to analyze all the new data.

Joe took full advantage of the opportunity and got field promoted to be one of TSA's lead intel officers, but because they had no secure facilities, he worked out of the FAA's office, walking over to the DOT to brief Michael, Secretary Mineta, and TSA boss, John Magaw. The infrastructural confusion of the essentially homeless TSA only magnified the chaos and angst still present at the end of 2001. Joe used a special locked briefcase to carry classified material down the five or so blocks between the FAA and the DOT, well outside the security cordon. One of his first trips over to the DOT was to share intel suggesting that there may have been a twentieth or twenty-first hijacker. A few weeks later he ran down Independence Avenue with info about the multiplying discoveries of white powder that alarmed the nation after powdered anthrax was discovered in a letter sent to Senate majority leader Tom Daschle's office. Hundreds of people who suspected they were exposed to the disease lined up for hours to be inoculated. DOT's involvement deepened once a suspicious white powder was reported on board a flight. Joe also hustled down the street with a copy of the first Osama bin Laden video tucked inside his briefcase. Finally, in December, Joe was on watch during the Richard Reid incident, the so-called Shoe Bomber tackled by passengers on board a Paris-to-Miami flight while he tried to light an explosive hidden in his boot.

The terrorists were still coming at TSA from all angles, and with the organization's limited operational and intel capacities, the threat overload forced it to assume everything was a real threat for the next six months. The FAA and the TSA were now privy to a higher level of information, but most of the major intelligence agencies themselves had been caught flatfooted by the attacks and were in the process of reinventing their capacities at the end of 2001. The CIA's organization was secret and not even officially acknowledged. The FBI didn't have adequate resources dedicated to counterterrorism, or "CT," in the industry, until 2002. And within those organizations' counterterrorism departments, Joe didn't have many personal connections to facilitate the flow of information to the TSA.

Nor did he have any capacity to chase down leads or educate himself by searching a computer database. Instead, his office would receive a printed stack of papers called cables that were intelligence reports on counter terrorism issues every night. He pored over the papers, but it would take years to create an intel capacity that allowed us a glimpse inside the terrorist training camps to detect attacks before they were launched. With these limited abilities, the FAA also fretted over what action it could take if there were more hijackers.

Joe remembers the conversations within the FAA, "Let's put out an SD," or security directive, Joe suggested in his clipped Rhode Island accent. "We'll let the airlines know who we think the hijackers are." So a directive was drawn up listing twenty-five names or so and dates of birth culled from the database. The airlines were told that if any of those people tried to book flights, they must not issue the tickets and should instead call the FAA immediately. This was the first iteration of the now-iconic no-fly list.

AS 2002 MARCHED ON AND THE TSA CONTINUED TO NAIL ITS DEADLINES, many of us who had volunteered for the stand-up mission trickled back to private industry. I left in May 2002 and returned to my family and job in California. As with any venture taken with such haste, the early TSA had flaws, but all of us were proud of what we had accomplished.

As a federal employee, Michael ploughed ahead, along with a growing career team of new TSA civil servants. By the end of 2002, the TSA had taken over screening at all the nation's airports. New Year's Eve was the last mandate: delivering and positioning the final few eight-ton EDS machines for screening checked baggage.

Anticipating success, Michael and Secretary Mineta sent a letter to President Bush to be delivered at his ranch on January 1, 2003. At about five o'clock on the evening of December 31, Michael stood on the ground floor of a Boeing command center several blocks from DOT's downtown DC headquarters, staring at the large electronic map of the United States that dominated the room. The screen looked like it might be tracking electoral returns, but instead of votes, the lights on the map turned from red to green as airports met all their criteria for operations.

"Jeez, that's a lot of red lights," said Michael. Turning around, he asked the room, "Hey, what time is it?"

Huge clocks covered the walls. Michael got no answer except for confused glances.

"No," Michael began again, "I mean what time is it in the earliest part of any physical geography owned by the United States—what is that, American Samoa?"

People scurried around, looking at the map. "Yeah, American Samoa is eight hours behind DC," someone replied.

"OK," said Michael. "Congress wrote that we have to be done by midnight tonight. They didn't say which time zone. So, if we need a little wiggle room, as long as it's not midnight somewhere in America, we're on schedule."

The extended TSA team made the deadline. But it would be a brief celebration.

FOUR

HOW TO LOOK WITHOUT SEEING

TOWARD THE END OF 2001, AROUND SEVEN IN THE EVENING,
a stout man with dark hair shaved back to a bristle and sparkling eyes was
checking the IDs of passengers boarding a Virgin Atlantic flight from Boston's Logan International Airport to London. A male passenger came forward
and presented the airline's security officer, Carl Maccario, with a brand-new
US passport. Flipping through it, Carl noticed that it hadn't been signed.

"You fuhgawt ta sign ya passpawt," Carl said in his thick Massachusetts
accent.

"Oh," replied the passenger.

"When did you get the passport?" continued Carl.

"Yesterday."

But yesterday was a Sunday, thought Carl. The passenger, realizing his
mistake, blurted out, "No, I got it in the mail."

"When did you get it in the mail?"

"When did I get it in the mail?" The man hesitated. "Friday, last Friday."

"Did someone bring it to you or did you get it in the mail?"

"I got it in the mail."

Carl paused. "Do you have any other ID?"

The passenger pulled out identification for a college in New Hampshire. Carl had grown up in Massachusetts, next door to New Hampshire,
and had never heard of the place. He began to get a feeling in his stomach

and, apparently, so did the passenger. The traveler turned around, ripped off his backpack, and threw it to two men further back in line, who passed him another backpack and ran off. Meanwhile Carl called the airport police.

"What did you have in the backpack?" asked Carl.

"Oh, just video games," said the passenger.

"Why'd you throw it to those guys?"

The man stared back mutely. He was running out of answers and eventually stepped out of the ticketing line. That ended the matter as an aviation security issue but other authorities pursued the international narcotics angle.

Carl had grown up in a working-class Irish-Italian family in the town of Melrose, Massachusetts. Until the age of thirteen, he shared an apartment over a hardware store with his mom, dad, and two brothers. To pay the bills, his dad frequently worked two jobs, while his mom worked to put Carl and his brothers through Saint Mary's grammar school. It was a tumultuous childhood, but both parents instilled a strong work ethic in their kids from day one or, as Carl would later put it, "my parents were never the kind to go to work and put erasers on the ends of pencils." By the end of high school, Carl had been voted class president in both his junior and senior years and was captain of the track team (a position his daughters, looking at the older, more solid version of their Dad, would later call into question).

Prior to the 9/11 attacks, Carl investigated financial fraud for the state of Massachusetts, but he had other interests, too. He managed to talk his boss into sending him to the State Police Academy to learn basic interview and interrogation techniques. The academy was a two-hour drive away, but Carl threw himself into the work and ended up re-teaching the material to hundreds of lawyers in his department. He also started watching videotaped interviews with serial killer Ted Bundy, studying what made him tick and how he tripped himself up both verbally and physically.

At the police academy Carl learned the classics of interrogation. People who coughed or repeated questions were often buying time, as the passenger with the brand-new passport had done when asked, "When did you get it in the mail?" There was also a long-standing "vocabulary" of tics that suggest a potential deception, such as avoiding eye contact; facial flushing; sweating; voice trembles; changes in voice pitch, volume, or rate of speech; choice of words; and a dry mouth. Another tip-off was when nonverbal gestures conflicted with a subject's verbal message; for instance, when the mouth says "yes" while a shake of the head says "no."

His studies made Carl an expert in reading the unintentional movements that signal emotions like anxiety, fear, contempt, discomfort, and deceit. He devoured academic books on the subject and was struck by reading that over 90 percent of human communication is nonverbal. Because we are unconsciously immersed in this second language every day, most of us are at least somewhat attuned to it, but Carl had taken his abilities to a new level. Carl also began to wonder if his cramped and sometimes rough childhood helped him develop his innate abilities after learning that people who grow up amid a certain amount of turmoil master these skills as a sort of survival technique.

Carl was in love with his new discipline. Although he was laid off from his state agency after 9/11 when funding was diverted from fraud investigation to counterterrorism, the attacks also prompted some airlines to make huge improvements in their private screening forces. They were looking for people like Carl with law-enforcement and investigation backgrounds. Carl interviewed for a security job at Boston Logan and landed a spot with Virgin Atlantic.

Like all of the new Virgin Atlantic screeners, Carl attended a one-week training course in New York led by a former Israeli agent named Chaim Koppel. Because of the political situation, Israeli aircraft—tempting targets for anti-Zionist terrorists—essentially fly around with huge bulls-eyes on their sides. So, starting in the 1960s, the country made a huge commitment to ensuring that the national airline, El Al, and the country's sole international airport—Ben-Gurion, just outside Tel Aviv—are the most secure in the world. Since 9/11, there have been recurring public suggestions to base US security measures on "the Israeli model." However, the term is often used imprecisely, and it remains unclear whether most people simply mean "tougher security" or are calling for expanded behavior observation, personal interviews, and ethnic profiling; or whether they imagine security as an integrated system encompassing the whole society.

Carl soaked up everything Chaim shared from these Israeli interrogation techniques. Chaim, who had a successful record of disrupting terrorist plots against Israel, claimed that reading people's nonverbal messages was the only way to do it; other techniques just caught the loose change. Carl didn't need further convincing.

At Logan, he would begin his shift with a printout listing the names of every passenger on the Virgin flight from Boston to London, roughly 400 people. His first step was to greet and briefly interview every passenger as they queued up for their boarding passes. The questions were simple and courteous, along the lines of "How are you, Mr. Johnson?" and "Where are you coming from today?" or "And who are you meeting in London?" Then Carl would wait silently for their answers. One of his core rules, he later told me, was that if he was going to ask someone a question, then "For God's sake, let them answer!" For it was in these answers, and the passenger's manner while giving them, that a distinction could be made between a harried but innocent traveler and those who had something to hide. Given enough opportunities via continued questioning, passengers in the second category often began tripping over their stories or projecting severe discomfort.

Once he finished the initial screening, Carl would affix either a red or green sticker to the ticket and send the travelers over to the check-in counter. It's no surprise that the red sticker signified that he had identified something suspicious about the passenger. And if that passenger were in fact up to no good, it would probably make him even more nervous, or convince him to leave the airport altogether.

Carl and the other screeners also worked on the departure side. Always experimenting, Carl would play around with the optimal position for screening. One night in 2002 he was working just outside the gate area with another security guard who was about six feet four and rail thin. Built like a fireplug himself, Carl was scanning the lounge and wondering how much the two of them resembled the cartoon duo Mutt and Jeff when a passenger pushed by.

"What are you guys doing?" he demanded.

"Gate screening," said Carl.

"Well . . . just don't get in our way," said the man as he stalked off.

Carl turned to his partner. "You might want to check that guy."

"Why?"

"Because he lit up like a Christmas tree when I told him what we were doing."

Carl and some agents on Virgin's security team approached the man near the gate, questioned him some more and eventually opened up his briefcase to find it stuffed with envelopes of money—well over the $10,000 allowed to cross international borders without a customs declaration. But the money wasn't a security concern, so they called in an officer from US Customs and Border Protection.

"You might want to have a look at this," Carl told him.

"How much money is it?" asked the CBP officer.

"Fifty-five thousand," said the passenger.

"Who are you bringing it to?"

"A bunch of guys."

"Where's your paperwork?"

"I don't have any. I've never had any."

Carl watched as the CBP agent led the passenger away for additional questioning and potential prosecution. While passengers didn't always signal their guilt so broadly, Carl discovered that by simply approaching and engaging people, or even observing them from afar, he was remarkably successful at sniffing out activity that no magnetometer or x-ray was ever going to catch. Over the months he found people carrying hundreds of thousands of dollars—an unexplained $100,000 in one briefcase alone, tens of thousands taped to the small of another passenger's back—as well as large caches of marijuana and cocaine, and even people fleeing arrest warrants.

Despite his skill at catching criminals, Carl was always aware that he was hired to stop terrorists. There are infinitely more smugglers and crooks passing through airports than there are operational terrorists, Carl figured, but both display similarly nervous and evasive behavior. Even though most of these suspicious characters pose no threats to their fellow passengers, it's still worth paying attention to their odd behavior—it's hard to distinguish the actions of a passenger smuggling cocaine on board from another who was concealing a bomb

Eventually, Carl met several other screeners with a 9/11 story that further strengthened his convictions. On that morning, several of the passengers boarding American Airlines Flight 11 were acting so strangely that the gate staff at Logan airport took notice and decided to hold on to the men's ticket stubs. After that flight flew into the World Trade Center tower, the travelers that they had observed were identified as part of the team of five hijackers led by Mohamed Atta. But at the time, the alarmed employees had no authority to pull them over for questioning based on behavioral observations.

Playing cat and mouse with airport passengers was engaging and rewarding work, but about half a year after he started at Virgin, Carl watched with contempt as the Transportation Security Administration came to Logan and slowly began assuming control of the checkpoints. A dedicated cigar smoker, Carl would take his breaks out front near a billboard put up by the Samaritans that proclaimed, "People hear but they don't listen."

Yeah, thought Carl, *but here it's more like "People look but they don't see."*

IN 2002, TSA BECAME THE SOLE EMPLOYER OF THE NATION'S TENS OF thousands of airport screeners. The exact transformations that Carl was eying suspiciously at Logan were spreading simultaneously across the nation. To avoid disruptions at the checkpoints, the TSA initially left the existing private screeners in place. The first step was simply to take over the existing contracts between the airlines and the security companies. But, before 2002 was out, all airport screeners would have to pass enhanced testing and training on their way to becoming federal employees.

Before this massive personnel transformation, America's screeners had always been private employees, usually working for large contractors. Security services were outsourced to companies who answered directly to the airlines that paid them. The FAA, and, thus, the government's only role in airport screening was when the Federal Aviation Administration issued mandates regarding security to the airlines. If FAA inspectors noticed a breach in these security protocols, they'd try to fix the problem with the same tool they used to correct an improper deicing procedure—slapping the offending airline with a fine. After such a penalty, carriers would, at least in theory, lean on their security contractors to fix the problem. In short, on the morning of September 11, airline security relied on a series of regulations just like those used to prevent any other potential aviation problems, from aircraft maintenance to flight scheduling. Like most regulatory schemes, over time, this approach to security bred flat, uninspired thinking and produced only bare-minimum efforts to meet the legal mandate. Protected from criticism by being able to state that they met the government-approved standards, the airlines' main security considerations revolved around controlling costs.

Similarly, improvements and updates in FAA mandates—whether in maintenance, personnel training, or security—were mostly reactive measures developed in the wake of notable failures. While this slow-growing collection of rules had its shortcomings, it was a very successful approach for the aviation operations in which problems were easy to predict and define. For example, it is always true that without x number of bolts, a wing will fall off, or that below y velocity, a 747 will not achieve liftoff. And when new problems arise, if they are knowable, then they can be fixed with a high degree of success according to science-based principles. When the FAA decides that, say, airlines spend money to maintain their wing assemblies, these regulations based on physics or engineering are likely to work pretty well.

But when it comes to hijacking and counterterrorism, eliminating the causes of previous failures is far from adequate. If a terrorist attacks with x technique, the FAA might, in the aftermath, take measures to eliminate that problem. But once airtight precautions are in place, the most likely source of future attacks becomes anything except x. Only the most incompetent operative (and yes, there are many) would rely on a known technique instead of selecting one of the nearly limitless alternatives. While regulations based on science are very successful at solving knowable problems, terrorism is by nature unpredictable.

Yet introducing measures based on the known plots of yesterday was the mainstay of pre-9/11 security. When increasing numbers of guns came on board in the 1960s, metal detectors were introduced. After Lockerbie, passengers were required to travel with their luggage. And none of these measures did a thing to dissuade the 9/11 hijackers. Nor did the rules hastily enacted after the disaster. Three months later, the ban on box cutters and other sharp objects left the door wide open for the Shoe Bomber's attempted attack—one, it bears noting, that was ultimately prevented by alert passengers and the operative's own haplessness, not stagnant regulations.

A more subtle shortcoming of pre-9/11 security was how it discouraged responsibility in the face of failure. When something did go terribly wrong, the FAA could blame the airlines for providing insufficient security, while the airlines blamed the contractors for faulty execution. The contractors, in turn, claimed to have met the government's "specific requirements" and pass the blame back to the FAA for not setting appropriate measures. The punch line was that *all three of them could be right.* But this was cold comfort for the families of dead passengers.

At the bottom tier of this flawed system sat the frontline workers who, no matter how intelligent they might be, were generally poorly trained and working in jobs with very little chance for career advancement and no performance incentives—almost no external motivation to do anything other than not get fired. While many of the screeners were committed to what they saw as important jobs, the fact remains that on the morning of September 11, 2001, the safety of almost all of our aviation system was in the hands of people who were selected based on the minimum bid.

Despite the low per-capita wages of screeners, the bill for taking over the entire workforce's contracts was not cheap. After about a week and a half on the job, Mike Restovich, the athletic, silver-haired Secret Service veteran who had driven up from Dallas as a volunteer, walked into his boss Kevin Houlihan's makeshift office with the purchase order for the airlines' existing screening contracts. Kevin hurriedly signed it and got back to his other work. Mike started to walk away, glanced down at the purchase order, and then turned back.

"Kevin, you might want to look at this," said Mike.

Kevin glanced up from his desk. "Why? What is it?"

Mike passed the paper back over to Kevin, who stared down urgently. "What do you want me to look at?"

"Well, try that number down there," suggested Mike. "You just signed a requisition for over $800 million."

Kevin looked up, bewildered. "Do I have the authority to sign for this?"

"Ain't nobody else around I know of who's going to," said Mike flatly.

"Well . . . will you give me a copy of it?" asked Kevin.

"Yeah, that's a good idea. I'll get you a copy."

But as stunningly large as that requisition was—the TSA's entire budget at the time was around $1 billion—the agency's payroll costs continued to balloon. Soon the Office of Management and Budget, the watchdog on federal spending, began showing up every Friday to ask why we needed so many people. It was a fair question. For years, about 20,000 private employees had managed to screen the traveling public. Now we needed 30,000, and would ask for 60,000 by the end of the year. But the answer was simple: the TSA was not created to provide pre-9/11 security.

When Congress created it, the TSA was working off the estimated number of airport screeners employed in September 2001. But Congress also mandated that the agency screen every piece of checked luggage, much more than the 5 percent of bags screened previously. Even fully automated models of the massive explosive detection system (EDS) machines needed operators on one end and inspectors to hand-search suspicious bags on the other—essentially a second workforce behind the scenes.

Likewise, the TSA wasn't planning to leave the normal screener operations untouched. We wanted more screeners at checkpoints, and needed them to be motivated and focused, to help us reduce the astronomical attrition rate of private screeners (then around 125 percent annually.) We enhanced screener testing and initiated a much tougher vetting process, including a requirement that all screeners be American citizens—which eliminated a surprising amount of pre-9/11 screeners. At many airports nationwide, including Washington's Dulles, a substantial number of foreign nationals had been manning the airports' checkpoints.

The hiring and payroll process for this massive new force was outsourced to NCS Pearson, Inc., an education and testing company. Pearson rented huge military reserve facilities and sent teams from city to city to do physical exams, drug testing, and other assessments. Employing the higher standards, the applicants for screener testing had about a 40 percent washout rate.

Once the first screeners were hired, their training became not only a logistical question but also a philosophical one. Congress required at least one hundred hours of in-field training before screeners could become instructors, but we couldn't certify the first screener with nonexistent instructors. We quickly decided to ignore this circular logjam, hired an initial group of screeners in early 2002, and packed them off to Oklahoma City to train in a simulated environment. Two weeks later, the team was at Baltimore/ Washington International for their first on-the-job experience. From that "seed" group, we created a mobile screening team of 3,500 people to go around the country and begin training what eventually became a force of nearly 60,000.

At least there was no shortage of applicants. When the company the TSA hired to advertise the jobs put up their announcement online in early 2002, the flood of responses grounded all their servers. In the midst of a recession and soft job market, TSA eventually received over a million applications from people representing every walk of life, from marines to doctors to teachers to retirees.

IN MID-2002, BOB BURNS, A TALL, BEEFY MAN WITH SIDEBURNS AND A relaxed demeanor, was watching his local Cincinnati television news when an upcoming job fair was announced. After partying his way out of college, Bob had started a band called Big in Iowa, recorded several albums for a German label, and toured around playing a blend of garage and roots rock similar to that of Neil Young and The Byrds. Bob was the singer, rhythm guitarist, and default publicist for the group, but he was beginning to wonder if plowing all his money back into promoting the band was worth it. He was heading into his late twenties, he and his wife had talked about having kids, and Bob was having trouble reconciling the notion of touring and starting a family. He also recognized that he had a pretty thin résumé. He'd done a three-year stint in the army's Third Armory Division in Germany and Southwest Asia during the first Gulf War, returned and slipped from a 4.0 to a 1.9 grade-point average while failing out of school, then spent the past few years playing with his band—not exactly a prize candidate. The TSA looked like an attractive way to build that résumé while helping to protect the country, so he applied online. Soon a series of emails arrived, asking him to come to an assessment and then an orientation.

After his first week of training, Bob reported for his first day of work at Cincinnati's airport—referred to by its airport code, CVG, after nearby Covington, Kentucky—on September 11, 2002. In addition to the eeriness of starting work on that date, Bob noticed that checkpoint operations were still a bit rough a year after the attacks. But once he got his feet under him, Bob became determined to overcome his subpar qualifications by volunteering for any extra work he could do to strengthen the system.

MEANWHILE, ACROSS THE COUNTRY IN PUEBLO, COLORADO, JEREMY Trujillo, a short, muscular young man with dark hair and a quick smile, noticed an advertisement for new positions at the small local airport. He applied, got no response, and had completely forgotten about the job when he got a call out of the blue from a representative of NCS Pearson.

"Can you be in Denver on Monday?"

"Um, OK," responded Jeremy, realizing that this must be in connection with the security gig.

"You'll be there a week," explained the voice on the other end of the line. "You'll be going through a series of training exercises before we send you back to work at Pueblo Memorial Airport."

Jeremy took well to his new position at Pueblo's airport. Like Bob, he wanted a little job security and a chance to prove himself. But there were few opportunities for advancement at his small stopover, so he began volunteering to take on work in nearby Colorado Springs as well.

WE KNEW MOTIVATING THE TSA'S FRONTLINE EMPLOYEES WAS CRITICAL to the nation's safety, but we were surprised when their enthusiasm began to affect the leadership in Washington. In 2002, after an official photo-op event with the governor of Arkansas, Michael Huckabee, my colleague and DOT Deputy Secretary Michael Jackson flopped back into his seat for his return flight to DC, pulling out a notebook to get some work done. It was a tiny commuter jet, and once the plane was airborne, the woman seated across the aisle, about three feet away, looked at Michael and said, "I'm going to Washington."

"Yeah," said Michael. It was a nonstop flight; everyone was going to DC. He turned back to his work.

About two minutes later, the woman piped up again. "I'm a little nervous about flying."

"Big changes," agreed Michael. "But I think things are getting stronger. I wouldn't worry about it."

A beat later the woman added, "I got a new job."

"That's great," said Michael, annoyed. "The economy's coming back." He flipped the page of his notebook, trying to look busy while thinking, *She's gonna be a talker and I'm not going to get anything done. I don't want to be rude, but I've gotta find a way to shut her down.*

"Yeah," continued the woman, "I'm working for the Transportation Security Administration. I'm going to Norfolk, Virginia."

"Oh?" asked Michael, closing his pad. "Are you going to participate in the EDS pilot program down there?"

"Yeah, yeah, we're doing this—wait!" she stopped. "How'd you know about that pilot test?"

"Well, I work for the same company you do," explained Michael.

"Oh yeah? What do you do?"

"I'm the deputy secretary of transportation," said Michael. He could see from her face that his title was lost on her, but he'd rather hear about her anyway. She was the first TSA employee he had actually met, minus those he'd bumped into in the hallways of the DOT.

Her name was Melanie McCann, and she had dropped out of high school, had two kids, gotten divorced, and was working to get a GED. She wanted to join the Marines but had physical problems that ruled her out, so after the attacks she got a screening job in Arkansas as a way to give back to the country.

"You know, Mr. Jackson," said Melanie, "people in airports these days tend to be pretty grumpy."

"You could say that," allowed Michael.

"But," she continued, "whenever I feel like I'm getting grumpy, I straighten up, turn around, and look down toward the gate area at someone who's just left our checkpoint. I follow them for eight or ten steps, long enough to remind myself that if I do my job right, that person is going to get home tonight to be with their husband or wife or daughter or mother or friends. I think 'I've got to do this.' And I turn around, put a smile on my face, and get back to work."

Needless to say, Michael has retold that story more than once.

LATER THAT YEAR, AS THE TSA CONTINUED ASSUMING CONTROL OF LO-gan's checkpoints, Carl Maccario, the Virgin Atlantic security officer, was still not impressed by what he saw. "Mass mayhem," he muttered to himself. But soon Virgin, along with other airlines, abandoned its private security program, both because the TSA was taking over operations and because of concern about being exposed to accusations of racial profiling based on the subjective observational techniques Carl and his colleagues were using. The most obvious example of ethnic profiling is for security people to look extra hard at young Middle Eastern males because statistically, so many discovered terror plots involve them. While a data-driven analysis would say that this could make sense, there is virtually no cost for al-Qaeda to use women, the elderly, infants, and blond-haired or balding middle-aged people of any ethnicity. If spending more attention on people who appear to be young Middle Eastern males means less attention on people who look like "us," that could be a dangerous vulnerability.

Soon Carl faced a choice. He could try to stay with the Virgin security team, which was being sold to a larger outfit in New York, or apply for a job with the TSA. He chose to remain at Logan and was soon wearing a TSA uniform and working with the assembly of retired cops, PhDs, lawyers, and others who wanted to do something after the attacks. Some of Carl's new colleagues impressed him, while others were real duds. Most of the second group weeded themselves out early, at least—by doing something stupid, like bringing a gun to work, as one of them did early on.

Carl never had a problem dealing with the frequently annoyed travelers at the checkpoint. In fact, he once goaded the passengers waiting at a gate for a seriously delayed flight into singing "If You're Happy and You Know It." He wasn't naïve; he knew that standing at a checkpoint could be a monotonous job, but he didn't see any point in complaining. When colleagues griped to him in the break room, he'd say, "Hey. When you get up in the morning is there someone standing over your bed with a gun to your head? No? Well, then go get another job or quit bitching and moaning to me."

Carl also noticed that the same strong emotions that drove people to patriotic service also had a dark side. Some screeners, he told me, seemed to be waiting for someone "with a turban and a bomb to jump out from around the corner." For months after September 2001, there were threats, assaults, and even shootings attributed to racial motivations. In Carl's hometown, cops stood watch outside the wastewater treatment facility—thought to be a potential target—with shotguns. During its early grappling with the full threat of terrorism, the nation chased solutions good, bad, and unsustainable. Screeners were not immune to this destructive fervor.

Though he had thrown in his lot with the TSA, Carl's negative opinion of the efficacy of the checkpoints didn't change, even after a few months at his new job. Beyond the lackluster operations, he also felt the TSA had an obsessive, blinkered focus on technology. There was a machine for every problem—or maybe a problem for every machine. He had seen during his time with Virgin how well engaging people in conversations worked in picking out suspicious characters, so the TSA's singular technological bent frustrated him. After all, the Israelis, world leaders in passenger interviewing and behavior recognition, hadn't had a hijacking in decades, and their system relied much more heavily on human interaction than technology. During his research, Carl had come across a professor named Paul Ekman, one of the recognized experts in reading people's emotional states as well as the inspiration for the TV show *Lie to Me*, who told Carl that the "best machine to find a guilty person is another person," because "you've been through every emotion already." But, as Carl found out, behavioral science was a tough sell. It was much easier to tell the public and Congress, "Hey, this thing's got lights and wires, it detects things and it creates jobs."

The checkpoints' bag-scanning technology at that time produced horrible-quality images, too. Much of a screener's workday involved peering at a dim screen on the legacy x-ray equipment, trying to make out vague shapes, and then ordering a check on any bag that might have wires or something opaque. Screeners were not encouraged to use their observational skills. Leaving a shift one day, Carl thought, *You could walk through this checkpoint in a ball of flames and so long as you didn't set off an alarm, you'd still get on a plane.*

What screeners were encouraged to do was follow the rules laid out in a one-hundred-page manual simply referred to as the Standard Operating Procedure, or SOP, which outlined every checkpoint technique from scanning procedures to addressing passengers to conducting a pat down. The initial idea behind the SOP—to create some sort of common operational framework for airports across the country—made sense. But continually providing good security isn't the same as opening a McDonald's franchise and then just making sure you don't run out of French fries. The SOP's demands for precise uniformity quickly dampened the enthusiasm of new screeners, who felt that under it their function was little more than a robot's.

In fact, by focusing on narrow and inflexible security measures like meticulously searching passenger's luggage in order to remove all butane lighters, keychain jackknives, or sharp objects larger than a pin, the SOP encouraged these newly minted TSA employees to evolve along the same lines as the old FAA regulatory system. Screeners were again trained to look for yesterday's threat according to an SOP imposed from above, leaving little operational flexibility. If something went wrong, a screener would be absolved of personal responsibility as long as she or he had followed the SOP to the letter. As long as the screener meticulously observed the written procedures, everybody all the way up the chain was off the hook. Individual initiative outside the lines was unprotected and dangerous territory even if security was not compromised.

The more time Carl spent at the checkpoints, the more this unswerving fealty to a manual in an operationally complex environment struck him as both funny and scary. One day he watched a guy walk through a metal detector, look up at the security camera, and pull his hat down over his face, obviously evasive behavior. He turned to his manager, and said, "Someone's got to talk to that guy."

"Did the alarm go off?" asked the manager.

"No," said Carl.

"Then let him go."

That by-the-book mentality played out in the other direction as well. Another day, the screener positioned at the carry-on baggage x-ray machine hit the stop button and called him over: "We've got a suspect item in the tunnel."

Carl looked over at the bag's owner in line, a father waiting with his two little girls.

The father began, "I think that's . . ."

"Don't touch anything, sir," warned the screener. "Do *not* touch anything." He then called over the state police Explosive Ordnance Detection officer, the man tasked with confirming and disposing of any suspected bombs.

The father tried again. "I think it's my . . ."

The line was now stopped and Carl peeked at the image on the screen, which showed an object with wires and power supply that looked like a portable compact-disc player. A minute later, the explosives officer pulled out the offending object: a pink Dora the Explorer bag with one of the girls' Discman inside.

Carl fumed. The father was with his daughters, everything about the scene made sense and there were no warning signs of deception or alert on the man's part, and he was also completely calm while the bag was being searched. But the TSA mindset was to focus on the items, not the people carrying them. It reminded Carl of the classic Three Stooges sketch in which Moe looks sternly at Curly and asks, "What are you doing?"

"I'm thinking," replies Curly.

"What'd I tell you about thinking?" retorts Moe. "Every time you think, you weaken the nation!" The SOP, in effect, sent Moe's message to the TSA's entire frontline workforce.

Nevertheless, Carl found ways to rely on his own techniques. During his shift one day scanning bags in the x-ray tunnel, he saw what looked like a jumble of wires and two prongs. He turned to the screener who was checking bags and said, "Check that one." After a brief search, she pulled out a Taser.

"Gimme that thing," said Carl.

"That's mine," argued the passenger.

"You can't have this on a plane," said Carl. "Do you have any more of these things in your bag?"

"No?" replied the passenger with upward tilt to his head.

"Check his bag again," said Carl.

By this point, the Assistant Federal Security Director for screening, Carl's boss' boss, had arrived. "I thought you said you already checked the bag," he said.

"We did," said Carl, "but when I asked that guy if he had anything else in his bag he said 'No,' but the answer was 'Yes'—he nodded his head at the same time."

The screener checked the bag again and found Taser components with a range of thirty and fifty feet.

"Jesus, Carl," said the AFSD.

"You can't turn it off," said Carl, smiling.

CARL WAS A TALENTED SCREENER BUT, DESPITE HIS EXPERIENCE AT VIR-
gin, he had started with the TSA at the base-level position and salary. One
day, a number of the Federal Security Directors, or FSDs—the people in
charge of operations at various airports around the country—visited Logan,
passing through Carl's checkpoint. That night he went home and told his
wife, "By the time I'm done, they're going to know who I am."

FIVE

AFTER THE PARTY

AFTER THE EUPHORIA OF MEETING ALL OF ITS MANDATES BY
New Year's Eve 2002, TSA woke up with an organizational hangover. The
unconventional, nonhierarchical, and results-oriented approach that got the
organization on its feet had left the agency with very little infrastructure and
some real accounting nightmares. And although the airport screeners had
been successfully hired, trained, and deployed on schedule, the human resources operation kept getting uglier.

By 2003, Bill Hall, the veteran of the World Trade Center evacuation
during 9/11, had moved over from the Port Authority to become the Federal
Security Director at John F. Kennedy airport in Queens, New York. His old
contacts came in handy, though. One morning in 2002 Bill received a call
from a friend at the New York Police Department: "Bill, I'm trying to confirm
a guy's story. We found him sleeping on a park bench downtown. He says he's
got a job with you and starts today." Turns out the new screener had drove
in the night before from his home in Illinois and didn't have a place to sleep.

JFK was one of the first airports to be fully federalized, so Bill experienced the full force of the TSA's growing pains. After getting his workforce
on board, Bill was trying to figure out how to keep them. Across the country
there were screeners who hadn't been paid for weeks, some who'd mortgaged
their houses while waiting for a paycheck, and others who, after waiting for a
check, simply quit on principle.

Bill arranged for a representative of NCS Pearson, the company in charge of hiring and payroll, to meet with employees so they could ask questions and hopefully find some solutions. The meeting was well attended; quite a few people weren't getting paid, and the event nearly tipped out of control with people yelling, "You owe me money!" as the hapless Pearson spokesman tried to drown them out.

When the meeting was over, Bill went over to the company's representative. "Why don't you meet with some of these people face-to-face?"

The man looked back at Bill and shook his head. "Sorry, there's not enough time. I fly back to Washington tonight; I don't even have a shirt or clean underwear."

Bill turned to his assistant. "Hey, Sal," he barked. "Take this man to Kmart and get him some underwear and a shirt because he's not leaving 'til he talks to everybody."

"You can't do that," protested the Pearson rep.

"Just watch me."

He stayed on for two more days, meeting with everyone who couldn't get paid and giving them a receipt noting the complaint. But the problem was bigger than anything a few town-hall meetings or proactive FSDs like Bill could handle. By the end of 2002, the TSA put Pearson's massive contract up for rebid. Accenture won it and tapped its employee, Stephanie Rowe, the old friend of the agency, to confront this enormous task.

A veteran of the asbestos-contaminated General Services Administration basement and a key player in the reinvention of the checkpoint at Baltimore/Washington International, Stephanie had worked with the TSA almost from the agency's beginning. By the end of 2002, she was exhausted. She thought Accenture was crazy for wanting the job. But she had thirty days before her company took over in January 2003, and there was an office to set up. So in late 2002, Stephanie walked into the Reston, Virginia, building that would become the TSA's personnel processing center. She was greeted by a nearly empty room with a few desks and no computers. This was just the tip of the iceberg.

Throughout 2003, TSA's human resources mess continued to unravel. Pearson had run up hundreds of millions of dollars in excess costs. Incorrect information in databases meant that some current employees weren't getting paid while other "ghost employees" still were (Stephanie still wonders where some of that money went). And the messy expenses were somehow leaked to the media, who pounced on the juicier episodes, including a Pearson conference held at a ski resort. The pricey holiday venue was selected primarily to schedule a last-minute meeting in a location with necessary infrastructure, like armed guards and T1 lines. But in stories like *USA Today*'s July 15, 2003 article "TSA contractor spending under scrutiny," the message much of the country picked up on was that the TSA was putting posh lodging ahead of homeland security.

Stephanie and her team also had enormous difficulty communicating with the tens of thousands of employees in the field. There was no phone or email distribution list to contact the 450 airports; only the FSD at each airport had a known email address; and at some airports, the TSA didn't even have a dedicated computer or phone. Stephanie couldn't make the necessary fixes—for example, updating and correcting personnel data so the right people got paid—without some direct contact with the frontline workers. Hamstrung, she resorted to a completely paper-based process. Stephanie printed thousands of forms, stuffed more than 400 of these "care packages," and FedExed them to FSDs across the country. But the job wasn't done. At most airports, the distribution of information relied on one or two people in upper management to get the word out to staff that could number in the hundreds, all working multiple shifts on various weekly schedules. To verify that people were actually receiving the hard copies they had mailed, Accenture employees traveled to the airports—not exactly a cutting-edge model of data transfer in 2003.

Stephanie then begged the TSA's human resources manager to have an open conference call with the airport-based human resource and administrative officers around the country. The HR manager was reticent; he feared the call might result in pointed or direct questions that they couldn't answer. In fact, he wasn't comfortable with any communications that might slip beyond the TSA leadership's control. And he was not alone: The top-down flow of information was part and parcel of the bureaucracy becoming increasingly dominant within TSA. In this case, Stephanie eventually prevailed, and the series of conference calls opened the door for small problems in isolated field locations to get back to headquarters for action before they spread agency-wide. They were reminiscent of the end-of-day meetings from TSA's earliest days: an open forum with open dialogue, where people could state their progress, address their problems, ask questions, and work together to find solutions. But this type of interaction was becoming increasingly rare.

ONE DAY IN 2004, LEE KAIR, A TALL, CORPORATE-LOOKING MAN IN HIS thirties, with dark brown hair and a relentless grin, walked into his new job as the TSA's chief procurement officer to find a crowd of Defense Contract Audit Agency personnel poring over roomfuls of invoices and contracts. That wiped the smile off his face and would later gray his hair.

Lee had been brought in to help clean up the TSA's accounting and procurement mess, a knotted heap of problems that went well beyond the payment debacle with which Stephanie had been tasked. During the TSA's standup, lots of contractors had gone about spending hundreds of millions of dollars based on what were somewhat oxymoronically called "undefinitized contracts." These were basically loose agreements in which the TSA said, "Here's what we need done, don't spend more than this amount," and the contractor went off to do the work without much oversight, expecting to be paid in the future. Now the government auditors reviewing these opaque records were trying to figure out what the contractors had spent, what they had delivered, and what costs were allowable before recommending how much the TSA should pay the companies to settle, or "definitize," the agreements.

By the time Lee arrived at the TSA from the Department of Homeland Security, he had logged over a decade in procurement, almost all of it with the federal government. He had loved planes since his childhood on Sanibel Island, off the coast of Florida, and of course he wanted to help keep the nation safe. But he couldn't deny that his new agency was an accounting disaster.

The TSA was started by people who thrived in chaotic and demanding environments, including John Magaw, its first leader, who earned the fierce loyalty of his team but ran afoul of the complex conflicting relationships among the agency's stakeholders and overseers in Congress and the administration. Magaw, once described as possessing the arms of a stevedore and the wardrobe of a CEO, had embedded bedrock values in the nascent agency and successfully melded disparate people from all over to focus as a team, but left TSA after just six months at the helm in June 2002. The just-retired Coast Guard Commandant, Jim Loy, who had a deep wellspring of support around town replaced Magaw. Loy led TSA through the completion of ATSA's deadlines and, in 2003, shepherded TSA into the newly formed Department of Homeland Security. He was subsequently promoted and Loy was DHS Deputy Secretary until Michael Jackson arrived on the scene in early 2005.

TSA experienced high turnover not just at the top. While many who left were underperformers, TSA lost some top talent who got fed up with the chaos and just left. But the truth was that the skills needed at TSA probably changed after the initial burst of energy in 2002. Many of the high quality, results-oriented pioneers who got the agency on its feet might have been lost in a more structured environment. What might be called the "core businesses" of the TSA—the 50,000 airport screeners, for one—were in place, but the infrastructure was either ad hoc or nonexistent. And it was now up to people like Lee to make the transition from start-up to steady state. He had to design a sustainable structure for the future, real accounting, a competent HR department, and to update checkpoint equipment and technology from the 1980s holdovers. The question for Lee was, "Where are we going to be in ten years?"

IN THE SUMMER OF 2002, ANDREW COX, A SLIGHT, UNASSUMING twenty-four-year-old with wavy black hair, quit his job at a DC–area IT firm to play jazz bass on the streets of Europe. Taking off with a musician buddy he'd grown up with in Raleigh, North Carolina, seemed to him an excellent way to escape his less than thrilling job in tech support and computer programming.

In Europe, he had two unsurprising realizations. First, while he might not starve as a street musician, it wasn't exactly lucrative. Neither, for that matter, was playing jazz anywhere, except for a lucky few who struck gold. So that fall Andrew briefly returned to his old job, limited himself to gigging once a week at local clubs, and began studying public policy at George Mason University. A little over a year later, walking out of class one day, he noticed a posting for a program analyst at the TSA. He sent off a paper he'd written at his old job, was hired, and began work there in May 2004.

At TSA headquarters, Andrew worked alongside a group of people with the jumble of backgrounds that typify the still-evolving field of transportation security: ex-Coast Guard employees, former ship captains, security providers at shipping companies or railroads. But much of Andrew's job was to travel around the country and evaluate Homeland Security training exercises. In one simulation, a dirty bomb was detonated in a port, requiring a coordinated response effort from the TSA, the Coast Guard, and Customs and Border Protection, plus local shipping, trucking, and transit companies, as well as city and state authorities. It was up to Andrew to determine the yardstick by which their performance should be measured.

It was on one of these exercises in Portland, Oregon, that Andrew came in contact with a few ex-Coast Guard officers who completely changed his way of thinking about transportation security. Instead of just focusing on specific assets—a boat, a shipping depot, a railway line—he began considering the larger system in which those parts functioned. In contrast to the single-minded response then prevalent at the TSA, Andrew began seeing the importance of managing the massive, interlinked transportation system to maximize its strengths, an approach known as network theory. Suddenly he was engaged in his work on an exciting new level.

Andrew began educating himself on the security applications of network theory, drafting memos and short papers he circulated within the TSA, none of which registered with his superiors. After the agency's wild first year, to many TSA staffers, "organizational maturation" meant modeling the agency on the same bureaucratic command structure prevalent in the Federal Aviation Administration, military, and the federal government. Ideas flowed down, not up. Andrew's papers were broad and strategic, unrelated to the operational and hypertactical concerns of upper management, and he gained absolutely no traction within the organization.

It is ironic that one of the dangers Andrew was trying to flag for his superiors was the precariousness of highly centralized, inflexible systems like the TSA's stratified chain of command. For example, the stock market or national power grid are two structures that share many of the same vulnerabilities. Electricity flows to millions of individual consumers from a relative handful of power plants. There is a low probability of failure, so normally the system works as intended and power flows unimpeded. But when there is a major disruption in the grid, the collapse is tremendous, much worse than it would be in a system based on many smaller, dispersed plants. Likewise, millions of stockholders expect and earn fairly regular returns on their investments. But because our financial system is tightly centralized, one big failure can drag the whole system down with it, destroying billions of dollars in value worldwide and leaving many individuals financially ruined.

Andrew saw the vulnerabilities inherent in the FAA's regulatory approach to aviation security. Its model was top-down, slow moving, inflexible, and binary: it either worked exactly as planned or suffered horrible failures. The TSA, the agency birthed specifically to prevent another massive failure like 9/11, apparently hadn't taken the lessons of the past to heart. Frontline screeners performed their duties within the narrow confines of the Standard Operating Procedure. Checkpoint security was focused on stopping the banned items like knives and guns that had previously been used for hijackings. Andrew knew that to get ahead of the terrorists, what the TSA actually needed to do was innovate. The time lapse between thought and action had to be lightning-fast. But instead of allowing new ideas to percolate upwards, the idea-killing bureaucracy trapped Andrew in its stubborn maw.

Outside of the TSA, other groups had intuited the advantages of an adaptable approach with more operational flexibility. The open-source Linux computer operating system is a classic example of success predicated on a system being readily available for local adaptation. Linux relies on a large number of geographically dispersed and often anonymous contributors, a nonhierarchical mode that has made the system much more resilient in the face of failures. More ominously, another group had learned these same lessons: al-Qaeda. The radical Islamist terror organization had successfully spun off indigenous groups in Iraq, Indonesia, Germany, Britain, and elsewhere, making it hard to track, let alone squelch the larger network. The group was innovative, quick moving, and opportunistic. And while al-Qaeda certainly had a hierarchy, there was nothing resembling a bureaucracy. Many operatives were supported without having their efforts micromanaged.

A horrifying illustration of these efforts came just a few months before Andrew began at TSA. On March 11, 2004, al-Qaeda–inspired militants carried out a series of coordinated bombings against Madrid's commuter train system, killing nearly 200 people and wounding 1,800. If Spanish security officials had been focused on suspicious-looking Egyptians, Saudis, or Pakistanis, they would have missed these Moroccans, a more locally integrated nationality and as-yet-unused operatives in al-Qaeda–linked attacks. Moreover, two members of the Spain's Guardia Civil police force were also implicated in the plot. The devices employed in the attack were a collection of rudimentary backpack bombs with a plastic explosive and detonator, but the effectiveness of even this simple operation suggested that a sluggish bureaucracy might have a hard time keeping pace with innovations.

MEANWHILE, LATER IN 2004 AND BACK IN THE USA, THE TSA HAD FInally found a home in two dark brown corporate-looking towers in Arlington, Virginia. And while Andrew was in his office on the tenth floor of the east building, Lee Kair and Joe Salvator, the stocky ex-Marine who had been drafted into the FAA's nascent counterterrorism unit, were now TSA employees sitting in a sixth-floor conference room and getting an earful on the agency's operations. Every morning, the agency's entire senior leadership, roughly thirty people, crammed into a sensitive compartmented information facility (SCIF) and reviewed a logbook that noted every incident at every airport in the United States. For three hours, Lee and Joe listened to the head of intel go through details like this:

> *At 02:11 hours on May 23, an Oakland TSA Operations officer reported that at 23:10 hours on May 22 Southwest 142 OAK/PHX passenger Michael McGrady (DOB 8/10/80) stepped on a toothpick while entering the WTMD* [walk-through metal detector]. *The toothpick was embedded in McGrady's foot. EMTs responded and took McGrady to the hospital for treatment. There was no impact on airport operations or media interest.*

Reports might also cover such disturbances as two drunk passengers on a United Airlines flight who began elbowing each other in a dispute over a shared armrest, a single pocketknife confiscated by security, a passenger in Burbank warning that his checked baggage was very valuable and if it did not arrive he would "kill someone," an incidence of vandalism to an EDS machine in Tampa, or an "artfully concealed lipstick knife" with a one-inch blade.

In addition to almost never hearing anything interesting or useful in the meetings, Joe found the conference room uncomfortable and intimidating. The administrator, the TSA's third in three years, was David Stone, a youthful looking, athletic former US Navy admiral and the first federal security director at Los Angeles International. The traditional head-of-the-table position in the cramped room put him right in front of the door so that others had to squeeze right behind the boss if they needed a "bio break" over the course of the three-hour meetings.

Not only was it hard to step out of the room, it was hard to enter the conversation. The head of intel, a decorated former general, would read the daily intelligence logbook while another agent might switch slides; there was very little back-and-forth during the meetings. Discussions tended to be along the lines of "Someone brought a knife to a checkpoint in Seattle? OK, who was that person? How old are they? Where are they from? Is there any record of them? How big was the knife? How sharp was it?" Sitting on the tenth floor, Andrew Cox had no idea that these meetings existed, but they bore out perfectly his fears surrounding the TSA's reactive focus on narrow tactical approaches.

To follow up on some incidents, the leadership would call the airports and ask for more details. For example, if a shell casing was reported found in the bottom of a carry-on bag in Dallas, someone in the crowded briefing room might say, "Wait a minute, wasn't there another shell casing in Denver last week? It was a .40-caliber. That's an unusual size." Then someone from TSA headquarters might call up Dallas/Fort Worth International and ask, "Was that the only shell casing? What manufacturer was it—Remington or Winchester? It's important, the one in Denver was a Remington round."

These questions often struck the frontline workers as ridiculous. *I saw the gym bag,* they'd think. *He had a shell casing in his bag, but so what? This is Texas. He picked up the wrong bag. He's not a terrorist.* It was communication of a kind, yet the obsessive demand for information of no consequence only served to hurt the credibility of the TSA's headquarters leadership with the people in the field.

The stagnant daily ops-and-intel meetings also reflected a more generalized inward turn for TSA. Almost at its inception, the new agency assumed the most prominent and hands-on role with the public of any branch of the government. What other federal organization has employees that interact with you *every single time* you walk through an airport? The TSA knew this public exposure could lead very quickly to intense criticism. After all, within weeks of the agency's creation, Secretary Mineta's honest comment that he didn't know exactly how TSA would meet its first deadline had unleashed the first of innumerable firestorms from the media and Congress.

The agency's initial launch wasn't popular in airports, either. Bill Hall remembered the hostile reactions the TSA first got as it set up operations at Kennedy. Some mornings he came in to find a piece of TSA equipment damaged, unplugged, or spray-painted with "TSA Go Home!" Only airport employees had access at those hours and, until matters were eventually smoothed out, the disapproving message was painfully clear. The agency was also constantly scrutinized by the Government Accountability Organization and was the regular target of Internet conspiracy theorists. By 2004, after two years of being kicked around, the agency's primary focus was on what it could control: information on checkpoint operations. But these ops-and-intel meetings also marked a spreading feeling of hopelessness within TSA.

The daily marathons that consumed the mornings of most of the top brass were also piped into a room on the TSA's secure sixth floor for the lower-level intelligence personnel to follow. But for these people, who were tracking al-Qaeda and other terror threats as best they could, the meetings produced very little of what could reasonably be called "intel." Two million people passed through America's airports a day; of course there were going to be incidents. But it was the hundreds of people training at terrorist camps in Pakistan or recruiting new operatives in England who were the real threat, and they were absent from the TSA radar.

ON MARCH 8, 2005, FRANCOIS LAMOUREUX, A FIFTY-NINE YEAR OLD Frenchman with silvering hair and reading glasses called up a Slovenian minister-level official named Marjeta Jager to offer her a job as a senior official within his department, the European Commission's Transport and Energy portfolio. Watching on from his director general's perch, Lamoureux had been impressed by Marjeta's energy, intellect, and the sheer merciless perseverance while negotiating Slovenia's entry into the EU the previous year. For her part, Marjeta, over two decades Lamoreux's junior, saw the career advancement as risky. She was already a major player within Slovenia's representation at the EU and knew that accepting Lamoureux's offer meant she'd be bound to the Brussels-based organization, possibly for life. Lamoureux's call had come coincidentally on International Women's Day, but gender mainstreaming in the EU was often more talk than practice, and Marjeta would be working in an organization otherwise dominated by older men from longstanding EU nations. Nonetheless, Lamoureux was compelling, had the fresh energy of someone half his age, and was a brilliant conceptual thinker.

In his capacity as head of transportation security, Lamoureux set mandatory procedures for member states like the UK, Germany, and France but he was frustrated with the United States, a diffident partner in aviation security. At times Lamoureux perceived the United States as not just vehemently disagreeing with certain EU policies, but treating the huge block of nations with outright disregard. He wanted to change that equation and hiring a security director like Marjeta, someone who was impossible to ignore, was part of that strategy. Marjeta accepted his offer and three days later, a Friday, left her office as Slovenia's Deputy Representative to the EU. She arrived Monday as a senior EU official, carrying a four by three foot framed photograph of former Yugoslavian President Josip Tito's black Bentley limousine, a parting gift from her Slovenian colleagues. Struggling with the huge picture, Marjeta, who only stood about 5' 2", then found the door to her new office was locked, and the interior was dark and empty. After momentarily second guessing her decision, Marjeta made some calls and within a few hours got her office open, well-lit, and staffed with two secretaries on staggered shifts.

WHEN ABDULRAHMAN HILAL HUSSEIN RETURNED HOME TO VIENNA from Cairo in the spring of 2004, his family was scattered. His mother, Samia, had divorced his father and moved back to Egypt, while his father was busy tending to his Europe-wide religious network. Abdulrahman's brother Ahmad was also back in Egypt; his sisters were still relatively nearby in Austria. But even if Vienna wasn't the same place he'd left a few years earlier, Abdulrahman's concept of home had changed during the last three years. Abdulrahman had made several trips during his student years to a growing Salafist center in southern Germany. Through his interaction with the older scholars and young German recruits there, he found a spiritual home. And he was ready to start his own family with Sonja Blinzler, a German convert to Islam in her late thirties, whom he'd met at the mosque earlier that year. They were married on June 1, 2004, and nine months later, on March 1, 2005, the firstborn son of Abdulrahman, himself a firstborn, arrived.

Abdulrahman also started working soon after his return to Vienna. His skills would have made him a strong applicant to the numerous technology-intensive companies headquartered around Vienna, but he wasn't looking for that kind of job. Instead, Abdulrahman had a mission: realizing the radical teachings of his Salafi jihadist scholars in Egypt and Germany. Once his son and heir was born, Abdulrahman was ready to be a warrior.

Also on March 1, 2005, the day Abdulrahman Hilal Hussein pledged to pursue violent jihad, the TSA announced that it would ban lighters from passenger aircraft. The measure was intended to prevent terrorists from lighting the wicks on bombs, but for Abdulrahman, a resourceful, technically skilled and patient man, this new rule would not present much of a challenge.

Initially he worked his network of friends and mosques near Vienna to recruit a team that he could take to Pakistan and train. Through his father's Ayman Zawahiri connections and people he had met in Egypt and Germany, he already knew he was being groomed for big things. He was a native-born Austrian with verified European Union travel documents. Now twenty-two years old, Abdulrahman bore a bit of a resemblance to the movie star Nicolas

Cage. He spoke fluent German, English, and Arabic, and he was not even a blip on the security authorities' radar—a key criterion for senior al-Qaeda leaders in evaluating future talent.

With this impressive résumé and pedigree, Abdulrahman could attract a top al-Qaeda sponsor once he got his group of young Austrians together. Just underneath Ayman Zawahiri in al-Qaeda's management structure was another Egyptian named Abu Hamza Rabia, the man charged with major operations against Western targets in Europe, the UK, and the United States. Abu Hamza Rabia soon would take note of Abdulrahman.

SIX

YESTERDAY'S AGENCY

BY EARLY 2005, THE TSA WAS BEING REGULARLY THRASHED
in the media. It hunkered down; its only defenders seemed to be at TSA itself. As Sara Kehaulani Goo reported in the February 9, 2005, edition of the
Washington Post, "The Transportation Security Administration, the primary
government agency entrusted with protecting travelers from terrorist attacks
aboard commercial airliners, faces a large-scale dismantling under President
Bush's 2006 budget proposal." Just two years after the agency assumed full
responsibility for transportation security, the wave of negative publicity and
the resultant institutional inertia at the TSA was so damaging that large and
formerly supportive sectors of the government were ready to scrap it and
start over.

But I was back in California, fully occupied with things like long runs
around my scenic surroundings, going on dates with my wife, Janet, enjoying
work, and being home for my younger son's junior year of high school. I'd
done my spell at the TSA, but that seemed distant and I rarely thought about
the agency except when I traveled, and I thought TSA was doing just fine.

In February 2005, I got a call from Michael Jackson. He'd just moved
over to the two-year-old Department of Homeland Security as the deputy
secretary. Michael was an old friend and I didn't think twice about going
out to Washington for a chat with him and to meet his new boss, Secretary
Michael Chertoff, who had taken over from the department's first secretary,

Tom Ridge, that month. I knew that TSA had organizational problems and, since the agency had been transferred from the Department of Transportation to the DHS in 2003, it was once again Michael's responsibility. But before leaving California, I decided that I would volunteer for a few weeks at DHS headquarters, perhaps stay with the Jacksons again, but if something else came up, I would decline anything more than that.

In Washington I got a chance to catch up with old friends, including Ashley Cannatti, my friend and invaluable assistant from the TSA start-up days, who was now counselor to the deputy secretary and had an office at DHS directly outside Secretary Chertoff's. We chatted about her adorable baby daughter until Chertoff was ready for me, and I passed through his office door into the unyielding gaze of his eyes. Secretary Chertoff was about my age, lean, and bald, with sharp features that accentuated his alert brown eyes. Withering under the laserlike focus of his stare for the first time, I stumbled backwards slightly and plunked down on a couch. He was an intense, fast talking, and brilliant former federal appellate judge, someone with qualifications on the level of a Supreme Court nominee. He didn't parse words or pussyfoot around, launching straight into an analytical discussion of what strategic changes he wanted to make at the DHS and the TSA. Michael Jackson was also in the room, but he didn't get a word in edgewise—the only time I'd ever witnessed that.

Chertoff's rapid-fire pitch revolved around a compelling approach to security predicated on the use of a combination of threat, vulnerability, and consequence as a framework for risk management. I'd just read a speech he'd given on the topic and although the meeting moved quickly, I was with him every step. My private-sector experience and familiarity with transportation and information networks were a natural fit with Chertoff's orientation. After forty-five minutes, I left his office and shut myself back in Ashley's office. "I *love* that guy," I said as I sat down. But although I felt we were on the same page, and Chertoff had laid out a good case for a revitalized TSA, I still didn't want to leave California and I hadn't been offered a job.

Before leaving town, I had breakfast at the Old Ebbitt Grill, the domain of the DC power lunch, with Ralph Basham, another friend from the early days who had left the TSA in 2004 to become director of the Secret Service. Ralph has perfected the ability to maintain a modest and unassuming appearance until he delivers a brutal blow. Just after my scrambled Egg Beaters, whole-wheat toast, and tiny strips of bacon arrived, Ralph lowered the hammer.

As I was describing how much I was looking forward to being home during my son Chris's senior year of high school, Ralph cut me off. "Kip, there are a lot of dads in Iraq and Afghanistan who are missing their kids' school years, so don't sing me the blues about that. It's your turn to serve and you need to step up. The TSA didn't need you last year and they might not need you next year, but they sure as hell need you now. Kip, it's your turn to serve the country; you've got to do it." At "Afghanistan," I started folding my napkin. By the time he had finished, the restaurant's wood-stained interior had faded away and I was left wordlessly waving the napkin around, the white flag of surrender. A week or so later I was offered the job.

Back home, Janet, Chris, and I discussed my career change, and both were unequivocal: "Don't let us hold you back. We'll just call that our way of serving. It's an honor, go do it." So, after being formally nominated for the post of TSA administrator by the White House in May 2005, I moved into Pentagon Row, an apartment building situated on top of a horseshoe ring of restaurants and cafés around a green courtyard. Directly opposite, at the intersection of South Hayes and Twelfth Street South near a mall grandly named "The Fashion Centre at Pentagon City" sat the TSA headquarters. The job seemed a good fit for my experience, especially considering that I had been present at the birth of TSA and knew its history well. I also felt I had the advantages of great air cover at DHS in Chertoff and Jackson and, since I'd been in the field for more than twenty years, reasonable support from the transportation industry. I expected to work insane hours, do some restructuring, apply metrics, and narrow the focus. My experience told me that it would take a solid year before real change would sink in, and then another year to get to where Chertoff wanted it. It was hard work, but the cause couldn't have been more important. My radar was tweaked a little when I went on my first round of Senate courtesy calls and heard from one senior Republican member of the Commerce, Science, and Transportation Committee that he was getting tired of having people like me come around every year and promise to fix TSA: "I'll be surprised if you're still here in a year."

ONE DAY IN MID-MAY 2005, ABOUT TEN MONTHS AFTER SHE'D STARTED working at the TSA's policy shop, Alison Clyde was late for work and in a bad mood. She'd been house sitting, had a sinus infection, and was already sweating in the unusually hot May morning. By a quarter past nine, when Alison got up to the seventh floor, one of the executive assistants pounced on her, yelling, "Where have you been?"

"I don't feel well," said Alison. "Why? What's going on?"

"They're waiting for you in the conference room!"

Really? thought Alison. *I'm a lowly policy analyst. Is this some sort of joke?* Confused, she ambled over to a corner office in her flip-flops and opened the door. Inside were four people in deep discussion—her immediate boss, her boss's boss, two other people she worked with, and a guy she'd never seen before (me). She quietly took a seat, waiting for a cue.

"What would you do about air cargo policy?" I asked the man sitting next to her.

He answered in a crisp military cant. "Yes, sir. The TSA's policy is to leverage the Known Shipper program with the development of the Freight Assessment System and introduce a risk-basis rubric to cargo screening. We are also monitoring the industry on their obligation to triple the amount of packages they screen, sir." His answer was so letter-perfect that I wondered if he had authored my briefing book.

I turned to Alison and said, "What would you do about this policy decision?"

She started to dutifully recite the TSA's official policy. Having played this game before, I cut her off. "No, I asked what *you* would do about this policy."

"Oh," she replied. "I'd nix that. I'd do it this way."

For the next ten minutes her bosses looked on wide-eyed as Alison contradicted one TSA policy after another. I ate it up. At the end of the meeting I stood up and shook her hand. "Hi. I'm Kip Hawley."

After the meeting, Alison's boss approached her and made sure she was aware how badly she'd screwed up any chance of becoming assistant to the administrator-to-be. She shrugged and went back to work. Later, walking to her car, Alison received a call on her cell phone asking her to return to the office. She wondered if she had been fired, but when told that she would be my new aide, she instead wondered what was wrong with me.

Alison arrived at the TSA simply because she had needed a job, but her résumé intrigued me. She'd earned a degree in third-world studies at Sewanee, a small Tennessee school with castlelike buildings sitting in the middle of a forest on top of mountain: "Harry Potter, without the robes," as she described it. She then worked three years at CNN's national desk in Atlanta (remarkably, her first day on the job was 9/11). I figured this work experience had taught her how to operate in the manic pace of a newsroom. After a few years in Atlanta, she left to pursue a master's degree in international relations at the Saint John's University campus in Rome, where she also did charitable work. Even after she arrived at the TSA, she continued to present papers at academic conferences on such topics as "Diplomacy and its Place in the Post-9/11 World." And after she showed up to our meeting late and wearing flip-flops but relatively undaunted, I knew she was somewhat iconoclastic. But her academic interests also signaled a curious, intellectual bent, unlike the strictly contained linear thinking that I feared had become ingrained at TSA. While I was waiting to be confirmed, I was allowed one assistant to bring me up to speed, and wanted it to be her.

Alison admittedly had no idea what an assistant did, but as a policy analyst, she knew how to plug me into the big machine that pulled expert advice out of a dark reservoir crowded with acronyms. Alison's job in the policy office had been creating TSA's official line on various issues. As she churned out "q-fers," or questions for the record, which are intended to guide TSA leadership during congressional inquiries, she got up to speed on the ins and outs of aviation security. But by the time I brought her on board, she was sick of spending her days that way.

PARTIALLY TO KEEP ME FROM BEING A DISTRACTION FOR THE OUTGO-ing management at TSA in advance of my Senate confirmation hearing as the new administrator, I was given an office in the old General Services Administration building, the same run-down facility where TSA's old start-up team had resided three years earlier. But once ensconced, a parade of TSA experts appeared in my doorway to instruct me in the finer points of budget and policy. I was trying to gauge the existing leadership team and get a consensus on our priorities going forward, but these meetings often left me feeling like a freshman being tutored on how to get around campus. One longtime department head handed me a large binder and then kept directing me back to its tabs during our discussion. I flashed back to the ill-fated meeting during which Walter Pankow kept trying to lead Michael Jackson down the prescribed PowerPoint course. Because my vision for the TSA lay outside the prepared material, the institution gently attempted to guide me back to the "correct" path: In this world, there *were* right answers. And since the agency was so accustomed to being criticized, the normal alarms failed to go off when Congress, the media, or the public dismissed the agency's circular talking points as bureaucratic double-talk. It was simply business as usual.

I decided to use some of my preconfirmation time to poke around the status quo. I asked for a meeting with the website team since I knew that the TSA's web presence needed a radical overhaul. I also knew that once confirmed I wouldn't have the time for web design—but I did for the moment. The website at the time was stiff and impenetrable, and worse, the team's proposed new digital architecture was about as simple as Bismarck's theory of statehood in nineteenth-century Europe. I suggested that they log on to the Apple website, the industry standard for user-friendly interfaces, and mine it for ideas. Then, I decided silently, should I get confirmed by the Senate, to ask the group's outsider—a graphic artist who was about to leave for a design job in New York—to lead the project.

One Sunday morning I hosted another mass-transit strategy meeting that quickly went sideways. Because we were convening outside normal office hours, the GSA's lights and air conditioning were in the energy-saving "off" position. Maybe roasting in the dark just put me in a bad mood, but it didn't help when I was informed by another one of the experts that further developing the TSA's then-limited role in mass transit was off the table. Increasing our involvement meant navigating gray areas of transportation security, and the agency wanted to avoid activities that might create controversy. *Wow!* I thought. *Since when did we retreat for fear of being criticized? What happened to the old "We're On a Mission!" TSA?* Even in the dimness of the room, I could see plenty of competent and smart faces, many from the old TSA, but the confidence node in their brains appeared to have been bypassed and hardwired directly to the pain center.

In the early days everyone was well aware of the operational ambiguities left by the Aviation and Transportation Security Act, the agency's founding document, but we had taken this vagueness as permission to get on with the job of protecting the public rather than as a hazard to avoid. Now the TSA was steering clear of these gray areas, and it seemed to me, important parts of its mission. Unless an action was clearly mandated by specific language of law, it did not appear to be a priority. It was in that stuffy, dark setting that I decided not to sit back and take the remaining briefings. Browbeaten, the agency had retreated into a dark recess, emerging into the light only to complete its most basic legally required functions. But this wouldn't be nearly enough.

DURING THE SPRING AND SUMMER OF 2005 I WAS STILL WAITING around for Senate confirmation while trying to stay under the radar. With no official status or prerogatives, and subject to the singular experience of full-on Beltway scrutiny during the confirmation process, I decided to get out of town. Alison scheduled a trip on July 7 up to the FAA labs in Atlantic City, New Jersey, to visit the agency's tech center firsthand.

At five that morning I got a call at my apartment from the TSA operations center, the first time I'd heard from them. A serious electrical fire had ripped through parts of the London Underground, but it wasn't clear that there was an attack. At six, I got an update: It was a terrorist bombing and people were dead. My trip to the FAA labs was cancelled.

I hustled across the street to the office. Although I wasn't allowed to do anything other than ask questions and make suggestions, I was curious to observe how the agency would respond. As more information came in, we learned that London's transportation system had been hit by four separate bombs. Three devices were detonated within a minute of each other on London's Underground, with a fourth attack on a city bus an hour later. The bombs were relatively simple homemade devices carried in backpacks, but they were extremely effective, destroying or damaging the train cars and surrounding tunnels while killing fifty-two people and injuring more than 700.

It turned out that the TSA, hamstrung by fear of involving the agency in the unfamiliar world of mass transit, wasn't prepared for possible follow-up attacks here in the United States. We had lots of capacity at our local airports, but we couldn't realistically rush 1,000 airport screeners off to cover New York's sprawling subway system. Our best available tool was coordinating with local police, and since the TSA hadn't made a priority of developing strong ties with local authorities, I called up my friend Jenna Dorn, who was then the head of the Federal Transit Administration (FTA) at the DOT. Her agency gave money to state and local transit agencies and she had open lines of communication and pretty good relationships with them. "Why don't we team up?" I suggested to Jenna. "TSA could use your communication system and we will provide you the security information." As we talked, I silently added "building local partnerships" to my to-do list. Since I lacked official standing to make any of that stick, I gave Jenna's number to the TSA operations head and they put together a working arrangement.

Around the TSA buildings, others were arriving at similar conclusions. Joe Salvator, our deputy head of intel, learned about the London attacks while watching CNN. (Even today, cable news is often the first to provide an enormous amount of information to the TSA.) As the screen showed footage of the damage, Joe's face tightened. *Shit,* he thought. *This could happen here next and very soon! And we're too busy looking at planes in the sky.* Like everybody else, Joe knew the agency's operations were too aviation-centric, but now those vulnerabilities were seriously exposed. The TSA didn't even know whom to call at the country's major transit systems—let alone their phone numbers.

For others in the TSA's intel shop, the attack, quickly dubbed "Britain's 9/11," served as a different kind of wake-up call. As the scope of the War on Terror narrowed to focus on the increasingly divisive two-year-old war in Iraq and alarms were raised over privacy issues involved in surveillance, America's 9/11 was slowly moving into the rearview mirror. There had been no major terror attacks in the United States in nearly four years, and people's confidence in flying had rebounded, even as the TSA and its efforts were regularly excoriated. This sense of stability reached far up the ranks at the TSA, too—until the July 7 London attack ripped everything back open again. Terrorists had attacked the largest city of our closest ally, and there was no doubt that the same type of attack could be just as deadly on American soil.

July 7 also signaled the start of a new and even more insidious terror paradigm. Instead of sending a bunch of foreign nationals to hijack planes or using incompetent criminals in suicide attacks, these operatives were British-born, with "clean skins"—i.e., no rap sheets. Two were married with children; another worked with his dad at a fish-and-chips shop. One was Jamaican, while the other three were Pakistani, at first glance indistinguishable from the one in eight Londoners of South Asian descent. Thus integrated with British society, all of the operatives would have been essentially invisible in a crowded train. For intel officers like Joe Salvator, the lesson was that the next attack on the United States wouldn't be carried out by nineteen guys who flew here from Saudi Arabia or Egypt, it would be nineteen guys who grew up down the road from the TSA in Arlington, Virginia. And that was a game changer, if we picked up on it.

ABOUT A WEEK AFTER THE LONDON BOMBINGS, I TOOK SEVERAL DAYS to go see what our frontline officers learned during their aviation security training. At the time, the TSA's acting director was Ken Kasprisin, the Federal Security Director from Minneapolis-St. Paul, and he enthusiastically suggested his hometown: "We'll put you in screener training, I've got just the place for you!"

After introducing myself to the TSA staff at Minneapolis-Saint Paul International Airport and watching checkpoint operations, I sat down at a computer with Gary, a solidly built African American guy in his forties with a mustache and shaved head. The TSA didn't have specialized trainers, so all the teaching was done by frontline screeners.

Gary pointed at a screen that simulated the carry-on bag monitors at checkpoints. "What do you see?" he asked, a half smile on his face.

I stared at the series of colorful, ghostly images that Gary froze on the screen and tried to pick an easy one. "Well, that's a computer or some electronics, there are wires, maybe a battery." The sharp edges were easy to pick out, and the recognizable pattern of a motherboard jumped out. "But I don't know about that big orange blob on top of it."

"Right," said Gary. "And the orange-colored part? That means it's organic. Anything made of organic material—clothes, shoes, food—it's all going to register orange here. Now see these shirts?" he continued.

I peered at their faint orange outlines.

"They're not as intensely colored as this book, right? This machine also shows you density. The darker the color, the denser the object."

Gary showed me a bottle of water, recognizable by the faint outline of the plastic shell and the telltale waterline that reorients itself depending on which way is up. Metallic objects were blue or greenish. There were also shades of gray in great abundance.

As a confidence boost, Gary gave me a series of images with guns and knives in various positions. Knives lying flat were giveaways but when viewed length-wise, they had very little visible surface. I missed quite a few of those. Guns were comparatively easy. Grips, springs, and triggers don't always jump out, but gun barrels are solid steel, and bullets are also hard to hide. Gary sent through an Uzi image as well, just to see if I was awake. As I started getting the hang of it, I was amazed. These were legacy scanners, pretty much unchanged since the 1980s, but I could see how a skilled operator could visually pull out almost anything in the bag.

Then we looked at explosives. Plastic explosive like C4 was organic and dense; it showed up as a heavy orange mass. Explosives made out of powder had a completely different appearance, a sort of lighter metallic hue. To simulate what the Shoe Bomber's boots would have looked like, the TSA put some balloons inside hollowed-out heels. On the monitor they show up as a medium-density orange boot outline with a noticeably darker inner heel where the explosive would be packed. Finding a working bomb also means identifying its other components, so if you spot, say, a potential organic explosive, you'd look for a trigger switch, power source, detonator, and connecting wires. Each of these components was detectable, although I found detonators—as small as a pen cap, without much telltale explosive, and possibly nonmetallic—nearly impossible to locate.

There were also plenty of possibilities for false positives, alarming items that were actually harmless. For example, cheddar cheese is dense and organic, and virtually identical to C4 on the monitor. An iPod has a battery and wires and, packed next to cheese, is going to arouse suspicion. It's these in fact innocuous combinations that make working at a checkpoint so nerveracking. Gary warned me that I would get points deducted from my test for too many false positives; a paranoid, overcautious "hair trigger" strategy would get me flunked.

After Gary was satisfied that I had the basics, he upped the ante: "Now let's try it with the belt moving." I got to control the belt speed but I soon felt the unsaid pressure to keep the belt moving. Images with guns took roughly one second to identify. Clear bags took about five seconds to double-check the sides for blade edges. But cluttered bags with their multihued oranges, blues, greens, and grays jumbled together in partial and vague shapes were killers. I soon found there was a discipline to reading an image. My approach was to first take in everything to see if my eye was drawn somewhere. Then I worked the quadrants, from left to right and top to bottom. After that, I gave a special look at the edges and seams. I might get a density hit, maybe a battery or a decent-size explosive main charge, but it took ten to fifteen seconds. I could almost feel the line backing up. I was also worried about whether or not I'd catch a bag with nothing but a hard-to-detect detonator or basic wiring.

"We only test on completed bombs," Gary assured me.

That made the test a lot easier; I could ignore the hard-to-identify detonators and only pull the alarm on a bag once I saw other components like explosives, batteries, wires, and switches. But while this technique made sense as a test-taking strategy, the TSA's training policy towards partially assembled bombs set off my internal alarms. How hard could it be to undergo security with bomb components divvied up among multiple bags and then reassemble the devices on the other side?

While in Minneapolis, I also got to walk around a few checkpoints and talk to people who I was pretty sure had not been handpicked by management. After years in transportation and logistics management jobs, one picks up on workplace vibes ranging from "high energy" to "I hate life." From these conversations, I got the strong sense that many screeners were committed to counterterrorism, but that almost all of them felt overwhelmed by operational constraints, criticism, and a growing sense of doubt. On the bright side, they didn't have very high expectations for me, the fourth TSA administrator in three years.

Finally, I sat in a lecture room and was instructed on the same Passenger Screening Standard Operating Procedure that was driving Carl Maccario to distraction up in Boston. There's an awful lot a screener needs to know before performing security operations on hundreds of people a day, and from that perspective, the SOP made sense. But I was still amazed at how the training took the phrase "doing it by the book" to a whole new level. While it may be necessary to tell new recruits, "In order for us to stay within our legal authorities when searching a person or his belongings, you must stay within these boundaries, both in what you say and what you do" or "In order to find cleverly hidden items and use the technology properly, you must be disciplined in how you conduct your search," it shouldn't stop there. The twenty of us sitting in the classroom were asked only to digest a tremendous amount of detailed procedural knowledge, and very little else, in order to become certified. A lot of my fellow trainees' faces seemed to be saying, "OK. But when are we going to get to the security part?" Large numbers of them—police officers, musicians, businessmen, plumbers, lawyers—had enthusiastically joined the TSA with a simple goal: Stopping terrorist attacks. I had to wonder what they made of this training. A rallying cry of "Compliance!" was not quite as effective as "Never Again!"

As I gathered my clutter of materials at the end of that training day, I struggled with a fundamental disconnect. Those who had been certified would soon be working at one of 450 different airports around the country, dealing with the nation's two million daily passengers. But while our training was detailed and professional, it had no rejoinder to the complexities of the real world. There would certainly be times an officer would face a situation not covered by the SOP. How would a workforce utterly discouraged from taking personal initiative react? I later learned that screeners were annually recertified by outside contractors who had never actually worked at a checkpoint environment. The testing to determine who kept working for the TSA did not include field observation; it was all precise regurgitation of the SOP. Apparently once you'd logged hundreds of hours, practical learning still wasn't part of keeping your job.

There was one other employee-related item eating away at me. After I finished the day of classroom training in Minnesota, I said a few words of thanks to the group. One of the officers stood up and threw me a softball: "What will your top priority as TSA administrator be?" Hmmm. I hadn't formulated a tight sound-bite answer to this pretty basic question. "Injuries," I blurted out.

My reasoning was partly personal. Back in 2002, I could have lowered our injury rate significantly if I had put more of a focus on designing ergonomic ways of working. We had fifty Go Teams, one of them should have been workforce safety. Most injuries are preventable. Three years after its creation, the TSA had the worst injury record in the entire federal government. In fact, the agency's injury epidemic significantly nudged upward the Department of Labor's workers' compensation figures for the entire federal workforce. That meant thousands of officers, most often those people tasked with moving heavy checked baggage through the explosive detection systems, were getting hurt and losing time to injuries every year, And as bad as those numbers were, the more important statistic was not the total dollar amount of claims and the compounding costs of extra payroll costs to make up for the lost worker, but the number of incidents, serious and minor. A friend of mine from my time at Union Pacific once told me, "The difference between an ankle sprain and a fatality is luck—which way the guy fell." By focusing on reducing the seemingly cheaper and less severe problems, you will, in fact, bring down the number of more serious injuries as well.

Injury rate is also one of the best metrics of effective management. A high rate doesn't just mean bad ergonomics and twisted bodies; it reflects the demeanor of the workforce. A well-motivated, engaged worker with a lot of positive energy is less likely to become injured. But in Minneapolis in July 2005, this technical answer to the priorities question seemed only to confuse my audience. I'd have to work to find my inner George S. Patton, legendary motivator of his troops.

I returned to Washington with some new questions and my screener certificate. During the length of my tenure at the TSA, it was the only professional decoration that hung in my office.

BY JULY 20, I HAD HEARD FROM DHS, FREQUENTLY JUST CALLED "THE Department," that the Senate was likely to consider my confirmation before August recess. I'd also received a call from Dave Stone, my predecessor, who gave me the best single piece of advice I got on my job. Discussing the London bombings, Dave told me that I needed to pick up the phone and call my counterpart in the UK, Niki Tompkinson, the director of transport security. He suggested I offer condolences for the attack and see if she could tell me a bit more from her perspective. Waiting for the international briefing would take forever, he warned, and Niki would be a key relationship to cultivate.

That night, back at my Pentagon Row apartment, I got a call from the DHS operations center telling me that Secretary Chertoff had invited me to an intelligence-related secure video teleconference (often abbreviated to SVTC and pronounced "civits") the following morning. I called Alison to confirm I had a ride and also asked her to look into getting Jenna Dorn's deputy from the DOT's mass transit department invited to the meeting. That was reciprocity for their help putting us in touch with local transit groups on July 7—it was never too early to start building relationships.

Created in 2003, the Department of Homeland Security had found a home in a repurposed Navy facility in the tree-lined and wealthy northwest part of the District. After arriving to the secure operations center, one of many buildings scattered around the DHS campus, I walked up three flights of stairs and found a seat in the surprisingly cramped conference room used for videoconferencing. Along with Secretary Chertoff were about a half dozen people I couldn't place. At exactly eight o'clock, Frances Townsend, President Bush's Homeland Security adviser, appeared on the monitor and the meeting began. A woman in her forties with a lean face and a blonde bob, Fran had become a well-known figure on cable news channels, but she quickly handed us off to an unnamed CIA briefer who dazzled me with an enormous number of specific reports on global al-Qaeda activity in the past twenty-four hours. This was an entirely different category of intelligence briefing than I was getting at the TSA. Then Fran suddenly cut off an intel analyst, saying, "We're getting something in the Sit Room, hang on a second."

Moments later, she returned on screen and read a short dispatch. London had been hit again; there were several explosions reported; the number of casualties was unknown. Fran suggested that we tend to that issue first, and the SVTC was over. Chertoff and I walked out into the open floor of the DHS operations center where he was mobbed by aides and I peeled off to get to a secure phone. A bank of large TV screens hung along the front wall overlooking a room with filled with watch officers from every DHS entity, including the TSA. CNN had good live video and while I called back to TSA's intel office, I saw the detailed map of London outlining the bomb locations.

In contrast to the month's earlier bombings, these were relatively ineffective. The detonators had gone off but the bombs had fizzled, filling the trains with acrid smoke. When the suspects were arrested and al-Qaeda claimed responsibility, it was clear that the group was purposefully switching up its modus operandi again: All four of the men were East African. Any officer in the subway looking for Pakistanis or Jamaicans with backpacks would have been profiling yesterday's threat.

NINE HUNDRED MILES EAST OF LONDON, IN VIENNA, THE JULY BOMBings gave Abdulrahman Hilal Hussein fresh material for recruiting. A month later he was ready to depart and on August 26, 2005, Abdulrahman and four other al-Qaeda volunteers left Austria, heading for training camps in Pakistan. Because all five had authentic, clean identities and credentials they flew to Pakistan like anyone else, from Vienna to a European hub, on to Abu Dhabi and Pakistan, where they were met and driven to their final destination: training camps run by Abu Hamza Rabia. Abdulrahman would be learning his trade at the hands of the mastermind behind the London bombings.

SEVEN

BETTING ON CHAOS

FOR LEE KAIR AND JOE SALVATOR, MY FIRST DAY AS ADMINIS-
trator began just as every other day had for months. At eight A.M. on July 28,
2005, they packed themselves into the seventh-floor conference room with
the rest of the senior leadership for another marathon ops-and-intel meeting.
With all the top people in one place, the meeting was the perfect opportunity
to introduce myself.

There is a well-worn template for this sort of situation: walking into the
meeting, smiling, shaking hands, and telling everyone, "We have an important mission, and it is a great honor to be working with you." This was exactly
what the TSA didn't need. I had been around long enough to know I was taking over an excessively cautious and beleaguered operation that appeared to
be stalled, the organizational equivalent of a deer in headlights. So I prepared
a tough love presentation intended to break the trance.

Halfway into my spiel I put it directly to them: the agency was viewed
as a rigid, Soviet-style bureaucracy, a purveyor of words without meaning, a
house with nobody home. I also used the phrase "brain lock," along with an
image of the Three Stooges, to make myself clear.

Then I launched into my vision for the TSA and its leadership going
forward. I looked at out at the thirty faces that comprised TSA's leadership.
"We are no longer going to stand still and take it; we are going to get up and
go on offense," I promised. "I would love for you all to jump on board, but

I understand if you're not up for it. It will be very hard. All I ask is that if you are *not* going to fully commit to the direction I outlined, let me know in advance and we will get you comfortably placed elsewhere in the Department of Homeland Security. But do not sit here slowing the rest of us down." Then I left.

For a second, Lee and Joe sat silently with their stunned colleagues.

Then Joe said, "Holy shit!"

"Wow," someone else echoed from another part of the room, which was suddenly bubbling over with excitement—and perhaps a bit of shock. Like the others, Lee and Joe knew that the TSA faced huge image problems, that we'd lost a sense of our larger mission, not to mention the confidence of Congress and the American public. But unspoken in everyone's mind was either, "Here we go again," or "It's about time."

I knew some of them thought I was crazy and that the last thing TSA needed was a leader tilting at windmills. Others, savvy government careerists, figured they'd bide their time because I'd probably be gone in a few months or quickly worn down by the process-driven bureaucracy. But since I'd offered an easy and attractive out to the senior leadership, I expected several volunteers. Figuring I'd soon be filling a lot of vacancies, I also had a meeting with the junior leadership soon thereafter. And sure enough, within a year or so we had replaced about seventeen of the top twenty-five people.

After introducing myself to the staff, I walked back to my office, all too aware that some of the TSA's difficulties could be traced back to the agency's hurried birth. And I was personally responsible for some of these structural mistakes, such as the agency's abysmal injury numbers. But there was no use wringing my hands now. London had been hit twice by major terror attacks in the space of a month. I had barely glimpsed how the terrorists were out-evolving and out-maneuvering us, but I knew that we weren't prepared to deal with them.

Our shortcomings were not due to the agency's lacking the statutory power to do its job. Congress had heaped plenty of powers—and expectations—on the agency while 9/11 was still a raw wound. The government gave the head of the TSA powers like designating federal law enforcement officers and authority to coordinate all US domestic transportation during an emergency. With nothing more than a signature, the person in my job could designate information sensitive and not releasable, a remarkable feat. Even at the CIA, information goes to a review board before becoming classified or top secret. But "TSA–1," as the TSA administrator is known on routing slips, has the last word in deciding what was security-sensitive information, or SSI, a unique designation that was not appealable in court. One of the first things I saw when I arrived on the seventh floor was a trash bin like the ones found at McDonald's. But instead of "Thanks," the swinging door read "SSI." Every night someone would come by to empty out and burn the papers.

I went down the hall looking for a replacement for my inherited heavy, dark furniture until I got to the office of Justin Oberman, one of the first people to join the TSA in 2001. He was then an Assistant Administrator and had a light-colored, high-tech office with pine tables and an open setup. Perfect. I called Justin and told him he was getting a promotion, at least decorating-wise. After grabbing his furniture, I hung a picture of my old jogging haunts on the California coast and got rid of the curtains, revealing an unobstructed view of the Pentagon. Now at least my office was bright and open, even if the organization itself was still choked with rules, regulations, and risk-avoidance. Looking north at the very wall into which American Airlines Flight 77 crashed, our mission crystallized: Not only should we "never forget," we had to break out of our complacency and fight back. Chertoff was right, it was about risk management; and part of managing risks is taking them.

Having shaken up my leadership team, I began looking for people who were ready to step up and buy into risk-based security. Each of the previous heads of the TSA had introduced personnel drawn from their own circles. John Magaw came over with some good people from the Secret Service, Admiral James Loy brought in other Coasties, while Admiral David Stone leaned on his years' worth of Navy contacts.

I didn't want to simply install a team of former associates. Just as only friending your closest acquaintances on Facebook limits the impact of your postings, bringing in people I knew who were already members of the Kip Network wouldn't spark a profound transformation in the agency. I needed to engage with people who were new to me but known in the organization and leverage their networks to access different knowledge bases, personal contacts, and novel talents.

At the time, the TSA certainly had a few people who fit the stereotype of federal deadwood—people who were unwanted at other agencies or simply running out the clock until the government's generous retirement benefits kicked in. And to be honest, there wasn't a whole lot of top new talent lining up to join an agency widely perceived to be on the ropes. Fortunately, the vast majority of employees came to work every day fully committed to our mission, from the frontline screeners at hundreds of airports to the administrative staff at headquarters. The problem was that many of their unique skills were being suppressed by the agency's top-down structure.

I thought the best way to incite change at TSA was from the bottom, that broad and disparate swath where the majority of our 50,000 employees worked. But, when I moved into the administrator's office, information at TSA only moved downwards, closely hewing to the hierarchal chain of command. Reversing this flow was critical, but I was hoping for more than a democratizing of communication. TSA needed to open up its all but forgotten neural pathways, allowing ideas to press sideways, skate diagonally, and tramp every which direction, unfettered by department, geography, or seniority. If we were going to be a thinking and agile organization, we had to be prepared to relax the agency's near stranglehold on data flow. I wanted to make it as easy as possible for good people to float upwards and new ideas to spread exponentially. I wanted to promote from within, reaching deep into the organization for fresh energy. And I wanted change to go viral within the TSA.

Of course, a transformation of this nature wouldn't be initiated by throwing a dusty switch hidden deep in the recesses of TSA's executive floor. My experience had taught me that the one way to do this was to generate opportunities for agents of change who would self-select and step forward, so I did a series of town-hall meetings in which I seeded a little complexity theory among the more basic questions on TSA employees' minds, like "Do we have a future?"

SOON THEREAFTER, ONE OF THOSE HIDDEN ASSETS STUCK HIS HEAD out and came across my radar. Up on the eleventh floor, street musician–turned–network theorist Andrew Cox was increasingly frustrated with his attempts to break through the administrative ceiling above him. Then, in mid-2005, he heard that the new administrator was promoting openness within the agency, holding informal talks throughout the building—he had even read a coworker's paper and returned it with comments. Though some of his colleagues were unsettled by these unbureaucratic leaps of communication, Andrew decided to give it a whirl. *Screw it,* he thought. *I'm just a program analyst—I've got nothing to lose. I'll send my paper straight up to the top."* Needless to say, when Andrew's bosses later discovered his breach of the chain of command, they were not amused.

One night, Alison walked into my office with Andrew's paper. "You have to read this," she said.

After giving it a look, I was impressed. *Holy jumping Moses!* I thought, echoing my grandfather. *Who is this guy? He really lives and breathes network theory.* Unlike some well-meaning enthusiasts who simply worked new buzz-words into old thoughts, I could tell Andrew was the real deal. I convinced him to give up his old job and join a new TSA strategy team I was putting together.

Personally, I saw applications of network theory everywhere, and was excited to have an overarching strategic framework for the TSA that tied together its diverse activities. But I soon found that the term scared some people off and reinforced the Don Quixote image. One especially disastrous evening in August, I concocted an informal get-to-know-you meeting with the TSA beat reporters. Over freshly delivered pizza from Armand's, I consistently failed in my attempts to explain how the theory worked and what it meant to what TSA did at checkpoints. *Dynamic security measures* and *connected networks* fit into the TSA doublespeak stereotype that I was trying to dispel. When I later briefed some key congressional staff, they tartly advised me to lose the complexity theory and just give clear direction about expedited screening programs like the Registered Traveler program.

I had only slightly better luck within the TSA. There was the unique Andrew Cox who brought advanced theory to me. There were people like Alison who, after I sent her an email on network theory, wrote back, "Never heard of it, but love it." But plenty of others simply began mouthing the phrase, or worse, staring back blankly. For those interested in reading, I offered up websites on complexity theory and *The Logic of Failure,* a short book by the German cognitive psychologist Dieter Dörner illustrating how too much faith in well-designed systems could blind smart people to the signs of impending catastrophic failure. Another personal favorite was Ross King's tome about the building of Florence's great Duomo, *Brunelleschi's Dome: How A Renaissance Genius Reinvented Architecture,* which chronicles Filippo Brunelleschi's efforts to deliver on a contract to build a mammoth unsupported dome, inventing both the process and the tools along the way. But when none of these worked, I finally settled on the story of my own personal conversion.

IN 1992, I WAS WORKING AT UNION PACIFIC, THE RAILROAD COMPANY that then owned almost 19,000 miles of track across the western United

States, as well as the surrounding land, the locomotives, and the train cars. Each month, all the senior executives met at the corporate headquarters in Omaha in a large, beautifully catered conference room with a view of the placid Missouri River and, in the distance, the old cattle stockyards of the cowboy days. I dreaded these meetings because Mike Kelly, the head of field operations and I had to present data on the previous month's on-time, efficiency and customer-delivery performance. Despite the fact that Union Pacific owned and controlled just about all the components of rail transport and had very sophisticated computer software and highly experienced personnel dedicated to enhancing train performance, I just couldn't make the trains run on time.

This wasn't for lack of trying. Local operations managers from Pocatello, Idaho, to New Orleans were allowed to identify specific critical trains and give them priority by clearing tracks across the country. But while we could fix these individual problems, the overall schedule was still off. A system-wide fix remained elusive, and I felt like I was playing a giant game of Whac-a-Mole every month.

Neither could the problem be ascribed to Union Pacific's lack of commitment to problem solving. From boardroom to locomotive cab, the company's focus on quality process management bordered on the maniacal. But unsuccessfully following UP's well-documented performance improving technique, using data to peel back the layers of the onion until the root cause was found and attacked left me increasingly flustered. One day, frustrated by my lack of progress, I asked myself, "What if the problem is not in the onion?"

Then, in 1993 after an internal restructuring, I was named vice president of reengineering and given a reprieve from the maddening daily roulette of flooded tracks in Missouri, washed out right-of-ways in Texas, snow slides in the Sierras, and busted locomotives in Chicago. Not long after, while on a business trip, I picked up a book titled *Chaos: Making a New Science* in an airport bookstore. After I had anguished for so long over train performance, the book offered an apparent answer.

One of *Chaos*'s precepts was that things happen at a given juncture not necessarily because of identifiable causes specific to that time and space, but rather because of some other seemingly unrelated factor not fundamentally linked by temporality or proximity. This phenomenon's best-known metaphor is the butterfly flapping its wings in China and causing a thunderstorm in Iowa. It certainly sounded like our travails at Union Pacific. We had dived deep into every aspect of operations and searched exhaustively for flaws, but never came away with the fix we needed. If this book was right, maybe the problems in train performance were not in the onion, maybe it was the surrounding environment. And ripping ever deeper into onions would never make things better. Soon thereafter, I had one of the great epiphanies of my career.

The Powder River Basin was the single biggest leverage point for increasing profitability in Union Pacific territory. It sits in the semi-arid rolling grasslands of Wyoming, in an area that nestles up to Yellowstone National Park to the west and is about a two-hour drive from Mount Rushmore to the east. Sixty million years ago, the land around the basin began rising out of the shallow inland sea that covered North America, eventually becoming one of the most important coal-producing areas in the United States—a place where our trains always seemed to get bottlenecked at a single line of rail leading to the coal fields while transporting coal to many of the nation's electric power plants.

Because on-time performance from this particular spot was so important—a serious delay in delivery could endanger the supply of electricity to the entire city of Atlanta—Union Pacific spent enormous energies trying to improve efficiency. We rushed high-priority coal cars to a continuous queue just outside the single-point entry to the basin. We advanced new, empty cars right after the previous train moved out loaded with coal. But instead of maximizing efficiency, we were actually overdoing it. One of the consequences of focusing so much operational and tactical energy on wringing every last second out of the process is that we left ourselves precious little slack when something did go wrong. As with brain surgery, in our scheduling there was no room for error. Moreover, unlike the tightly controlled environment of a hospital surgery room, we faced complex challenges spread out over thousands of miles and dozens of terrains and microclimates.

Though Union Pacific was as vertically integrated as possible, we were still vulnerable to the whims of the weather, employee error, and mechanical breakdowns, making a sense of control a dangerous illusion. It is simply the nature of large, heterogeneous systems like a railroad network to have things go wrong all the time. And as soon as something went wrong with one train, the other trains we'd stacked up behind it were stuck. Lining up all the trains in a row, we realized, had effectively squeezed all room for error out of the system and was slowing down our delivery schedule.

After letting that conundrum soak in, one of our brainstorming teams proposed a solution that directly contradicted the time-maximization mode we'd been toiling in. What if, rather than rushing the empties to the gridlock point, we staged the coal cars far away from the troublesome intersection and then flowed them in, so they arrived when the intersection was clear? Rather than trying to cram in as many priority trains as possible, we dispatched the cars to a collection of holding points dispersed across the railroad, making sure that the Powder River Basin's access point wasn't idle for very long. It worked. Not only did it clear up the gridlock, it also increased the number of daily coal trains by 30 percent. Over a year, that improvement was worth hundreds of millions of dollars, and enabled the largest single-year jump in coal shipments during the company's 150-year history.

Another way of thinking about that solution was that railroad dispatchers were building resilience into the process. Previously, we'd put all our eggs in one perfect basket, leaving us no viable secondary options if the basket filled up. It was true that our new system of flowing in trains was not technically as time-efficient as the first system, but by accounting for the time eaten up by unpredictable problems that plague any complex network, it was ultimately more successful. Contrary to decades' of management logic, it was only by *accepting* some *error* that could we create a more reliable system. A few years later, when I had moved to an executive position in a supply chain management company owned by Union Pacific, I saw the same phenomenon at work in the high technology industry. Dell Computer built its computers according to real-time demand at its assembly facility in Austin, TX and our company had the contract to present the right parts to the assembly line with less than two hours' notice. Using the same philosophy as staging the Powder River trains away from the bottleneck, we kept a small buffer supply at a warehouse in Austin but most of the inventory flowed in transit from points all over the world, sped up or slowed down according to Dell's demand. Resilience, it seemed, was the secret ingredient to delivering reliable results in a chaotic, unpredictable world.

When I arrived at the TSA I realized that the agency's internal and external operations were plagued by the same phenomenon that I had grappled with at Union Pacific: futilely trying to maintain a viselike grip on problems that reacted poorly to such control because they were by definition unpredictable. In 2005, after a decade's research, chaos theory had evolved into complexity theory, a discipline that brought a set of tools to explain and influence what they called complex adaptive systems. These networks consisted of independent but interactive pieces that behaved according to a set of general rules but whose individual interactions were unpredictable, a little bit like the difference between building a pyramid of Lego blocks versus building one cheerleader-style with people. Lego pyramids are standardized and endlessly interchangeable. Designing a human pyramid means negotiating individual subjects' weight, height, strength, personality and willingness to be part of the effort in the first place, an almost endlessly spiraling array of variables.

In trying to explain this to my TSA colleagues, I would sketch the coal-train problem on a napkin or the back of a memo. Then, wondering if I'd already lost my audience, I'd bring it back around to aviation security and make the pitch of Why Network Theory Mattered to the TSA. Just as Union Pacific was trying to avoid crippling backups on its tracks, TSA's main operational challenge was to manage a similarly complex adaptive system at its checkpoints. Not recognizing those characteristics, TSA issued specific rules to passengers and trained our TSA people to behave strictly according to the Standard Operating Procedure. The "Lego Model" was simplistic and had little to offer in the daily interactions between millions of unique air travelers and tens of thousands of TSA personnel. Although the control mentality endemic to the agency had worked so well in setting up its initial operations, it was now stifling the talents and abilities of our workforce, frustrating travelers and choking checkpoints from coast to coast.

At the bottom of this hierarchy sat the frontline workforce, straitjacketed by the Standard Operating Procedure. Just as Union Pacific had wagered on stacking up its train cars at the tight entrance to the Powder River Basin, the TSA had put all our chips on the single, catchall moment at the checkpoint. Then, because we'd imbued that moment with disproportionate importance, we sought to insure its success by amping up system-wide rules, aiming for fine control. Not only did that approach engender near universal frustration at airports, it represented serious security vulnerability as well. If someone made it through our incredibly predictable checkpoint, they were basically home free.

Now, just as Union Pacific had embraced resilience, accepting the certainty of error and spacing out their trains to achieve better results, the TSA needed to accept that stopping attacks required less rigidity and predictability, and, while adding more layers, that granting some latitude in managing the system was a good thing. We had to encourage some autonomy and improvisatory ability among our screeners to counter the barrage of unpredictable

SOP-busting situations our frontliners faced every day. The new efficiency would also save money by lowering failure costs, such as overtime and the resulting absenteeism. If we could do that, then we would have money to invest in adding further resilience in the form of additional security layers before or beyond the checkpoint.

Because network theory is so broadly applicable, people could view it through the lens of their own experiences. For example, Andrew Cox's years of playing jazz had already revealed to him the difference between strict control and looser, improvisatory techniques. While classical music will vary in interpretation and style, classically trained musicians tend to perform music almost exactly as it appears on a score. They follow this guidebook as precisely as the TSA's screeners were instructed to follow the SOP. But in the cavernous silence of a concert hall, a few wrong notes from the second violins spells disaster for the piece. Why should we expect our frontline workers to follow a strict SOP note by note while surrounded by the noisy hubbub of a major airport?

In jazz, musicians don't follow a score. Instead, Andrew explained to me, "We spend years building up a shared vocabulary of modes, classic songs, and styles so that when we play together there's a loose framework to work within. This way we can play together without a conductor—in some bands, each player briefly leads the group." Ultimately Andrew's jazz training became my model for our screeners: thinking, engaged people working within a common framework, able to adapt in the face of unpredictable attacks and other problems. Within a few months of taking over at the TSA, I sprung Andrew from his analyst job and convinced him to join a strategic group looking at less hierarchical and more adaptable models.

EVENTUALLY I HAD TO GO UP THE LADDER AND EXPLAIN MY STRATEGIC approach to Secretary Chertoff. He was a very intelligent, curious, and quick-witted man, but I still had misgivings about marching into his office and prattling on about chaos or network or complexity theory. So I took a different tack, starting my presentation with a slide of a football game. Football is a sport with set plays in which each player sticks very closely to his assigned role. Normally, the playbook is drawn up by coaching staff and signaled to the quarterback from the senior leadership on the sidelines. The quarterback, in turn, is generally the team's leader in the field, an operations manager. And the rest of the players simply follow the tightly designed plays. But in football, just one mistake, like an offensive tackle momentarily slipping on muddy turf, can ruin a play. It is a game predicated on command and control.

Then I flipped to a slide of a basketball point guard—another sort of operations manager, but one working within a much different strategic environment. Basketball coaches also call set plays that rely on precise execution, but the game is also much more fluid than football. Except for opening tip-offs, teams do not begin every play by lining up in the same place. With defense suddenly switching to offense every time there is a change of possession of the ball, the game develops in an uninterrupted field of continuous play. Basketball requires players with good court vision who can improvise autonomously within a team framework. These are the abilities people are referring to when they talk about "basketball IQ," a highly valued intangible that doesn't have a football equivalent. In basketball, the most valuable team members are able to absorb the complexity of ten bodies nearly constantly in motion while avoiding predictable decisions. But neither can these players allow the game to slip into a disastrous absence of control. Larry Bird and Michael Jordan were known for pushing the envelope of improvisation while keeping teammates involved at all times. Their genius was the opposite of the heroic lone figure carrying the team to victory—it was engaging the team network to victory. The greatest basketball players constantly ride on the edge of chaos, but never alone.

The point I wanted to communicate to Secretary Chertoff was that the TSA needed an interactive team approach at all levels. And it was with that metaphor in mind that we began developing a set of operational guidelines for working with local airport law enforcement called Operation Playbook. The idea was to get away from imposing regulations on the people who actually had to do the work and replace it with locally derived "plays." We would have given up paper control but would gain actual improvement in security results. But in order to successfully implement Playbook, we needed a sense of trust between headquarters and the field—and between the field players and their host airports. Without that relationship, Playbook would be passed down like traditional football play: constructed by headquarters, handed down to each FSD, and communicated last of all to the frontline staff. In the absence of trust, Playbook risked becoming just another control mechanism.

IN JULY 2005, IN THE STAFF BREAK ROOM AT PUEBLO MEMORIAL AIR-port in Colorado, Jeremy Trujillo looked up and noticed that the picture of the TSA Administrator had changed again. But this time it wasn't a picture, it was a mirror.

It was different, sure, but what did it really mean? Jeremy had been with TSA since the end of 2002. The start-up had been rough. Plenty of his co-workers hadn't been paid during his first month, around Christmas. And since then they'd had to endure the regular beatings the TSA received anytime one of his 50,000 colleagues made an error that went public. Jeremy knew it wasn't personal; mistakes were easier and sexier to report on than successes. But the negativity was wearing down all the agency's frontline workers. Jeremy had been working hard over the past few years, taking on extra duties to try to move up to the next level, but he was still at a fundamental remove from the revolving portraits of administrators that stared back from the break room walls. Jeremy had never been to Washington, and it sometimes seemed like no one in DC even knew where Pueblo was.

The mirror portrait was part of an initiative I launched in October 2005 called "I Am TSA." Rather than looking up at another anonymous leader, I wanted the screeners to see themselves as critical to the agency's mission as anyone at headquarters and take accountability for their work. The agency was defined by what they did more than what I did, so to fix the TSA required their active involvement. But I knew it would take more than a few shiny plaques to bridge the disconnect between my room on the seventh floor and the tens of thousands of people receiving paychecks and directives with my signature.

AFTER A FEW WEEKS, I INSTRUCTED MY ASSISTANT, ALISON, TO GET OUT of the office and meet the "real TSA," those working on the ground. Alison took off for Philadelphia, LaGuardia, and Kennedy, and at each airport, she went to the TSA break rooms and met with the screeners to listen to their perspectives and explain our new priorities, including injury reduction and performance-based advancement. After her presentation at LaGuardia, she stopped for questions.

"How's he different from any other administrator?" asked one disaffected screener.

"Yeah," piped up another. "We've had three in four years. Who *is* he?"

Blushing, Alison tried to convince her hostile and doubtful audience that we really were worth listening to. But the lack of trust ran deep. A few hundred miles from the TSA's towers in the Washington suburbs, Alison found herself on the other side of a very serious breakdown between headquarters and our front lines. Until something tangible happened, she was just one more Washington schmuck spouting off promises to the people who spent eight hours a day on their feet, confronting the gripes and snipes of an increasingly disaffected public and the media.

After being called out at LaGuardia, Alison stopped at the gleaming headquarters of Bloomberg, the information services company founded by New York mayor Michael Bloomberg, which is housed in a tower glistening over the east side of midtown Manhattan. There she got a personal tour of the company's unique work culture and building. "Transparency" is a corporate buzzword, but at Bloomberg it was manifested physically: The building's internal walls were transparent glass, with fish tanks spaced along the halls to encourage a sense of calm. Food and coffee trays lined the hallway.

As they entered one workspace, Alison's guide turned to her and pointed. "Over against that wall is the senior producer of the nightly news." The program's associate editors were clustered around him in concentric circles, but Alison could not discern a real difference between the producer's workspace and that of the others. The whole staff sat in the middle of a totally open space, no cubicles or barriers whatsoever, at beautiful workstations with huge monitors. This was an arrangement that Bloomberg liked to call the "beehive," and it was replicated in all the different teams throughout the building.

Another innovation at Bloomberg was the ID card worn by employees and attached to a sort of internal company directory or Facebook. Logging onto the website allowed a user to locate anyone else in the building. This system not only created links outside individual teams; it turned the entire building into one virtual room, enhancing collaboration and openness. If someone was interested in a particular topic, they could find out when a related meeting was being held and attend. Network theory in application!

From there Alison traveled over to Mayor Bloomberg's offices, where she found the same concepts replicated on a micro level in his modest office. A racing bike hung over Bloomberg's desk, and his office always had an ample supply of food, which he explained with the dictum, "If you have food and all the drinks your people want, then there's no reason for them to leave."

As a TSA policy analyst, Alison had worked alongside plenty of smart people, but mostly in traditional, top-down work environments. When she returned from New York, I encouraged Alison to replace the cubicled policy shop with what we called the Info Center, a workspace housed in the room that immediately greeted people exiting the seventh floor elevator. Outside the room was a board listing the TSA's top priorities for that day—maybe an air cargo summit or a security incident at Denver International. Anyone in the agency could come by and get a feel for the top issues for senior leadership that day.

The Info Center's exterior wall was glass, a nod to the Bloomberg building, and buzzed with ever-evolving stories. The room was also mapped out in a beehivelike orientation, key people in middle with other team members arrayed around them, surfing the web or following cable news. At intervals, they would trade jobs so that no one lost focus or felt disconnected from the rest of the team. While the Info Center was used for congressional testimony and interdepartmental communications, its purpose was now bigger. The TSA's core business was managing information, from reports of a novel explosive to communicating with our frontline staff. Getting reliable, timely information to security personnel in mass transit, general aviation, and everywhere in the transportation sector would, over time, produce better security results than a library full of instructions. Information is what drives operations, from LAX airport to the Long Island ferries.

MEANWHILE, ABDULRAHMAN HILAL HUSSEIN ARRIVED IN AFGHANISTAN at the beginning of September 2005. After being driven to rest stops and safe houses for several days, he arrived in the mountainous, heavily wooded area near Miranshah, in North Waziristan. He and his Austrian recruits surrendered their passports and other identification to their hosts for safekeeping and went about learning the basics of military training. Their courses were physically grueling, and the accommodations, from meager meals to extremely rustic facilities, were Spartan. Abdulrahman soon realized that the training was meant to not only teach his team hand-to-hand combat skills and get them into shape, but also to instill mental toughness.

Abdulrahman excelled at all three elements and was soon separated from his fellow Austrians and brought to a smaller camp near Datta Khel, close to the Afghan border. There he met an Egyptian named Abu Abdulrahman al-Muhajir, a legendary bomb maker and the director of al-Qaeda training operations. Al-Muhajir's terror credits were deep and impressive: He had created the explosive hidden inside a video camera that killed Afghan Northern Alliance chief Ahmad Shah Massoud. The assassination, carried out two days before 9/11, was a preemptive assault on the group that al-Qaeda presumed

would soon be the United States's primary local allies in its forthcoming invasion of Afghanistan. Al-Muhajir also created the explosives used in the devastating October 2000 attack on the USS *Cole* and the lethal 1998 attack
on the US embassy in Nairobi, Kenya—and was the tutor of Shoe Bomber
Richard Reid. Al-Muhajir was brilliant, creative and, for obvious reasons,
considered a top target of American forces. In a very short period, Abdulrahman's talent and promise had brought him to the highest levels of al-Qaeda
operations. Sponsored by Abu Hamza Rabia, he was now learning bomb
making under the storied Abu Abdulrahman al-Muhajir.

EIGHT

WHERE'S THE ACTION?

ONE LONGSTANDING WASHINGTON TRADITION THAT CLEARLY makes sense is getting out of town during the city's hot, swampy Augusts. The last weekend in August 2005 was no exception, as large parts of the downtown evacuated and business slowed to a crawl. But I had only been on the job a month, and even though the corridors outside were emptied and quiet, it seemed like a good time to put in time with the TSA's strategy team.

Further south, the muggy weather had created a large hurricane that was expected to hit land somewhere along the Gulf Coast over the weekend. I had been briefed and the TSA's standard precautions were all in place. At the time, TSA did not have major assignments in hurricanes other than to keep its security checkpoints in sync with local airport operations and protect the electronics of its scanning machines from leaking roofs. Local management looked after its own personnel and the TSA Operations center in Virginia was available for support as needed. Over the weekend, I kept track of the hurricane while sitting in my air-conditioned office translating some of our new strategic goals into actual checkpoint operations. That Monday, as I was on my way to the briefing room to get the latest storm update, Gale Rossides burst from her office, her face blanched white, and headed toward me.

Gale had been a longtime employee of the Bureau of Alcohol, Tobacco, and Firearms before coming over for the TSA's start-up. I'd convinced her to come back as our culture champion, helping to transform the agency's stagnant work environment. "Kip," she said tautly, "it's Mike on the phone. It's sheer bedlam down there."

Mike Robinson was the Federal Security Director at Louis Armstrong International Airport in New Orleans. While I'd been getting regular reports on the Mississippi and Louisiana coasts from our watch desks at the operations center near headquarters, they never communicated the sheer magnitude of what was happening. Apparently Mike had spent hours frantically trying to contact headquarters but couldn't make himself heard through the implacable layers of our normal reporting process. Even though he was calling from a crisis zone, the official channels at the TSA kept dampening down his SOS and converted the escalating human tragedy into the dry factoids of briefing slides that conveyed only that the airport was closed to incoming and outbound flights. Finally, as Hurricane Katrina thrashed the city and his airport began to fill with evacuees, Mike had had enough, and called Gale's cell phone.

"I can't get any returned calls," he had told her in a pained voice. "It is absolute chaos. We've got thousands of people showing up here. There are only three parish cops and they got called away. I've got screeners who lost everything to the storm. They had to leave, and now I can't get in touch with them. And the airport director wants to know when we're going to open up and accept flights again."

"What!" I stopped in my tracks. "What do you mean? Get him on the phone!"

Grabbing a few people, Gale and I stormed into the briefing room, where a few hours before, a PowerPoint summary of hurricane information had been recited for us. As Mike described the situation unfolding at the airport over the speakerphone in the center of the dark wood conference table, his quavering voice underscored the uncontrollable situation he was facing: "You don't understand. The city is gone." It was heartbreaking and terrifying. We, the leadership of the TSA, were stunned. How had the situation at this airport gotten so bad while headquarters went on with business as usual? A few minutes into the call, Tom Quinn, by now the head of the Federal Air Marshals, jumped up and walked out into hallway, where we could hear him pound his fist against the wall in anger as he was talking on his Blackberry.

New Orleans was falling apart. At the convention center, people were channeled by local officials on buses out to the airport, but no planes were coming in. Even if planes had been sent, the air traffic control tower had closed, and the runways were littered with large chunks of debris. The airport was overrun with wet, sick, injured, and homeless evacuees. Most of the screeners, exhausted, had left to rescue their own houses and families. Despite his son and daughter having lost their houses, Mike had stayed at the airport, but even there, law and order were slipping away.

We knew that as soon as it was possible to get planes down, we would need lots of feet on the ground, so Gale put out a call to nearby airports asking for volunteer screeners. Tom came back into the room, and even though the FAMs would not officially become part of the TSA for another month, Tom was all in with us now. Law-enforcement presence at the airport was nonexistent while the local authorities were in emergency lifesaving mode elsewhere. In the following hours, the agency's senior leadership worked with the FAA, the airlines and FEMA on airport issues like air traffic and ground conditions. After the head of Customs and Border Protection agreed to fly in some armed law enforcement to cover the night ahead, Tom pledged to get several dozen armed FAMs on site the next morning. We also asked the airlines if they could fly our volunteers on otherwise empty planes into New Orleans. And then I called Mike Restovich.

AFTER PLAYING A KEY ROLE IN THE TSA'S LAUNCH, MIKE HAD MOVED back to Dallas to take over our operations at the city's Love Field Airport. Tanned and trim, with a shock of white hair and sharp blue eyes, Mike had been a star athlete four decades earlier, even defeating a high school team led by future NFL Hall of Fame quarterback Terry Bradshaw. He went on to serve several decades in the Secret Service. Mike already had plenty of experience with high-pressure situations. He would need it.

Mike picked up my call just as he was getting off a plane, returning from a federal security directors' conference in Utah. He went home, grabbed some supplies and a few trusted TSA colleagues, and drove overnight into Louisiana. The highway was closed about an hour and half outside of New Orleans to prevent additional looting, so Mike and his team slept on the floor of the TSA office in Baton Rouge. Early the next morning, they got a police escort into the city.

By the time Mike got to Armstrong International, it was just about hell on earth. The huge terminal offered shelter for thousands of homeless evacuees, but that was about it. Inside, throngs of people sat clutching their belongings, waiting for an evacuation that had yet to begin. There was no plumbing or electricity in the whole building, except for a small amount of generator power that was being used for medical gear. Roasting in near hundred-degree heat, the whole complex stank of rot, decay, and human waste. It cooled a bit at night, but without lighting, most of the building went pitch black.

The Coast Guard had organized the fastest federal response to the crisis, plucking stranded people off the tops of houses with choppers, but once in the airport, all the refugees could do was sit around, hungry and tired, while others lay on carts waiting for doctors. Much of the airport had been transformed into a makeshift hospital and morgue.

Mike Restovich found Mike Robinson with the twelve other TSA employees who had stuck around to help manage the crisis. Robinson hadn't slept or changed clothes for days, and there was scant food and water in the airport. "I've got some stuff out in my car," said Mike Restovich, and grabbed some snacks, water, first-aid kits, and clothes. After a day or two, the TSA team did get some MREs and bottles of water, but they had to hide them out of concern that their presence would ignite the already tense situation with the near desperate evacuees.

Mike Restovich and the TSA team got busy making the airport operational again, dragging debris off the runways and communicating with headquarters when they could. Landlines were all dead, most cellular service was out, and even the satellite phones were having problems. No one slept for the first forty hours.

MEANWHILE, A PETITE BLONDE WOMAN IN HER EARLY TWENTIES WAS surveying the wreckage of the city from a helicopter. Rebekah Williams, a member of the Department of Homeland Security secretary's scheduling advance team, had talked the DHS leadership into sending her as a local contact in the crisis zone. Rebekah was not a high-ranking official; she worked out of the advance team's little closet, but she had successfully argued that her local Mississippi roots, knowledge, and connections made her the best choice.

She was right. Federal operations were a mess. When Rebekah told a Federal Emergency Management Administration officer that her boss, Secretary Chertoff, wanted to get his FEMA team, along with the TSA, the US Immigration and Customs Enforcement, and the special agents in charge of the US Customs and Border Patrol, together for a conference call, he scoffed, "Nobody knows who all the special agents in charge are."

After a few more conversations like that, Rebekah phoned the DHS in Washington. "None of them know each other," she explained to her contact in the Secretary's office. "They don't have each other's cell phone numbers and most of them are working off of satellite phones anyway. Getting them together is going to be difficult."

As the DHS representative, Rebekah was also fielding calls from people in the Office of Congressional and Legislative Affairs trying to arrange visits by elected officials to the region with little understanding of the situation on the ground. One DC-based congressional aide, while discussing the route for one such disaster tour, unhelpfully told her, "I've looked up on Google where you can get over from Bay Saint Louis across to the rest of Mississippi. It looks like a better route than what you're suggesting."

Rebekah was standing on the point where said bridge used to exist with a member of Legislative Affairs' advance team. They exchanged annoyed glances. He jerked the phone out of Rebekah's hand. "The f-ing bridge no longer exists! What do you not understand about that?!"

Rebekah's family connections had also come in handy. She ended up sleeping in her cousin's camper in Mississippi, and as she looked down from the helicopter, he was identifying the cities and towns below for the pilot, who was from Georgia, and the other out-of-town observers. Around them, the sky was crammed with choppers. Because there was still no air traffic control, the pilots were in charge of their own navigation. The rushed rescue effort around the water-choked city was done entirely by line of sight. *Thank God no one's trying to control this,* thought Rebekah. *It'd be even more chaotic. It's good they're just letting the experts do their jobs.* Finally, Rebekah decided they had taken up their portion of the sky for long enough: "We've seen enough. We're not rescuing people off rooftops, so let's go."

ON MONDAY, SEPTEMBER 5, I TOO FLEW DOWN TO GET AN ON-THE-ground sense of things and support our team. I will never forget the horrid stench and the putrid green cast to the air, indoors and out. But on that trip I got an inkling of what the TSA was about below the surface. Flying in on one of Delta's 757s with a relief crew of screeners and air marshals, I saw the faces of a different TSA. These were people to whom personal sacrifice in the name of mission was nothing. Walking through the airport, meeting the people who had been on duty and were about to be relieved, I saw in their faces deep lines of fatigue and noted a salty locker-room scent, but nowhere among the

FAMs or screeners did I detect a trace of hesitation. Every one of them would have stayed until we dragged them out.

Although the arrival and coordination of federal resources was uneven, other agencies' teams eventually began to arrive. The Department of the Interior sent in personnel who had just been fighting fires in California and Nevada. They parked their well-outfitted eighteen-wheelers outside, and suddenly the airport had had warm showers and a full kitchen. And by the fourth day, there were more MREs at the airport than anyone knew what to do with.

The air marshals had really come through after Tom gave the order, and I was glad to have them on the team. Facing a powder keg of angry, hopeless people short on food and sanitation, the marshals not only kept order but also literally carried the sick, dirty, and injured to their evacuation planes. The only condition I had asked for before becoming administrator was for the FAMs to return from Immigration and Customs Enforcement, where they had been working for the past few years, to the TSA fold. The switch hadn't happened yet, but they were well outfitted, rolling in to New Orleans in overnight coaches with sleeping berths, bathrooms, air-conditioning, and kitchens.

Those SOBs, thought Mike Restovich when he saw their jealously guarded gear. He'd been sleeping on the floor for the past four days. The TSA had nothing to offer in terms of basic emergency supplies—no food, no water, no cots to sleep on. While the FAMs may have carried some unnecessary swagger, I had to admit they had something I didn't see elsewhere at the TSA: when everybody around is frozen in place, they were already in motion.

With their help, along with too many other organizations to mention, Mike Restovich and Mike Robinson were able to put the airport back in order. Southwest Airlines flew screeners in from DFW and Love Field to begin the evacuations, while the FAMs filled the security vacuum created when the Jefferson Parrish sheriff's deputies pulled out. After we reached about 200 volunteer screeners, we began a series of refugee airlifts.

Even that process wasn't simple. Once word got out that there were planes leaving the city the next morning, a queue of people who had been stranded in the fetid airport for up to seventy-two hours began to form. Overnight, an unspoken honor system developed where people ahead and behind in line kept watch to be sure nobody sneaked in who hadn't earned their spot. No one slept or left the line, so they simply defecated and urinated on the floor. Some people died waiting. Mike Restovich learned before dawn that the relief flights would only be able to pull up to a gate that was in a different terminal than the one in which the evacuees were lined up. Worse, the new gate was nearer the end of the line than the front. Quietly, Mike briefed several FAMs and paratroopers from the 82nd Airborne and they slowly walked back along the line asking the people there to calmly gather their possessions and stand by. Incredibly, all eight hundred tired, hungry, and edgy people in line followed at a snail's pace behind Mike and the others and they reestablished the line, this time pointing toward where the incoming aircraft would ferry them away. When the FAA called ahead with the projected arrival times of the first flight, the line moved forward again, this time for security screening which was necessarily loose. Our team was basically making sure that no one got on board the plane with guns or large knives. Lots of people were so weak and disoriented that the ID requirement was also waived and a hand-written manifest was kept. In fact, a lot of people had to be hoisted by the screeners and marshals and carried down the stairs, across the runway, and up onto the planes. There were plenty of large bodies in the crowd, and it took a team of five or so TSA employees to lift those weighing upwards of 250 pounds.

Once we had packed the planes, FAMs in raid jackets on board covered for our less-than-thorough screening. It was crude, but if anybody caused trouble, we figured a couple our FAMs with visible guns could settle things down. When the planes took off, they often didn't know where they were aiming for until a message from the FAA came in: "You're going to Mobile." "You're going to Dallas." "Head for Atlanta."

AS WE BEGAN DIVERTING ALL THESE RESOURCES TO NEW ORLEANS, ALIson Clyde played devil's advocate. "What does a hurricane have to do with transportation security?" she asked me. "Sure, planes can't get in to evacuate people, but is this really a security issue?"

"Look," I responded. "If I'm a terrorist, I can see that something has gone wrong, so I may be thinking, 'How can I leverage this chaotic situation to initiate a plot? Maybe use it as a distraction?' But also, this is a *network* problem. Two weeks ago who cared about Mobile and Gulfport airports? Now they are among the most important airports in the country. Talk about complexity theory, this is resilience in action."

Beyond humanitarian concerns, there was also a strategic correction to be made. The book I'd given out, *The Logic of Failure,* dissects several large-scale industrial accidents—the nuclear meltdown at Chernobyl, the poisonous gas suddenly jetted out of a Union Carbide chemical plant in Bhopal, India—and draws similar conclusions about each incident. In each case, operators became overconfident while working within a complex, heavily regulated system. Annoyed or unimpressed with what they viewed as unnecessary rules and restrictions, they kept pushing the operational envelope until they made a fatal mistake.

In each case, "human error" is technically the correct diagnosis. But these mistakes were not made by incompetents but by expert technicians either chafing under, or lulled to sleep by a rulebook handed down from above. I was already concerned about this dynamic among our talented but disaffected screeners, and as Katrina unfolded, I had a front-row seat to the rampant dysfunction at headquarters.

We had received the reporting on the hurricane as it approached the city, but as the situation grew more dire, there was no mechanism to pick up on the growing sense of concern or initiate a new response. Instead, I continued to receive briefings from these very capable employees, many of them former soldiers or police officials, that the airport was closed, that some Transportation Security Officers were sick. Our inertia-weighted reportage process just kept taking data points and putting them into PowerPoint templates, rather than sounding the alarm that something outside the planning scenario was afoot.

The lesson for me was that, just as with the September 11 attacks, what works for daily federal operations is unlikely to work in a new kind of crisis. Communications were lost in translation even before cell-phone coverage collapsed; decisions stalled on the way up the chain of command; and the people at the top, myself included, didn't adequately understand the local conditions. It was clear that top-down agencies, once decapitated, are unable to make full use of their resources or adapt quickly to challenges. Whether the TSA was facing down threats presented by terrorists or acts of God, we needed to have people everywhere able and authorized to adapt and respond.

But there was a bright side. Once we overcame the communication failures, we realized that we could mobilize our committed frontline people very quickly. And we knew how they would respond. In a short period, we had found hundreds of TSOs and FAMs willing to volunteer for the New Orleans relief effort. We had successfully coordinated with private industry—the airlines that supplied planes—to move in our volunteers and evacuate the refugees. Afterward I twisted Mike Restovich's arm until he agreed to come up to

Washington and be our head of operations. After his team's enhancements, we were able to use subsequent hurricanes like Rita (2005) and Ike (2008) as training grounds to improve our readiness and crisis-management abilities.

AFTER KATRINA, I WAS EVEN MORE ENTHUSIASTIC ABOUT GETTING THE federal air marshals back at the start of the fiscal year on October 1, 2005. They added a unique, mobile, and powerful layer to TSA's security abilities. Of all the US special military and law enforcement forces, FAMs receive arguably the best and most specialized firearms instruction. If they have to use their weapons, it will likely be in very tight quarters surrounded by innocent passengers. This is critical, because when faced with actually shooting someone, even police officers and soldiers who are trained to do so, everyone experiences similar physiological sensations. Instinctively, blood begins rushing protectively to a shooter's vital organs or major muscle groups, causing them to lose manual dexterity. Their heart rate increases dramatically while they lose hearing and experience tunnel vision.

To simulate this real-world shooting environment, FAM training doesn't take place on a simple shooting range, but on an obstacle course. Marshals will run a mile, be asked to do one hundred pushups, or engage each other in hand-to-hand combat before drawing their weapons. Then a whistle blows, sending the marshals sprinting through a shooting range mocked up as an aircraft cabin. As they run down the tight aisles, they target and fire at ten-inch plates. Before they are certified, FAMs are trained to make a decision, draw, and fire within two seconds, knowing that any mistakes, including inaction, can kill an innocent person.

In addition to the specialized marksman training that takes place in Atlantic City, FAMs also learn travel-specific skills such as how to work out in hotel rooms. To stay in top shape while traveling, FAMs learn several different adaptable exercise disciplines, including Pilates. When not in the air, they are training at one of the many FAM training centers found in unmarked, innocuous-looking office parks around the country.

After visiting some of these training facilities, I was impressed. It would be nearly impossible for a hijacker to take over a cockpit with one of our air marshals on board. They were also well networked, constantly receiving and integrating real-time information into their daily work. Many of the FAMs I met considered their smart phone to be their best advantage, more so even than the Sig Sauer pistol hidden somewhere out of sight. The FAM control center located off the main watch floor at TSA's operations center, called the Freedom Center, near Dulles Airport does more than manage its teams' flights on US air carriers all over the world; it keeps a database of suspicious people and activities, sharing relevant information system-wide and pulsing out real-time reporting from FAMs all over the world. The FAMs have revolutionized air-to-ground communications, but I was just as excited by their versatility and how valuable they could be in nontraditional roles. In fact, their flexibility was so unique that I promised Secretary Chertoff that we could transport 500 FAMs anywhere in the country within four hours, at any time. TSA personnel are already in airports; they are constantly wired to headquarters, and in most scenarios, we could utilize existing commercial flights. If not, we are able to work with the airlines to transport them in an emergency. If we put out a call for FAMs and had, say, 150 covering flights in and out of Hartsfield-Jackson in Atlanta, we could ask Delta to load them up and fly them to wherever they were needed. No other federal organization—not the FBI, not the US Marshals, not the ATF—can deliver an infusion of law-enforcement personnel that quickly.

NINE

SEARCHING FOR A POCKETKNIFE IN A HAYSTACK

ONE EVENING A FEW WEEKS AFTER HURRICANE KATRINA, LEE Kair sat quietly in a corner of the seventh-floor conference room during an evening leadership session I had called. Lee, the acquisitions expert with a wry smile, was well aware of the agency's early failings. He had been one of the people tasked with patching up the budgetary nightmare inherited from our founding. Now Lee listened intently to my challenge to the senior leadership's ideas that we faced a dangerous security gap related to undetected bomb parts. I still felt the sting of having been blindsided by TSA's slow-moving incident management process shown during Katrina, but mainly I was concerned about the TSA's vulnerability to someone bringing a disassembled bomb through a checkpoint. Our process wasn't built to stop that threat, and I knew we needed to implement some new thinking as quickly as possible. By the time we wrapped up, Lee was impressed. *This could be really good for the agency,* he thought.

"Right," I said, looking around the room. "So who is going to lead this effort?"

Lee looked around the silenced room, thinking, *Some poor sucker is going to have to head this up. And those operations guys already have a lot to do.*

After looking around at the stoic faces and letting the room sit quiet for an uncomfortable period I said, "So, I think that we need a special task force drawing on all of your resources. This effort will report directly to me, and, Lee, you ought to lead it."

Lee's face was impassive, but I know he was thinking, *This is completely out of my league.* But he went home and talked to his wife about a major career change, moving away from the job in which he had gained years of experience and a master's degree. The next day he came up to my office and said, "All right. Let's do this."

Lee had no mentors since no one had had this position before. So he fell back on what he knew, containing problems with rigorous analytical discipline, sound project management, setting up partnerships, and cajoling people into do things they normally wouldn't. And it turned out that collaboration and discipline were not only perfect skills for the position, but also elements sorely lacking at the TSA. Lee set up his team in the Info Center, down the hall from my office.

At the time, the TSA was focused almost solely on finding prohibited items, an approach I suspected was not the best use of screeners' time. To get a sense of what this policy really meant, Lee led teams to several local airports and said to the employees there, "Give me all the prohibited items that you've collected over the past week." He then dragged the garbage cans of banned items off to whatever private space was available in the airport—an empty room, hallway or closet—and spent hours digging through the piles to see what was being seized. Cigarette lighters, scissors, knives, and small tools comprised almost the entire contents of the bins. Everything else was marginal, meaning that screeners were spending hours collecting relatively low-risk objects. And because they were almost always focused on these small objects, they eventually became conditioned to *only* expect to find these items. They were working within a system in which finding a small pocketknife or lighter became equivalent to finding a bomb, and therefore much more likely.

To test this theory, Lee's team ran carry-on bags through the checkpoint x-ray machines with a test item packed underneath a lighter, both visible to the officer positioned at the monitor. We got better at finding the lighters than finding the test items. Constant positive reinforcement on lighters had turned our checkpoint operations into an Easter egg hunt for minor banned items.

Fortunately, live plots to smuggle explosives on board are extremely rare. So, to give our officers the practice they needed, we used test kits to simulate what a terrorist might carry. As time went on, we also had screeners themselves try to sneak bomb components past checkpoints, packing the bags themselves and then handing the luggage off to unrecognizable accomplices. Not only were we getting our frontline workers more accustomed to seeing bombs, we were also training them to think like terrorists.

Just as important was reducing the amount of time screeners spent searching for these low-risk objects. Unfortunately, lighters were untouchable, having been banned by congressional legislation. And despite the radically reduced risk that knives and box cutters presented in the post-9/11 world—a small blade wasn't getting anyone through fortified cockpit doors—allowing them back on board was considered too emotionally charged for the American public. The Federal Air Marshals weighed in heavily against lifting the ban on knives but were open to supporting some other changes, such as small tools. We looked for a dividing line to separate "good" tools from "bad" tools, and decided to uphold the ban for larger tools or ones that could be used to bash or pry open the cockpit door.

Finally, we came to scissors, which are essentially two knives. A pair of scissors could probably do the same bloody damage at a crowded shopping mall as in an airplane cabin—they weren't going to take down a plane—but the potential violence could be limited by the length of the blades. Thus, the decision over allowable length became a classic application of the risk-management approach to security that Secretary Chertoff had endorsed: The amount of risk we were willing to take on versus the burden imposed on our screening staff and the traveling public.

At the time, 95 percent of the seized objects were less than four inches in length from the fulcrum. Allowing blades up to four inches would relieve our screeners of a tremendous amount of work and was a measure that seemed to pass the eyeball test as well.

"You know those Fiskars?" I asked Lee and his staff, during a discussion about allowable lengths. "That's about right." In fact, it turned out that Fiskars, the ubiquitous orange-handled scissors, were about three-and-a-half inches in length, readily available at any drugstore, and would make a huge difference in the number of scissors we had to confiscate. After 2001, they were not going to allow anyone to hijack an airplane. But then, right on time, internal politics intervened.

Our plan to change the regulations regarding scissors was leaked by someone inside the agency—not a planned leak, but a real tip-off from someone interested in killing the suggestion. In the following public debate, the TSA was slammed by, among others, Senator Hillary Clinton of New York and the Association of Flight Attendants, who warned that our recommendation would lead to "blood running in the aisles."[1] So then our deputy head of intelligence, Joe Salvator, had to go up to Capitol Hill to brief Congress on why scissors and lighters weren't serious threats. This put him in a tricky bind: Six months earlier, he'd also been sent there by the former TSA administrator, Dave Stone, to tell the same people why the exact same items should be prohibited.

Joe later told me that while leaving the second meeting he thought, *I wasn't lying either time.* The terrorists had begun to expand and develop new capacities that pushed scissors way down the threat chart.

Soon thereafter, Joe was walking through New York's JFK airport and spotted a screener doing a explosives trace detection on a wheelchair. Interested in seeing the procedure conducted in the field, he walked over to introduce himself to the TSO.

The officer responded sharply. "We don't get any intelligence on this stuff. We're getting everything from CNN."

Joe paused for a second. He got the same complaint everywhere he went; in fact, everyone in the intel community did. "You just checked that wheelchair," he pointed out. "You don't know why you did it, but I do. You did that check because we know from al-Qaeda training documents that terrorists are considering smuggling explosives in wheelchair wheels. Now here we are a week later, and you're checking the wheelchair. So I'm sorry you don't know why, but I'm damn glad that you're doing the check!"

The wheelchair was not the only worry. The TSA was also getting other intel regarding the terrorists' innovations, including remote detonators and more sophisticated concealment. Someone on the other side was proving himself to be a smart engineer, with elegant and simple designs. Whoever he or they were was very focused on aviation, and was spending a lot of time improving the shoe bomb, a device originally hidden in a heavy boot. Now the presumably same engineer had developed the technology to create a completely nonmetallic bomb. The new bomb also had an idiot-proof electric detonator—no matches necessary—that was suitable even for a bungler like Richard Reid.

It was Reid's December 2001 attempt that spurred TSA to take off our heavy shoes and boots at checkpoints. Three and half years later, I came into the administrator's office dead set on eliminating that requirement. I thought it was a confusing, overly reactive rule. Maybe, but as al-Qaeda's technology progressed far beyond the original boot bomb, I realized that they could take down an aircraft with an explosive device hidden in a normal street shoe, not a thick-soled hiking boot. We knew that street-shoe bombs were in the al-Qaeda labs, and we knew we couldn't stop them unless we x-rayed shoes. It is this advancement in their technology that makes shoes a serious continuing threat, and something passengers unfortunately still have to deal with at airports. And, as amazing as it sounds, requiring everyone to remove their shoes actually noticeably increased line speed, by removing the uncertainty of whether or not shoes would be inspected.

BACK AT EUROPEAN UNION HEADQUARTERS IN BRUSSELS, MARJETA Jager had gained some insight into her new boss, Francois Lamoureux, and his frustration with the United States as an aviation partner. Marjeta also wondered why American authorities were issuing security rules for Europe. For example, the security at Paris' major international airport, Charles De-Gaulle, (known as CDG) is controlled by the French government, but the EU also inspects the airport operations. CDG must also be in compliance with the United Nations's International Civil Aviation Organization as well as another group called the European Civil Aviation Conference. Then, on top of all this mix, the United States has its own independent regime of regulation and inspection that was not coordinated with the three other efforts.

Marjeta understood that the attacks of 9/11 drove the American insistence on inspecting all planes headed their way, but, if nothing else, all the different inspection regimes seemed a waste of resources. What's more, Marjeta suspected that the TSA's demand for "enhanced" security measures from European airports and airlines might not actually be improving the safety of those flights. The US requirements seemed more focused on creating a regular paper-trail that would allow the TSA administrator to tell Congress the agency was "conducting an independent review of European airport operations." It was a phrase that sounded great in testimony, but the reality was less impressive. TSA inspectors were required to give sixty days notice to an airport authority before an inspection and, once on site, the TSA was escorted on a carefully limited tour of the airport before heading to a conference room filled with reams of paper to verify inspection. To Marjeta the US technique seemed much less effective than the unannounced and boundary-less EU-authorized inspections.

Even more maddening, the TSA had developed the practice of issuing regulatory thunderbolts to Europe in the form of "Emergency Amendments" that had the immediate force of law. In a real emergency, Marjeta understood TSA's need to protect American-bound flights, but the TSA's refusal to divulge the intel behind threats to the EU only deepened the chasm separating the United States and Europe. TSA had also recently turned back a number of flights to the United States on the basis that a European air carrier had potentially allowed someone on TSA's No-Fly list onboard the aircraft. The airlines were furious with what they considered draconian treatment by the TSA, especially when flights were turned around, at a cumulative cost approaching the millions of dollars, for somebody who actually was not on the intended No-Fly list but had a similar name. But because the EU did not get a copy of the No-Fly list, there was little Marjeta could do.

Meanwhile, on the other side of the Atlantic, TSA officials were livid that the European airlines were doing such a bad job at just keeping a limited number of suspected terrorists off planes. In short, Marjeta found herself pursuing Lamoureux's cooperation offensive in an already poisoned environment. But since this initiative was one of her major responsibilities, Marjeta decided she would at least be un-ignorable and show up on the doorstep of her estranged counterparts in the United States. But to whom could she go? TSA had a competent set of representatives in liaison positions from their international office. Delightful and deeply knowledgeable, they could explain anything about the TSA's legal obligations under US law and they did listen, for hours sometimes, to the EU's side of things, but they were not going to drive fundamental transformations. In the first half of 2005 the group which *could be* an agent of change, the US aviation security team, was in transition. Homeland Security Secretary Michael Chertoff and his deputy, Michael Jackson, were both new. And the new TSA head, a California businessman named Kip Hawley, drew a blank. But Marjeta had learned from previous jobs that the first step to anything successful started by building trust, so she booked a flight from Brussels to Washington in August, 2005 to put faces to names.

At the TSA buildings in Arlington, Marjeta was greeted cordially by the head of TSA's international office and brought through security and up to a conference room on the tenth floor where, for an hour, Marjeta and TSA's international staff rehearsed the meeting. The hosts delicately informed Marjeta that the new Administrator was very busy and not quite up to speed on all the details of the relationship and that during this introductory meeting she might want to accentuate the positives in the relationship and defer discussion of the more complex topics. Marjeta looked out the windows and wondered whether they opened, because if they did, she might just take a leap. But an hour later, she was escorted by her cautious and amiable handlers down to the seventh floor, through double glass doors and a long series of hallways until she was admitted to the Administrator's office area.

Twenty minutes later, Marjeta stood to leave and thought to herself, "Why the hell did I come? I have just been talking to a blank wall."

As he ushered her out into the hallway, the TSA's international liaison turned to Marjeta with a smile, "I thought that went well."

Despite her frustration during her August visit to Washington, Marjeta was still optimistic when, on October 19, TSA's head paid a visit to Brussels. At least Kip Hawley was stopping here first before going to London for his first meeting with the UK authorities. The set piece meeting, where the two sides would sit across a large table from one another and march through a pre-arranged list of topics, was unavoidable but unpromising. As perhaps an exchange for behaving so cooperatively in Washington, DC, Marjeta had exacted the promise from the TSA international guy that she would have dinner with Kip, or "Keep" as she pronounced it. Marjeta wasn't going for the *moules frites*, she wanted someplace quiet where she could lay out her case.

ABOUT A MONTH AFTER HURRICANE KATRINA, I WAS STRIDING THROUGH Logan Airport on a quick trip up to Boston for my mother's birthday when a stout, excitable man ran up behind me.

"Mr. Hawley? Hello. My name's Carl Maccario."

"Hello," I said, shaking his extended hand. I recognized him as a TSA person but I couldn't quite place him.

"I'd like to talk to you about behavior detection."

I paused. I was hoping to get through the airport quickly and grab a cab, but Carl's pitch was intriguing, so instead I sat down with him in a Dunkin' Donuts for a coffee. I was already interested in the possibilities of behavior detection, but of course, Carl had a lot more to say on the subject.

Carl told me how in 2003, while working a screener job for which he felt overqualified, he had continued to develop his own behavior recognition techniques. Eventually he fell into conversation with a state police sergeant named Peter DiDomenica who was posted at his checkpoint.

"Where'd you do this before?" asked the sergeant.

"At Virgin," replied Carl.

"Really? Jeez, I'm putting together a program called BASS, the Behavior Analysis Screening System, for the state police."

Carl looked over. "You know, the TSA should have a behavior program too. But I'm just a pimple on the ass of the TSA."

Carl and the sergeant decided to pool their knowledge. To expand their research, Carl called the American Psychological Association, eventually getting in touch with some of the best-known and respected professors in the detection community: Paul Ekman, a colleague of Ekman's named David Matsumoto who had collaborated on a tool to identify microfacial expressions, and a Rutgers professor named Mark Frank. Carl pulled long hours, sometimes working the four A.M.–to–noon shift, going out to the parking lot to nap in his car, then coming back to the airport to work on his proposal.

Fortunately for Carl, Logan was one of the most forward-thinking airports in the country. (The airport had extra incentive for improving security; recall that on September 11, both planes flown into the World Trade Center had originated at Logan.) After his persistent inquiries, the FSD in charge of Logan allowed Carl to start a trial behavior-detection program. By this time, Carl had absorbed every related model he could locate: the Israeli practice, the Massachusetts State Police program, academic research, basic police interrogation skills, and his own experience. The net result was a completely novel discipline that Carl could now refine in the field.

Soon Carl's approach was getting regional attention outside of aviation. He was asked to bring a team and work with the Secret Service at Senator John Kerry's Election Day party at the Copley Hotel in downtown Boston in 2004. Carl positioned himself at the front of the barricades, scanning the thousands of faces in the crowd. The party was a big event, with Bon Jovi and Sheryl Crow performing, so there were innumerable innocent onlookers, but Carl zeroed in on one guy who kept moving with the crowd. Most people at these events fall into two categories: people with passes or people content to stand outside and watch the entertainment. But this guy seemed uninterested in anything other than scoping out the scene. It was, Carl knew, a classic type that the Secret Service looked for. Instead of being caught up in the pageantry and entertainment, a stone-faced person who shadows the dignitary is always worth watching. As the night wore on, the security team spotted two suspicious people displaying just that behavior. After Carl pointed them out to the police, they were questioned and then arrested, most likely on outstanding warrants issued by other law enforcement agencies rather than violent behavior that night.

By the beginning of 2005, Carl was ready to pilot a program called SPOT, or Screening Passengers by Observation Technique, that had some immediate successes. One day he saw a group of men apparently conducting surveillance on the checkpoint. Their faces obscured by hoods, the men kept moving furtively up to toward the checkpoint without baggage or boarding passes before dropping back. Carl watched them for a second and then walked outside. He lit up a cigar and thought about what he'd seen for a minute. Finally, he, laughed. "Ya gotta be kidding me!"

After stashing his cigar in a crack above the door molding, Carl called the police and went back inside to engage the group. Immediately, the suspects tried to take off, but were collared by the police. Carl went back outside, fished his cigar out of its hiding spot and imagined what it would be like if TSA made SPOT an official part of security. Carl was interrupted by a call from his boss who beckoned him upstairs to see his superiors. The small room was a mob scene crammed police and airport authorities. It turned out that members of the group, all Brazilians, were wanted on drug charges. There was only one question for Carl: "How did you catch them?" Soon thereafter Carl got permission to expand his SPOT pilot to Providence, Rhode Island, and Portland, Maine.

I sat listening to him recount all this, riveted. When I looked down at my watch, I realized that I'd been talking to Carl over two hours. I looked back up. "You need to come to HQ so we can do that program on a national scale."

THE STIRWEN RESTAURANT IS ONLY ABOUT ONE HUNDRED METERS from Marjeta's EU offices and is a commission favorite. Off a bustling square and along a bumpy gray brick sidewalk, the Stirwen's green awning makes it stand out. It has a few steep steps and then a dark reception area. Marjeta had arranged a table in the front corner with a nice view outside, but more important to me, a source of light for another hour or so to keep me going. Earlier in the day, we had met at her office. With her black hair pulled tightly back and precise business attire, Marjeta had steered us through an extremely professional and cordial meeting. But by the time I had perused the appetizers, I sensed that this was a whole different Marjeta, talking fast, puffing deeply on her cigarette and spicing her key sentences with tone-perfect American swear words. Her agenda wasn't the sub paragraphs of codicils or the nuances of bulleted talking points, Marjeta just wanted some-body to engage with her. We didn't talk a minute about California or Slo-venia, but bonded over a shared frustration with overly rigid processes that defied common sense. About midway through dinner, Marjeta said some-thing I didn't catch. "Keep, I see your sherrif du ciel is quite vigilant." I got "Keep," that was how my name came out in her near flawless but accented English. But "sherrif du ciel?"

Marjeta pointed out the window at a man crossing the square. It was Rich Stein, head of the international department with the Federal Air Mar-shals. Ah, "sherrif du ciel,"—my Air Marshal.

The following morning, I got an audience with Marjeta's boss, Francois Lamoureux, a distinguished and long-serving civil servant who worked out of a formal, stuffy office. I knew we had a major issue with the French over No-Flys, so I braced myself for a browbeating, but Monsieur Lamoureux was witty, charming, very cerebral and had a vision for harmonized security across countries and modes of transportation. I became so engaged during our talk that I broke my own rule and rolled out my complexity theory analogy.

After our big picture conversation we talked specifically about the trou-bled EU-US relationship, an issue that didn't enflame Lamoureux so much as sadden him. Then he paused and glanced at Marjeta before getting up from behind his desk and walking over to his credenza to pick up a folder. Walk-ing over to me, he said "Kip, if we are to trust each other, one must take the first step. I would like to give you a document that is considered confidential. I trust that you will know how to keep this document safe but I also think that you will find its contents highly interesting." I opened the folder to find a classified internal review of EU airport security audits full of specific de-tail, including weaknesses and corrective actions. Shortly after our meeting, Lamoureux became ill and passed away within the year, but his vision for harmonized security among EU and American partners came to fruition, and sooner than any of us expected.

TEN

WHY WE WATCH OUT FOR WEDDINGS IN CHICAGO

IN OCTOBER 2005, ABDULRAHMAN HILLAL HUSSEIN GOT A new name. During the upcoming operation he would be known as "Imran." Still living and training in alternately muddy and dusty camps in the hills of western Pakistan, Abdulrahman met the other two operatives in this elite group, both Britons of Pakistani descent. One was a stout, talkative man from the Manchester area named Rangzieb Ahmed. Ahmed was about thirty and, judging by their conversation, seemed to have been a longtime activist whose efforts had landed him in an Indian jail after what Ahmed described as hiking into contested Kashmir. Ahmed had been in training since arriving in Islamabad on May 26, but was not nearly as fit as the other operative, a quiet guy named Mohammed Zillur Rahman. Soon it became clear that the three of them constituted a cell in whatever Hamza Rabia's larger scheme was. Imran was put in charge.

The cell occasionally moved around from camp to camp for security purposes, but mostly the threesome followed the same routine: training drills involving fitness and combat skills mixed with long stretches of time—sometimes days—when they prayed, exercised, read, ate, and sat around discussing the Koran and jihad or argued about football. The Brits were dedicated to English Premier League soccer and barely acknowledged FK Austria Wien, even though Abdulrahman's team had reached the quarterfinal of a European cup tournament the previous season. It soon became a circular conversation. The group sometimes received messages from Hamza Rabia through a messenger. Occasionally al-Muhajir, the short, olive-skinned master bomb maker, showed up unannounced, sparking a palpable electricity. Al-Muhajir's abilities with explosives had made him a major celebrity within al-Qaeda.

Early on under al-Muhajir's tutelage, Abdulrahman and his accomplices had each received a silver Casio F91W-1, a classic digital watch featuring a calendar, stopwatch, alarm, and, once they rewired it, the ability to trigger bombs on a precisely timed schedule. Once wired to the detonator, the operatives could select a date weeks ahead or utilize that popular set piece of every thriller: a timer counting down to a deadly explosion.

But correctly timing the explosives was far easier than selecting the best option for a mission. Each of the many possible explosives offered its own advantages and drawbacks, ranging from power-to-size ratio, stability, what type of detonation was sufficient to make it pop, and concealability. Nitroglycerin, for instance, packed a tremendous punch and, by itself, they thought was virtually undetectable by airport security. However, the liquid was also very "jumpy" and needed to be stabilized with a tamping material, like cotton, to avoid a premature explosion if the device were dropped accidentally. And even when the explosive's volatility was under control, the cotton was easily detectable by airport x-rays. Nitroglycerin was also already on security officials' radar after Ramzi Yousef, the 1993 World Trade Center bomb maker, ignited a nitro-based device on a Philippine Airlines flight in 1994.

Al-Muhajir preferred working with plastic explosives because of their power, stability, reliability, and ease of detonation, as well as the fact that you could hide them almost anywhere. The biggest drawback to plastics like C4 is that they aren't very easy to source, so once a terror group got a supply, they would be quite possibly be pursued by tenacious security officials with global reach. Setting off these alarms was not an ideal condition for a terror cell operating in Europe or the United States.

But by 2005 there was an exciting new possibility: hydrogen peroxide–based explosives in both liquid and solid forms. Hydrogen peroxide bombs were powerful and easily composed from ingredients commonly found in hair dye and pool cleaner. A form of powdered hydrogen peroxide had been successfully used by the July 7, 2005 London subway bombers, but the later attempt by the July 21 crew fizzled, revealing the complications with some peroxide-based bombs. Making the explosives pop in their liquid form was even more of an art. But even with this drawback, hydrogen peroxide's stability, punch, and invisibility to security measures, made it a very intriguing option.

Abdulrahman loved these technical and creative challenges, and his measured intensity seemed to energize al-Muhajir, who told Abdulrahman that he should go by the code name "Waqas," meaning "the Warrior." The name stuck.

By early November, the men were well versed in coded communications and disappearing ink; they had learned how to prepare massive bombs that looked like everyday video-game equipment; and they had been coached by the hand-picked confidantes of Ayman Zawahiri and Osama bin Laden. On the fifth day of the month, the threesome learned actual details of their mission.

Having struck London in July, Hamza Rabia was ready to hit hard again, and Abdulrahman understood that this new operation was aimed at both Britain and the United States. Abdulrahman was only privy to the critical elements of his—Imran's—cell, one link in a larger global operation. But he was unsettled. While his spirits were lifted by the knowledge that he was doing important work, Abdulrahman's focus was jarred by the death of his fighting colleagues nearby. American and British forces just across the border in Afghanistan engaged with some of the young men with whom he had trained and killed some of his acquaintances. A missile strike the previous Saturday in Mosaki, North Waziristan, had killed the family of his mentor, Hamza Rabias. The unseen blow from above disturbed him—how had the Americans learned of Hamza Rabia's location? Did they know about this mission? What would happen if they killed Hamza Rabia? Al-Muhajir? Was he next?—but also created an air of invincibility. Hamza Rabia himself had escaped with a broken leg, and the mission would go forward despite the death of his family. Perhaps, Abdulrahman thought, his team was favored with the same god-given protection as Hamza Rabia.

Despite their excitement at learning the details of the imminent operation, Abdulrahman and his team soon found themselves back in the routine of waiting, eating, idly chatting, and sometimes breaking into fervent discussions of religion. Then, just before dawn one morning, a pair of dirty white Toyota 4x4s pulled up and idled outside their house. Abdulrahman rushed Ahmed and Zillur Rahman out the door. Outside, a stocky Egyptian whom Abdulrahman half-recognized but did not know jumped from the first truck and yelled, "*Steigen Sie ein!*"

Abdulrahman hopped in and the Toyota roared off, bumping along the rocky dirt road. Inside, the Egyptian continued speaking in fluent German, explaining that he had lived in Germany and developed lots of contacts in the country. Then, after a few minutes of chatter, the man got down to the business at hand, and Abdulrahman felt a surge of adrenaline. He realized that the Egyptian, known as Abu Ubaydah al-Masri, was an operational deputy to Hamza Rabia and obviously knew al-Muhajir because he used his nickname, Waqas. Abu Ubaydah also seemed to know a great deal about the London attacks and their bomb-making techniques. Abdulrahman guessed that this guy was now his boss. Not particularly handsome, with rough features and curly black hair, Abu Ubaydah looked a decade or two older than the other two men in Abdulrahman's cell.

This was the beginning of the mission. After the drone strike, Hamza Rabia had decided to put the team in motion and get out of the dangerous Waziristan area—which was also probably the most heavily monitored place on earth; emails and phone calls were regularly intercepted—and begin positioning them for their attack.

The Toyotas dropped the cell off at an airport in western Pakistan. Abdulrahman, Rangzieb Ahmed, and Mohammed Zillur Rahman took flights to China, where they stayed a few days. They had no real business there other than blurring their travel profile, creating a route that didn't immediately set off alarms and might throw anyone off their movements. The group then backtracked to Dubai, just off the east coast of the Arabian Peninsula. As team leader, Imran was the first to move into position, arriving in Abu Dhabi in the early hours of December 10. He needed time to secure the hotel rooms and make sure there wasn't an enemy reception committee on hand to compromise the attack. A day later, Sunday December 11, Ahmed and Zillur Rahman arrived at Dubai's sleek international airport. They gathered their bags and took the ten-minute cab ride to the Hotel Versailles, a luxurious building on 15th Street. Abdulrahman met them in the marble-floored lobby and the three men went to room 701 to review their plans for the next stage of the operation.

AT ROUGHLY THE SAME TIME, I WAS CHECKING MY BLACKBERRY AS MY government-issued black Chevy Suburban crossed the Potomac on the way to a meeting with Secretary Chertoff. Depending on traffic, it was about a twenty-minute drive from the TSA's vintage brown towers to the Department of Homeland Security's leafy, low-lying campus at a tony northwest Washington address. Because the buildings sat at the intersection of Nebraska and Connecticut Avenues, they were known as the NAC, which stood for Nebraska Avenue Complex and was pronounced "knack." Since my initial interview with Chertoff, I had been up to the NAC quite a few times, but I had no idea what this meeting was about.

My driver, Terry, maneuvered past throngs of American University students before turning onto a wooded road, a back entrance that wove along one side of the DHS campus. At the guard gate, I pulled out the massed badges around my neck—some for TSA access, another to get me past emergency roadblocks in the National Capital Area, and another for the DHS campus. Then we clunked over the steel barriers, passed through a shed used for vehicle inspections, and pulled into a parking lot behind the secretary's office. I hopped out and up the stairs, pulling out my badges several more times to gain entry. At the last barricade, I deposited my BlackBerry and everything else in my pockets into a locked wooden cubbyhole before passing through a six-inch thick door into the secure area with nothing more than my badges, a bottle of water, and a notebook from Staples. Nothing came out of the vault either. When I left, my notes would be confiscated and later couriered back to the TSA's intelligence floor.

Immediately inside the vault sat a mini operations room. Twenty watch officers peered intently at computer monitors and TV screens covering the wall. Several agencies, including the TSA, had personnel there around the clock to keep a finger on the world's pulse through both global news reporting and government-sourced material. If there was an episode in which, say, a stowaway climbed up in the wheel well of a 747 flying from Johannesburg, South Africa to JFK and froze to death as happened in June 2005, several people would be scrambling to figure out how that happened.

I turned right toward the briefing room. These types of secure facilities, which exist somewhere in nearly every major government agency, give new meaning to the phrase "controlled environment." The air was always kept cool and dry for the benefit of the huge number of computers, monitors, cameras, and other electronics. The floor, ceiling, and walls were impenetrable to monitoring and outside noise. The lighting was focused and artificial. The space below the floor was hollowed out to run cabling, and my footsteps echoed as I walked down the hallway. But for all their sophistication, the teleconference rooms I passed always seemed to be filled with a jumbled mess of unused telephones, monitors, and chairs stacked against walls.

After the brief walk, I turned left into a small room with colonial yellow walls, a monitor and camera for video conferencing, and a secure phone on a heavy rectangular wooden table. At the head sat Secretary Chertoff, framed by the American and DHS flags. To his right sat Michael Jackson; to his left, Charlie Allen, the 69-year-old DHS head of intelligence known as "the Legend."

Secretary Chertoff, who had light olive skin, a nearly bald head, and bright, probing eyes, started the meeting with a few words in his precise New Jersey accent. Then, after his brief preface, the CIA briefers sitting along the wall were introduced, first names only. Within minutes I was sweating bullets.

The CIA personnel laid out a series of tiny information snippets, each a puzzle piece that meant little by itself. Some of these bits of data were from human sources; some from electronic surveillance or intercepted e-mails and phone calls. But as the fragments piled up over the next twenty minutes, a picture slowly emerged: Operation Glidepath, a plot hatched at the highest levels of al-Qaeda and aimed at targets in the United States and the United Kingdom.

But that wasn't what made my palms clammy. While the threat was deemed real enough to bring all the top people at the DHS together, there were many details the intel community didn't know: who, when, how, and where they were going to strike. After the meeting, I walked back out through security, retrieving my BlackBerry and keys, climbed numbly into the Suburban and stared straight ahead. A few months earlier I had been sworn into a job to restructure and promote a new work culture at a stumbling agency. Or so I thought. But this briefing had ripped open a whole new universe of threats, plots, and possibilities. I felt like I was facing down my first genuine terror threat—with an empty gun.

I didn't know it then, but the conundrum I faced after the Operation Glidepath briefing was common in the intel world. Intelligence gathering doesn't consist of diligent analysts laboring until information explaining a plot drops into their laps. In fact, most intel veterans will dismiss data that explains the who, how, and when as *too easy* to be trustworthy. Real information is almost always obfuscated and incomplete. Understanding it is a painstaking process of guesswork and conjecture leading to hypotheses that are usually torn apart and discarded. Eventually, the shadowy outline of a serious threat may emerge like a constellation in a universe of data. But even when a compelling series of bright data points appear, how do you know if they describe a bear or a dog?

But in late November 2005, I was a neophyte in the world of intel, so I fell back on what I did know. I stepped up the deployment of Behavior Detection Officers (BDOs), one of the TSA's most effective assets for sniffing out threats while we were virtually flying blind. After our chance meeting at Logan, Carl Maccario had helped to set up a nucleus of trainers that went around to twelve of the nation's largest airports, known as Category X, and taught screeners to become BDOs. These new teams were all deployed before Christmas.

The BDOs were trained to refer to a sheet that scored various behaviors—distress, fear, fidgeting—on how alarming they were. BDOs used a cocktail of targeted emotions that drive the point-based system. By weighing different behaviors on a score sheet and confirming that they observed multiple alarming emotions, BDOs were able to incorporate a more objective approach to what is perceived to be a very subjective technique. Every day in America, 2 million people walk onto planes from every possible ethnic, religious, cultural, and racial background. The score sheet was meant to provide some sort of threshold before selecting people for additional screening or questioning, and hopefully protect us and the passengers alike from mistakes driven by preconceptions of what a terrorist looks like.

In accelerating the launch of the SPOT program, I told Carl we faced a real terrorist threat, but couldn't reveal anything else about it. Soon thereafter Carl again demonstrated a BDO's ability to detect unusual behavior. One day, Carl was outside the American Airlines terminal at Boston's Logan Airport wearing his white TSA shirt, looking, he figured, like a Good Humor ice-cream salesman, and generally watching for the watchers. After a bit, he spotted a woman and two men without bags, or any apparent interest in the arriving or departing flights.

What are they doing here? wondered Carl. The group was simply staring at the exit lane. He called a state trooper over and pointed out the group.

"Yeah," agreed the trooper. "What the hell are they doing?"

"Maybe some kind of surveillance," suggested Carl.

The trooper walked over to talk to them and then waved to Carl.

"Nice going," said the woman angrily as Carl arrived. "We're with the FBI. We're doing some surveillance. You just exposed the operation."

"Well, then you better go back to training," replied Carl. "My daughter could have picked you out."

"What's that supposed to mean?" she asked.

"You've got no luggage, no ticket, you're not even looking up to see if there's an arriving flight. You stood out like a sore thumb."

The FBI team walked away.

AGAIN USING STAGGERED TRAVEL ARRANGEMENTS, MOHAMMED ZILLUR Rahman was to leave for Johannesburg, South Africa, on December 13, where he would meet the contacts who were handling the logistics for the cell's onward trip to their ultimate target, the United States. Abdulrahman and Ahmed would wait a day or two longer to receive the green light from Hamza Rabia before joining Zillur Rahman in South Africa. A cleanup operative named Habib, who was a colleague of Ahmed's from the UK, was due to arrive from England, overlap for a day in Dubai with Abdulrahman and Ahmed, and tie up loose ends so that nothing of value would be found after the operation. On December 14, Zillur Rahman departed on schedule to Johannesburg. But the approval for the rest to move forward never came: Hamza Rabia had been killed by an American drone attack. The mission was aborted, the operatives told to get out immediately, go home, and lie low.

The next day, Habib flew home to Manchester via Schiphol Airport in Amsterdam, carrying with him code books and notes. Zillur Rahman flew to London Heathrow from Johannesburg. Ahmed stayed another week to let things cool off before he too flew home to Manchester on the December 21. Abdulrahman, showing his instinct for survival, was gone as soon as he received the order, leaving Imran's identity to evaporate in the Dubai sun.

WE GOT LUCKY WITH THAT ONE, BUT I KNEW IT WOULD BE A BRIEF REprieve. Drones wouldn't always take out al-Qaeda's chief of operations in the eleventh hour. The warning bells at the TSA were sounding at full volume, and to me, the amorphous, largely unknowable threat posed by Operation Glidepath meant we had to accelerate our departure from an rule book–driven, mechanical model of security, one that only worked when we could predict upcoming dangers. The sudden and unexpected menace of Glidepath scared the hell out of me, but it also pointed toward the necessity of what I called a threat-agnostic approach to security: We couldn't always know the threat; we just knew there was one. Effective security would not be built on bedrock assumptions about terrorist profiles and operational techniques, but on an agile response to blindside attacks.

Accepting all this uncertainty also pointed toward a risk-management approach to security. If all threats cannot be known or stopped, our resources would best be used recognizing, but not obsessing over, the smaller, known risks in order to focus on mitigating extreme threats. For example, we allowed small scissors on board because although they were theoretically a threat, they were extremely unlikely to bring down a plane. On the other hand, bombs were much less likely to make it through security and be successfully detonated, but that remote possibility would have a catastrophic impact on the entire aviation system.

These were among the operational changes that Lee Kair had already initiated. But Glidepath also spurred me to rapidly upgrade our intelligence capabilities. Although the TSA was in the crosshairs of many of the largest terror threats—attacks on airplanes, trains, subways, buses, ferries—that fact alone didn't guarantee us access to all the potentially relevant intel. With no real connections and a largely disregarded capacity within the larger intelligence community, TSA was often shut out, receiving pro forma reports, but unable to see the real game.

Looking for a fix, I turned to Charlie Allen. Charlie's storied career began at the CIA in 1958, the height of the Cold War. A workaholic, he moved up the ladder and gained legendary status after predicting Iraq's 1990 invasion of Kuwait ahead of time and being well ahead of the curve on the threat posed by Osama bin Laden. In fact, if his requests to go after bin Laden had been fully funded, there probably wouldn't have been a 9/11, a DHS, or a TSA.

"Charlie," I implored over the phone. "You've got to get me a head of intel. I don't care who it is. I want it to be your person. You pick them so you're happy and they can work with you. And you'll have access to the full TSA operations range." Charlie listened thoughtfully but made no promises. A little while later, in early 2006, he called back with a suggestion—and a caveat. "I'm not going to tell you anything about him, but I want you to meet him," said Charlie in his faded North Carolina drawl. "He's not everyone's cup of tea."

A week later, Bill Gaches, the head of the National Security Agency's counterterrorism unit on the morning of September 11, arrived for an interview. Mustachioed, balding, and dressed in an understated dark suit, he had a diamond stud in one ear and a belly full of fire. Bill had grown up in Pittsburgh, where he had wanted to be a history teacher. But as college graduation approached, his job search wasn't going anywhere, in part because teaching positions and their draft-deferral status were at a premium during the Vietnam War. So, in 1975, Bill unexpectedly ended up at the NSA, an agency he had never even heard of, even after four years of political science classes. Ensconced in "the Fort," Bill punched the clock for two decades without finding anything particularly out of the ordinary about it. Then, in the 1990s, his jobs, including a spell with the NSA's antinarcotics squad, suddenly got more interesting. In January of 2000, Bill volunteered to head the counterterrorism department, a position that radically transformed and expanded a year later. Since Bill had gotten into the terrorism beat before 9/11, he was suddenly an attractive adviser for what became a burgeoning industry after the World Trade Center collapsed. Bill found himself working a growing network of contacts, especially at the CIA and FBI. Notably, in 2003 he was drafted to help set up the new National Counterterrorism Center, or NCTC, a group that had responsibility for coordinating efforts between the FBI, the CIA, the NSA, the DHS, and an alphabet soup of other intel agencies.

Bill's appearance for a job interview at an agency built around the strait-laced, no-nonsense military and law enforcement cultures struck me as a bit odd. And Bill could immediately tell that although I was not someone with a depth of knowledge in the intelligence field, I appreciated the insights it afforded and wasn't going to tell him, as he colorfully put it, "how to cook an egg every single frickin' morning."

A few minutes into the interview, I tossed Bill one of our current briefings. He was unimpressed. I gave him a few more TSA intelligence reports, called "products" in the intelligence business, in one of the locked courier bags used for carrying sensitive information. As he got up to leave I asked, "Do you have the key for that bag?"

"Oh yeah," he said. "I've got the key, but in a pinch I usually just get out the scissors and cut the damn things open."

"You can cut them open with scissors?"

"I am pretty sure I am joking."

Soon thereafter, Bill assumed control of our vaultlike Office of Intelligence. When the TSA moved to its current building, a former office tower, virtually the entire sixth floor had to be gutted and rebuilt to the DOD's exacting anti-eavesdropping standards.

To enter the office, as at the inner sanctum of the DHS, visitors dumped their electronics into tiny, locked cubbyholes in a tall cabinet stuffed with cell phones that beeped and chirped plaintively all day. Next, they entered a well-lit anteroom under the watchful eyes of both a camera and a guard behind a one-way mirror. Inside waited a rabbit warren of cubes, a few offices, two large conference rooms, and a few smaller videoconference rooms. Just like in the movies, there were also huge banks of big-screen TVs, computer monitors, printers, and rows of secure telephones.

Soon after moving in, Bill realized that the TSA needed to be plugged into the National Counterterrorism Center SVTC, the secure video teleconference that served as a briefing between the major players in the intel community each morning. *The terrorists want to kill us,* thought Bill. *We can't be locked out of this. I don't want a whole bunch of dead people lying around because we aren't plugged into this critical daily intel show.*

So Bill, in February 2006, called his old colleagues at the NCTC and convinced them that the TSA should be part of the briefing—an enormous step forward for my agency. Under Bill's leadership we also started getting more of the right intelligence briefs and, just as important, the ability to chase up the underlying reports. Bill would milk his old Intelligence Community network and then come by to tell me, "We got a few more nuggets."

ONE DAY BILL AND I WENT OVER TO THE NCTC, HOUSED IN A BRAND-NEW campus west of the capital in Virginia, near Dulles airport. While we waited for one particular meeting, I wandered around, studying the conference room they'd stuck us in. It was familiar—fluorescent lights overhead, a solid wooden rectangular table in the center, a secure telephone on top and surrounded by ergonomic black rolling chairs. On a counter to the side sat one phone with thirty or so numbers of the heads of relevant intel agencies, plus the White House Situation Room, on speed dial. There were also a few computer monitors and various other bits of teleconferencing and video equipment. I stared up at the walls at some generic government pictures, a white board, and a clock. "I like that clock," I mentioned to Bill. Finally they ushered us into the meeting, which was relatively brief.

On the drive back to our office, Bill opened up his classified briefcase. "What are you doing?" I asked. It's considered a breach to open the bags up outside of a secured room. But as we pulled into the garage, Bill reached into the bag and pulled out a miniature version of the same clock I'd been admiring at the NCTC, one that he had secretly bought at the trinket store off the NCTC lobby. I laughed and then went up to my office and hung it on my wall, almost breaking my neck trying to balance on my rolling chair.

Bill could be playful, and liked to go follow what he called "the weird direction," pushing the envelope of the believable, with intel. But his interpretation also benefited from his 1990s experience in counternarcotics. When Bill first began to shift to the terrorism beat, he was surprised by the similarities "Shit," he said to himself. "These guys are just like the druggies. Whatever you think they're going to do, they do something different. Whenever you think you've got something figured out, screw it—you're probably wrong. And they're heartless."

As he learned more, the analogies between drug runners and terrorists multiplied. Both groups had a goal that bound them together—money or martyrdom—even if they didn't like each other personally. Rather than a clearly defined organization with a well-delineated chain of command, both groups relied on subversion, on being amorphous, and on quickly replacing individual players to maintain viability in their extremely violent operations. While there were some hierarchies and figureheads, the resilience of both groups' networks was derived from their dispersal. For example, security forces have repeatedly taken out the person holding the number-three position in al-Qaeda, like Hamza Rabia, but after a brief decline in activity, that person has always been effectively replaced.

The single biggest similarity was the opportunistic ingenuity of both groups. The efforts of drug runners are opposed by the DEA, Customs and Border Protection, the FBI, Interpol, and various national armies. In response to the operational power of these well-funded organizations, smugglers flew drugs hidden in planes, rode at night on speedboats, and used submarines. They might dig tunnels hundreds of feet long under borders or stick drugs down the throats or up the backsides of their human mules. The terrorists used some of the same techniques: just as you can get a bag of cocaine across a border, so you can a plastic explosive. And both groups stretched the human imagination in the quest for new ways to carry out their missions.

Likewise, Bill's thirty years in intelligence made him well aware that the forces which now represented America's biggest national security threats bore no resemblance to the cold war rivals against whom we'd squared off for most of the last century. Even in 2006, with terrorism having been moved to the front burner for the past four years, many people in the intel community who had cut their teeth on the Soviet menace were unable to make the switch to combating a more mobile, dispersed, and elusive target. "In the past," Bill observed, "We'd ask 'What's the Soviet army going to do today?' Well, pretty much the same thing it did yesterday: Wake up, put its uniforms on, drink, go to sleep. These guys aren't like that."

ONCE THE TSA GOT INVITED TO THE MORNING BRIEFING AT EIGHT A.M. every weekday and often on Saturdays, I instituted a new internal intel meeting at eight-thirty to follow that briefing. After Operation Glidepath, I wanted all of the TSA's networks to become intel-driven, so attendance was not limited to just the heads of operations or analysts but also included people from PR, strategy groups, or scheduling personnel. To drive our work with intelligence reporting meant bringing every department into the fold at as high a level as we could, but because of the wide range of security clearances, the briefings were also a good lesson on how intel was shared from the public all the way up to the top.

When a threat flickers across the US intelligence community's radar, even the most serious plot is first issued as a vague bulletin to state and local law enforcement. Later that morning, after the information is invariably leaked to the public, a DHS spokesperson will attempt to quell the ripple of media interest with the soothing mantra, "This information is of limited specificity and uncertain credibility." If the plot and media reporting continued to develop and expand, the next official statement might read: "The United States and its European allies are at risk of a terrorist attack, although there is no specific, credible threat at this time." Three words—*specific, credible,* and *imminent,* abbreviated "SCI"—were the threshold below which action was often considered imprudent.

I viewed this obsession with clearing the SCI barrier as a technique that many people in the intel community employed to cover their behinds and pass the buck. For any threat stream considered below the SCI hurdle, once the paperwork was reported and filed, any threat to the official's career was mitigated, if not the actual plot. The same paperwork could also be used to pass on the onus for actually protecting the country. If it wasn't classified, I would have hung on my office wall a letter from a senior CIA official informing me that there was reporting of active al-Qaeda plotting against American commercial aviation and that I should take all necessary precautions. It was like a game of hot potato: If a plane goes down, it's your problem now.

But the TSA wasn't the NSA or the CIA; we all had different roles, and given the uncertain nature of most intel reporting—most threats, real or fake, never reach SCI level—we often had act on our own by quietly inserting subtle but effective security measures against these half-seen, shadowy plots. Our mission was clear: Keep planes in the sky and trains on the track. I knew there would be no way to explain or do other than take the blame head-on after a successful attack on American transportation.

Meanwhile, at one of our morning briefings, we'd get the classified version of the threat intel: "Senior al-Qaeda operations planners have given approval to begin preparing a dedicated cell of Western operatives for a coordinated series of attacks on European passenger rail targets. They are believed to be in the intermediate planning stage." Next, after we shuffled everyone with bright red badges indicating a lower security clearance out of the room, we would continue with the final level of classification, Top Secret/Secret Compartmented Information, or TS/SCI: "Mohammed al-Masri, al-Qaeda's head of external operations, is believed to have met with chief explosives expert Naji al-Libi and three unidentified Western-looking operatives in a farmhouse in Swat, Pakistan, three weeks ago. The Westerners appeared to speak Danish amongst one another."

I had come over from the private sector with no intel background, but after a month or so playing catchup, I was soon obsessed with intel. In the wake of Glidepath's near miss, I was forced to abandon my naïve belief that I was simply the CEO at a 60,000-person organization. I wasn't just promoting work culture; I had been dumped into a sea swarming with sharks. And I wanted everyone around me to have the same fire to their feet and twist in their gut.

As the intel leadership realized how serious my interest was—I was the only agency head who sat in on the morning briefings—they created a special binder for me, and eventually a dedicated shelf in Bill's office on the sixth floor. Whenever I had the time, I'd go downstairs to "Kip's shelf" and pore over the binders and network charts. On Saturdays, when no official meetings were planned, I could spend hours ingesting the new and rereading the old reportage in the sixth floor's secure intel vault, beyond the constant chirping of text messages from temporarily abandoned BlackBerries.

ONE SUCH SATURDAY, I NOTICED AN ANALYST'S ROOM COVERED WITH Soviet and Russian posters, photos, and memorabilia. I had taken Russian in high school and popped inside to say hello to a man with a receding brown hair, a goatee, and glasses.

A military brat who grew up outside of Frankfurt, Germany, Tom Hoopes had spent the end of the cold war flying in an airborne listening post positioned just over the edge of Communist airspace. Hoopes had spoken German since he was a child, learned to speak fluent Russian, and could still recite every aircraft type in the East German air force, the location of every one of their airfields, what planes flew out of them, what their mission was, how they communicated—and almost everything about the ground forces as well.

The Defense Language Institute had taught Hoopes how to use mnemonic devices to memorize large tracts of information. But the testing also revealed his innate linguistic ability. Students at the school are quizzed on not only actual languages but also artificial ones based on the structure of real languages. For example, in the artificial version of the English sentence "He petted the brown dog," "He" may be replaced by another singular masculine pronoun; "petted" would be a verb conjugated into the third-person singular past tense; the adjective replacement for "brown" would precede the word it describes, et cetera. After artificial tests in Russian, Arabic (a language Hoopes did not speak), and others, Hoopes developed the tools to recognize patterns within a sea of otherwise confounding information.

The first step Hoopes used to process the immense amounts of data that flashed across the TSA's wires was evaluating credibility. Of course, with all the different information streams capturing all sorts of data fragments, this verification process is near impossible. So rather than discarding or randomly selecting these bits of data caught in epistemic limbo, Hoopes just assumed everything was a real threat. "It's very easy to say something's not true," he explained. "The truth needs to prove itself sometimes." So he would put the different bits up on a board and start playing with them. Based on these bites of data, he'd conclude *These guys are obviously trying to do this,* and then write out what was known to be happening before raising every possible objection to the original interpretation. It was a laborious process, but it did allow each possibility to run itself out.

Casting a wider net also gave us a better chance of catching a plot, technique, or operative heretofore unknown to us. The United States has never been attacked by someone we were watching, so it's the muddled, half-plausible hints that kept Hoopes—and, soon, me—awake at night. In this context, reliable info that a Pakistani-British operative will try to carry a plastic explosive on board an American Airlines flight in London is not all that scary. A report that a passenger on whom we have no history tried to carry a block of cheese wrapped in wires through a checkpoint, however, sets off the alarms. When a report like that came across Hoopes's desk, he would mutter quizzically, "Why in the hell is that? What is that?"

Another approach to the flood of information hitting the sixth floor was to place it into a larger contextual network. Below the top echelon of al-Qaeda, the organization becomes incredibly dispersed—more like a web of interactions and relationships than any sort of hierarchy. This meant that any one of a thousand intel fragments could acquire new significance based not only on what it said or who it was traced back to, but also whomever else that person was in contact with.

As Hoopes explained it to me, "If we heard some wacko at the adjoining table say, 'A bomb's about to go off,' and that's all you heard, you'd have to start evaluating the source, this person at the next table. Once you find out that that person has talked to such-and-such known operative on the phone, went to university with somebody else we were watching, had met a top al-Qaeda official in Pakistan, and trained in a camp with this other guy, then the original fragment expands rapidly in possibilities." He added, "Lots of idiots plan or threaten attacks, but based on this person's network you probably have to consider this a serious terror plot. Of course, it probably isn't, but you've got to walk down that path."

Further complicating an interpretation so heavily based on a broad context is that terrorists often speak in other languages, bringing questions of interpretation and nuanced meaning into play—an area where Hoopes, fortunately, had a leg up. But even English-speaking terrorists will likely use some coded speech.

For example, "getting married" was a frequently used code phrase for martyrdom. "Wedding" could refer to an operation. So when somebody we were interested in was heard to say, "I'm going to a wedding in Chicago," we might look at inbound flights to Chicago's Midway and O'Hare airports. Or the person may in fact be going to a wedding in Chicago. We once chased down some intel on someone "baking a cake"—cakes being a centerpiece at weddings. After more surveillance, the guy turned out to be preparing for an actual baking contest. We think.

Moments like these can either make you laugh or wonder when exactly paranoia replaced investigatory imagination. But the nature of the adversary necessitated our hair-trigger threat assessment. Three decades ago, if a squad of Soviet soldiers crossed over to West Germany at night, American intelligence would closely follow the incident while assuming the soldiers were lost or drunk: It was hard to believe that the Soviets would launch World War III with a single squadron instead of a well-coordinated assault. But because terrorists are by nature unpredictable, a small step or clue left behind had to be worried until it fell apart. So when someone under surveillance says, "I'm going to a wedding in Chicago," you have to pay attention.

ELEVEN

THE SPORTS DRINK'S SECRET

ON THE MORNING OF MONDAY, MARCH 20, 2006, ABDULRAH-man Hilal Hussein woke his two-year-old son with a gentle *"Aufwachen, mein Kleiner"* ("Wake up, my little one") and dressed him for the airport. Abdulrahman was going back to Pakistan and bringing his son and wife. Because his flight information had just arrived via email the night before, he had had little time to say good-bye to his mother. On the way out the door he handed her a disposable phone from a big bag. He kept the phones around for making untraceable calls, using them once and then throwing them out. Abdulrahman promised his mom he would call her on the phone when he could, but told her not to use it otherwise.

Like thousands of other parents in busy airports, Abdulrahman lost Sonja and Abdullah in a crowd. But when they didn't appear at the gate, he boarded anyway shortly after ten A.M. At 10:23, Abdulrahman placed a call to his mother's disposable cell phone, thinking maybe she had heard from Sonja. She hadn't, so Abdulrahman told her that he'd be back in a month. He was distraught over not being able to bring his family after all, but he was on a mission. It wouldn't be very professional to miss the flight or his handlers on the other end.

Abdulrahman arrived and waited impatiently in the boring guest houses for transport up into the Waziristan camps—every minute sitting around was time away from learning, teaching, doing. Setting up and running small cells in Vienna over the last few months had kept him occupied, but it wasn't the same as strategizing alongside al-Qaeda's top minds.

Back in the dusty mountains overlooking Miram Shah's wide valley, things started happening. Abu Ubaydah, the German-speaking Egyptian who had launched Abdulrahman on the busted December mission, showed up in the traditional garb of the area: loose pants, a long shirt, and a rounded hat. The two prayed together before Ubaydah brought Abdulrahman up to date. Rangzieb Ahmed and Mohammed Zillur Rahman, Abdulrahman's former team members, were back from England. Zillur Rahman had happily joined one of Ubaydah's old fighting units in Afghanistan, but Ahmed had his own ideas, and it was hard to figure out what to do with him. Ubaydah suggested that Abdulrahman might like to join a unit and sharpen his battle skills. After a moment of contemplation, Ubaydah abruptly stood up. Abdulrahman scrambled to his feet to thank him, but Ubaydah stopped him short by sticking a finger into his chest. "You, my clever young Austrian, aren't going anywhere near the front lines," he said. "We have something more interesting for you." Looking deep into Abdulrahman's green eyes, Ubaydah continued, "*Morgen früh musst du bereit sein,* Waqas"—be ready in the morning.

The next day, Abdulrahman found himself disoriented after an hour-long ride in a dusty pickup, but he was exactly where he wanted to be: in a room with the master bomb maker Abu Abdulrahman al-Muhajir, Abu Ubaydah, and their brain trust. Al-Muhajir, who was leading the technical conversation, exuded a humility that attracted Abdulrahman, speaking in a sometimes inaudibly soft voice.

Abdulrahman gathered that al-Muhajir wanted to craft a new version of the hydrogen peroxide bombs used in the successful London Underground bombings. The formula had worked, but several elements needed to be adapted. First of all, the authorities would be looking for similar backpack bombs; moreover, the powder hadn't ignited properly in the second wave of attempted bombings. Al-Muhajir was happy with most of the bomb components. The detonators, AA-battery casings that had been emptied and refilled with the chemical HMTD (Hexamethylene triperoxide diamine), were virtually impossible to detect in a normal security search. Ditto the small lightbulbs used as initiators and the battery power source. Al-Mujahir also favored a pepper additive that, through months of trial and error, he had discovered gave an extra pop to the bomb. Hydrogen peroxide was a divergence from al-Qaeda's previous explosives, which were mostly commercially available materials used for construction or military purposes. It was very easy to obtain, but the scientific literature on the explosive abilities and parameters for hydrogen peroxide was comparatively limited. The element of surprise was useless, however, if the concentrated end product wasn't perfectly balanced, as demonstrated by the July 2005 failures. Al-Muhajir wanted something new. Undetectable. High-powered. Reliable. Stable. Repeatable. Unexpected. They could really up the ante by making a novel liquid explosive.

Abdulrahman was mesmerized. When the men broke, he gravitated to al-Muhajir, who was talking with Ubaydah and a slender man with a long face and beard to go with it. Next to al-Muhajir and Ubaydah, the third man also looked extremely tall. As he walked over, he heard the technical discussion continuing: How could you attach the detonator to the liquid mix? Did it have to be inside the container or could it be immediately adjacent?

As Abdulrahman approached, al-Muhajir paused to introduce him to the tall man, Rashid Rauf. They exchanged greetings and Rauf remained quiet as the discussion continued. Abdulrahman remembered seeing Rauf with Rangzieb Ahmed the previous year, but quickly sensed that Rauf was smarter than Ahmed. After the meeting, Rauf and Abdulrahman left together to eat and talk in English.

Rauf grew up the son of a baker in the industrial city of Birmingham, England. He arrived in Pakistan in 2002 and was now well settled, having married into the family of the founder of a local Islamist group, Jaish-e-Mohammed. Rauf had also been busy. While Abdulrahman was completing his training in 2005, Rauf was using his native-born knowledge to help Ubaydah and al-Muhajir orchestrate the July 2005 plots. Now he was working on a successor mission targeted at aviation. Rauf had tagged a savvy young guy named Ahmed Ali Khan, known as AAK, from the outer London suburb High Wycombe, to lead the mission. Between the two Brits, they had plenty of contacts willing to be foot soldiers. Meanwhile, Ubaydah had been talking to his fellow Egyptian, Ayman Zawahiri, and was confident that money and support would not be a problem. The main hurdle now was developing the explosive.

Most days, Abdulrahman and Rauf went to al-Muhajir's testing area and worked with either him or one of his assistants. Simply concentrating hydrogen peroxide down to 30, or even 50 percent, from the standard consumer-grade 6 percent wasn't doing it. Abdulrahman ended the days frustrated, dirty, and with burns on his hands and arms. Aside from occasionally mentoring fresh recruits, or discussing sports and politics with the German-speakers arriving in the North Waziristan camps, Abdulrahman was completely immersed in the chemistry of explosives.

On April 13, a Thursday morning, Abdulrahman made his way to al-Muhajir's lab, only to be stopped by two men yelling and waving in a jeep. Abdulrahman hardly listened to their words before realizing what had happened. Late the previous night, the Pakistani army had attacked a house in the village of Anghar, between the Tochi River and Miran Shah. What happened next was unclear—either the house's occupants had been killed by a missile, gunfire from a Cobra helicopter, or an invasion of soldiers. Either way, al-Muhajir and his top assistant were dead.

Immediately after, every cellular and satellite phone in the camp was confiscated. Ubaydah vanished. Abdulrahman and the others laid low and waited. He hated losing his web connection, but after the bombing, nobody went near the internet. With everything silent, Abdulrahman missed his mother and Abdullah even more. He had called her only twice since arriving Pakistan, to tell her that he was safe, that he would be home in another month, and to make sure there were no money problems at home. He had also learned of his brother Ahmad's wedding.

After a period of cautious inaction, Ubaydah, Rauf, Abdulrahman, and a few others put their heads together once again, finally arriving at an explosive device that met their requirements: unpredictable, reliable, devastating. Meanwhile, Rauf sent his lead operative, Ahmed Ali Khan, back to the UK to organize a cell. AAK was competent, but by July Rauf had grown impatient with his operatives. There was a necessary rhythm to operations; once agents were trained, they had to move fast. The longer the lag time, the greater the chances of being detected.

Via his Yahoo email account, Rauf prodded his team to make progress. By July 13, 2006, he had given the UK team the go-ahead for a trial run. But he soon got messages back haggling over the price of hydrogen peroxide, which they called "aftershave." Rauf and Abdulrahman were worried that the team still didn't get it.

By July 31, things were getting dicey. AAK had picked up on possible surveillance and Rauf asked if their countersurveillance techniques had worked or if "skin infection" had gotten worse. AAK thought he was being observed when traveling around but was otherwise in the clear. Then, on August 4, Rauf sent a fairly direct message to AAK: "Do you think you can still open the shop with this skin problem? Is it only minor or can you still sort out an opening time without the skin problem worsening?"

Two days later, on August 6, AAK replied, "I will still open the shop. I don't think it's so bad that I can't work. But if I feel really ill, I'll let you know. I also have to arrange for the printers to be picked up and stored. . . . I have done all my prep, all I have to do is sort out opening timetable and bookings."

While closely following the details of the developing operation, Abdulrahman had been drawn into a tight circle with Ubaydah, Rauf, and a few others. He constantly played the operation's secret details through his head, becoming increasingly withdrawn. Because he had had no contact with Sonja or his mother for months, and no one called him by his birth name at the camps, "Abdulrahman" seemed almost like a different person. With al-Muhajir dead, he felt he could no longer go by Waqas. Looking for a new name, he settled on the al-Qaeda tradition of creating pseudonyms based on an operative's country of origin. As the operation approached, Abdulrahman Hilal Hussein was reborn as Zubair al-Masri, Zubair the Egyptian.

IN JULY 2006, BRITISH PRIME MINISTER TONY BLAIR CALLED PRESIDENT George W. Bush at his ranch in Crawford, Texas, to inform him of imminent terror attacks aimed at both UK and American targets. The call, across 5,000 miles from bustling central London, was not the normal channel through which such intelligence was passed but, in this case, it was the only option: MI5, the group responsible for Britain's internal security, hadn't wanted to share the intel with their American counterparts at all.

MI5's reluctance could be traced back to a year earlier when, following the 2005 London subway bombings, the British had shared a good deal of highly classified information with the American intel community. But as the information worked its way through America's counterterrorism channels, a lot of what MI5 considered confidential leaked out in the media, infuriating the Brits.

Despite this unhappy situation, and the resulting chill in transatlantic intelligence sharing over the previous year, Blair insisted that he had to inform the United States of the plot. But MI5 remained vehemently opposed. Not only was it local work that had revealed terror groups operating on their soil, they were doubtful that any promises from the Americans could be trusted. And a leak on either side of the Atlantic would spook the al-Qaeda operatives, costing MI5 its chance to further study and learn from the terror cells—not to mention preempt the attacks. As a result, during Blair's call to the "Western White House," he asked for Bush's personal assurance that he would keep the information highly confidential.

ON FRIDAY, AUGUST 4, 2006, I CONCLUDED AN AIRPORT TOUR IN PHOENIX and flew home to California to celebrate my wedding anniversary—also a make-up date for the one I'd canceled the previous year. But no sooner had I walked into my house, put my bag down, and inhaled some Pacific air than my BlackBerry went off. As I looked at my wife across the kitchen, Michael Jackson told me to return to DC. ASAP. I clicked off. This wouldn't be fun to explain.

Aside from having to apologize profusely, there was another snag with immediately hopping on an eastbound flight. I had a dinner scheduled that night with a congressman visiting California who was also on my appropriations committee, and it's always bad form to cancel on important lawmakers at the last minute. I also couldn't appear panicked without offering an explanation; it was his business to know what was going on. So, in an unhappy compromise, I went through with the dinner, stayed the night, and flew back early the next day.

As soon as I landed at Dulles, my BlackBerry sprang back to life and informed me that I had an appointment with Michael Jackson and Charlie Allen at seven that evening. My son Nick and his girlfriend picked me up from the airport and we had time to squeeze in an early dinner at a Mexican restaurant. Nick did an excellent job of acting unsurprised at my busted anniversary plans—as well as my request to be dropped off right outside the NAC. I said goodnight to Nick and passed through the gates, my brief attempt at normalcy over.

It was completely quiet on the Department of Homeland Security's wooded campus, a little odd, since something was clearly going on. Although I had received no official details about this specific plot, Bill Gaches had been working his network and clued me in to the telltale signs of an information lockdown among his peers in the counterterrorism community so I was not completely shocked to get Michael's call the previous day.

Michael Jackson had an office that was small, dark, and secure enough for even the most sensitive information. Crowded around a small, cluttered conference table with him were Charlie Allen, the department's head of intelligence, and Mary Connell, his deputy. With barely a "Good evening," Charlie began reading crisply from his omnipresent black marbled composition book, always stuffed with his handwritten notes, on a terror plot code named by British authorities, Operation Overt.

Prime Minister Blair's request was heeded. I had just become the fifth person among the Department's over 210,000 employees to be briefed on the plot. After the meeting, Secretary Chertoff crossed the anteroom separating his rather modest office from the Deputy Secretary's. Charlie and Mary then left and the Secretary, Michael, and I worked through different scenarios. After another hour, Chertoff had a rough game plan in his head and left Michael and me to work into the early morning on countermeasures for every potential scenario—from an orderly arrest of the operatives to planes suddenly disappearing over the Atlantic.

The next morning, Sunday, August 6, Secretary Chertoff joined Michael and me for Charlie's update, which was largely based on physical surveillance and intercepts from both Rashid Rauf, the al-Qaeda project manager in Pakistan, and Ahmed Ali Khan, known as AAK, the boss on the ground in London. Their type of bomb told us they were only interested in aviation targets. When we were told that AAK had started looking at flights from London to the United States and Canada, an electric shock coursed through my body. Our assignment was now to prepare contingencies that Secretary Chertoff could bring to the White House and recommend to the president that Monday morning.

I pushed to brief in some key people at the TSA and was flatly rejected. Michael explained that the DHS had only gotten permission to bring me in after repeated, strong urging from him and Chertoff. I later learned that my UK counterpart, Niki Tompkinson also applied some torque from her side of the Atlantic. The president had had to personally approve any individuals privy to Operation Overt's existence.

But Charlie and I decided to get a few TSA intelligence and operations people thinking about options with a plausible cover story. We settled on a tale of "undetectable bombs" related to the Lebanese civil war, and to provide a sense of authenticity Charlie invented a series of "disturbing intelligence dots" that indicated serious plotting against aviation from the region. After more than forty years with the CIA, Charlie had honed his gift of cloaking euphemisms inside jargon while surrounding them with buzzwords and important sounding caveats, like, "This is strictly Red Stripe material." Within a few minutes, any audience would be completely confused by the torrent of facts emanating in a weathered, confident voice from his little notebook, but also absolutely certain was that the TSA was up against a very real, immediate threat. And they would also be very aware that any mention of the plot meant sudden career death – or circumstances much worse.

LATER THAT SAME DAY, SUNDAY, MO MCGOWAN, A MUSCULAR MAN IN HIS fifties with a white mustache, thick Texas accent, and a deliberate speaking manner, picked up a call from my deputy, Robert Jamison.

"Hey," said Robert. "We've got to go over to the DHS to work on the 2007 budget."

"Why?" asked Mo. He'd spent decades as a detective before becoming the TSA's deputy head of operations behind Mike Restovich, but anyone could smell something phony in this request.

Robert demurred. "They want us to come over—they want to talk to us."

"OK," Mo replied, and made his way over to Building 19 at the NAC.

I met Mo, Robert, Mike Restovich, and Dana Brown, the director of the Federal Air Marshal Service (who replaced Tom Quinn after his retirement earlier in the year), inside and confessed that the budget excuse was a ruse to call them in using unsecured lines. "If I could tell you everything, I would," I promised. "But this is the no-kidding real deal, however we dress it up. I need you guys to keep this to yourselves and know that I trust you and will let you know what you need to do your job."

I paused for a second, looking at each of their faces. "To put this in context," I added, "Chertoff and I are meeting with the president in the morning. We need to be able to count on you."

Soon after, Charlie Allen walked into the borrowed conference room and did a masterful job of fabricating a convoluted but convincing scenario that energized our team without giving away anything about the real plot. He ended with a stern warning: The president had issued a direct order that no one else be brought in on the plot.

With some of my top team now looped in enough to do some useful work, I went back to sketching out the president's briefing with Michael and Secretary Chertoff. Charlie produced the only electronics we could use for the presentation, a highly classified laptop and a dedicated inkjet printer to be kept in the massive safe in the rear of Michael's office. As we plugged in the special computer, which looked to me just like a normal Dell laptop, I began to wonder how one writes a memo for the president. "We're going to use

PowerPoint slides and the secretary is going to talk from them," said Michael firmly, although he was famously averse to the format. "The president is in Texas and it's going to be on a videoconference."

The next several hours combined urgency, succinct analysis, and editorial farce. Initially, we worked with Michael standing over my shoulder, giving me complex sentences to convert into bullet points while Secretary Chertoff paced around the office giving his thoughts. After about ten minutes, Michael gave up on me, grabbed the keyboard and started to type, more or less ignoring Chertoff. Within five minutes, Chertoff insisted that we "hit print" on the draft, sat down with a government-issue pen and added his improvements. The package complete, Chertoff left it on the table and ran off to a dinner engagement, maintaining his own appearance of normalcy, and Michael and I started to expand and "edit." Half an hour later, Chertoff's military aide phoned back from the dinner location and asked when he could get the final version of "the document." I stalled while Michael kept repeating to me that it still needed a lot of work and was missing some "critical details." Eventually, starving and anticipating a long night, I wandered off into the department's darkened hallways, looking for a vending machine. After I fielded a few more increasingly firm calls from the aide, Chertoff himself amiably click-clacked in to the office with his sockless loafers. "Let's have a look," he said with a cheery smile. After studying the presentation for few minutes, Michael locked away Charlie Allen's super-secret laptop, still muttering something about "drilling down into security directives on slide four." We left the NAC at about 10:30 and Michael dropped me off at my apartment in Arlington.

WHEN JOE SALVATOR, THE TSA'S DEPUTY HEAD OF INTEL, GOT TO THE Delaware coast, a necessary night away from DC's stifling humidity, he realized he'd mistakenly grabbed his wife's cell, a phone identical to his.

"Crap!" he said. "Ah well . . . it's only for a night."

A day later, the evening of that Sunday, August 6, Joe returned home and checked his cell. He had fifty-four missed calls. "Oh, shit!"

As Joe began scrolling through the calls he could see that most were from me, but there were also a few from DHS, and one that looked like a White House number. One of my messages was, "Going to the White House Sunday at ten. I need you to come with me." Because Bill Gaches was away in South Carolina, Joe was the acting head of intel—if he hadn't been fired. He called me up.

"Sorry about this," said Joe.

"I'll kill you later!" I said. "Just get your ass in here bright and early tomorrow morning."

"What time? Like five?" asked Joe.

"No! Four!"

Joe came in at three, with a knot in his stomach.

EARLIER THAT DAY, I CALLED ED KITTEL WHILE HE WAS ON VACATION IN Alaska. "When are you coming home?"

Ed was a solidly built former Navy and FAA explosives specialist from Long Island, now serving as the TSA's chief explosives expert. "Next Wednesday," he replied.

"What time?"

"Do you want me to go to the air force base or the FAA to get on a secure phone?" asked Ed.

"No. That's OK."

"Dave is in DC," Ed noted. Dave Resing was his deputy.

"Yeah, but when are you coming back?" I didn't know Dave as well as Ed. "If your flight lands at two, we want you in the office at three."

A day later, Ed got a call from Dave. "I just had the weirdest meeting with Kip," he said.

Because details about Operation Overt were so tightly guarded, those of us who knew anything about it had to make contingency plans without the expert help of our staff. I'd brought Dave into Secretary Chertoff's conference room at the DHS and, trying to be nonchalant, asked him a bunch of questions. I needed technical advice, but I couldn't ask anything that might tip him off to the plot. So I had to throw some head fakes to keep Dave from simply working backwards to decipher the highly classified technical material. And because everything I asked was theoretical, the questions were very hard for him to answer.

A few days later, Ed dragged himself into the TSA after his twenty-four-hour flight from Alaska and I briefed him in as best I could.

He listened and said, "It's like the answer for Bojinka." Bojinka was a 1990s al-Qaeda–backed aviation plot and a precursor to 9/11. "They might switch from a contact lens solution bottle to some other container. Until we know, the obvious option is to ban all liquids, gels, and aerosol bottles."

"But why aerosol?" I asked.

"It's not about whether it sprays or pours," explained Ed. "It's about the container. You can put anything into any kind of container. Don't focus on what it is—gel, liquid, or aerosol—it's about the container." The physics behind Ed's answer were fascinating, complex, and critical to our response but, in a nutshell, these explosives could only be a serious threat to an aircraft if detonated in a container with a sufficient diameter. Even as we talked, I knew that the TSA's head of operations, Mike Restovich, and his deputy, Mo McGowan, were developing specific responses to the threat while working under the same limitations of imperfect information and uncertain timeframe.

ONE OF OUR OPTIONS FOR STOPPING THE BOMBS WAS NOT BANNING liquids at all, but training our officers to stop any live bombs, a plan that was met with extreme skepticism at the White House (I will always appreciate Secretary Chertoff's support when I suggested this technique). But then the CIA made a mock-up of the bomb, which looked for all the world like a bottle of orange Gatorade. When it was first handed to me at the White House, I was thankful to get some rehydration in the midst of the draining summer. Soon thereafter Mike Restovich compared a real liquid bomb with a Gatorade bottle under an X-ray scanner and they were virtually indistinguishable. Once it became clear that it was impossible to tell a real bomb from water, soda, or Gatorade, we had to accept a complete liquids ban.

The countdown to Op Overt was a whirlwind, with demands that kept my head spinning in unfamiliar situations. After another presidential videoconference at the DHS, I took the short drive down tree-lined Massachusetts Avenue to the British embassy. Charlie Allen's counterpart there wanted to arrange a secure telephone call between me and Niki Tompkinson, and I soon found myself wandering around a nicely landscaped bit of British real estate in the middle of the American capital, looking for an entrance. A few minutes later, I spotted a large set of steel doors with the telltale bulletproof green glass and was soon handing over my phone and signing in. In exchange I got a badge numbered 007—I'm still not sure if they hand out that number to titillate every American visitor—and was escorted up a curving staircase, through sets of doors, up an elevator, down narrow hallways stacked with cardboard boxes, and through more doors until I arrived at a large office with an ancient rug and books and papers everywhere. My host, Ronald Ryan, said all the polite things as he moved me over to his UK-issued secure phone with a sleek gray plastic receiver and plugged it into a box with lots of wires.

"Have a seat; Niki's been looking forward to speaking with you," he said as I sat, trying to look relaxed and trustworthy. The past year had been a baptism by fire for the TSA's security and intelligence operations, but I was still more experienced with networking or supply-chain questions—and quite unaccustomed to sitting in the highly secure personal office of a senior member of Her Majesty's security services. After dialing Niki, Ronald handed me the receiver and smiled. "Kip, I am awfully sorry, but I have to run. Just let yourself out when you're done." I guess I passed the test.

During the ensuing forty-five-minute conversation, Niki and I agreed that it was important to have the same security measures in place, although we weren't exactly in accord as to what those should be. We agreed on a complete liquid ban, but she also wanted to ban carry-ons altogether. We also both wanted to bring in the European Union security regulators quickly. Our contact there was the director of security, Marjeta Jager, with whom Niki already had a close relationship. So I was tasked with calling the EU to enact an emergency ban on liquids for US-bound flights, while Niki would follow up with Marjeta.

AT 6:15 THE NEXT MORNING, TUESDAY, AUGUST 8, I WAS ALONE IN MY office when the White House called me in to a 7:30 briefing for the president in the Roosevelt Room and a 7:15 pre-brief in the Sit Room with Secretary Chertoff. Problem: I didn't have a car, and no one else would arrive at the TSA until seven. I took off outside and across the four lanes of South Hayes Street to the Fashion Centre at Pentagon City, where I managed to flag down a cab. Of course, I left anything classified at the office. It was already muggy at that early hour and I was beginning to sweat even before I was denied entry by the Secret Service checkpoint at the southwest gate of the White House. Whoever scheduled for the Situation Room hadn't entered me in the system, and I was left staring back at bulletproof glass, sweat running down my face and briefly contemplating being tardy for meetings with both Secretary Chertoff and, fifteen minutes later, the president.

The White House meetings were short. Fran Townsend, the President's Homeland Security Advisor, moved things along since the new updates were minimal and the list of to-dos for everybody involved was long. The CIA was pulling out the stops to find Rauf in Pakistan, the FBI was quietly scrubbing the intelligence for signs of any activity within the United States, and I went back to the TSA headquarters to make sure we could roll out, virtually instantaneously, whatever new security measures were needed. Those efforts were made easier when Michael Jackson called me shortly after noon to tell me that the President had authorized us to brief in Mike Restovich, and he became my point person back at the TSA. While I was running between the DHS and the White House, Mike got together Mo McGowan and Dana Brown and they worked late into the night, staring at spreadsheets that spelled out possible countermeasures based on theoretical plots.

We did eventually get some of the other operations staffers involved using Charlie Allen's "undetectable Lebanese bomb threat" to begin working up more contingencies for different explosives. That way, we could pull the relevant operations plan off the shelf when it was needed. But despite our best efforts to maintain secrecy, once the rest of the operations crew learned the real story, they were angry for not being brought in. (Mike later told me that, after five years, some people still haven't forgiven him.) A few days later I got Dana Brown's assurance that he could flood Europe with federal air marshals somewhat inconspicuously stationed near London. I knew that we had to cover every flight from the UK to the United States when the plot became public. As a result, a few hundred FAMs wondered why they were sitting around undeployed for a few days, sightseeing in European capitals.

ON WEDNESDAY AFTERNOON I WAS SITTING IN MICHAEL'S OFFICE AT THE DHS, completely exhausted. The plan was to hold the plot secret until Friday, when British authorities would sweep up the terror cell. At around three-thirty I told Michael that I was going home to nap before heading over to my office for the evening. My driver Terry picked me up outside in the black Suburban and headed down Massachusetts Avenue. As we hit Ward Circle, the telltale sonar sound of my BlackBerry alerted us that either the secretary, deputy secretary, or the TSA's ops center was calling.

I answered. Michael. "Cold start," he said, meaning the trigger was pulled, the endgame near. I looked up to tell Terry, but he had already made another pass around the traffic circle and was heading back toward the department's rear entrance.

TWELVE

MAKING WAVES

AT FOUR P.M. ON AUGUST 9, 2006, ALISON CLYDE WAS HAVING a surprisingly normal day in her office when her phone rang. "Meet me in the garage," said Joe Salvator. "If you have plans, cancel them."

Alison stared at the wall for a second. Then she got on her phone again and dumbfounded her closest friends by canceling a dinner party, the one she had planned to thank them for sticking by her during a year in which she'd all but disappeared socially. After rummaging around her office for a second, she grabbed a flash drive filled with her best guess of what might be useful and hopped into the elevator.

"Hi," Joe greeted Alison as she climbed into the TSA's black Suburban. "We're going up to the NAC." Alison nodded back as they pulled out into DC rush-hour traffic. Surveying the gridlock, Joe leaned back into his seat. "You know, I really miss the days when I had a flashing light I could put on top of the car."

After anther second Joe turned back to Alison. "We're not in a SCIF," he continued more urgently, "but it'll do. Here's what's going on. There's a cell in the UK that their people have been following and have infiltrated. The cell has figured out a way to make a liquid bomb that can be carried on board in energy-drink bottles. Now the cell leader has started looking at tickets for flights from London to the United States—there's a lot of 'em, so they could be targeting up to a dozen different flights. We raised the flag and now the

Brits are gonna move in and arrest them." Joe paused for breath. "That's where the TSA comes in. There may be other cells in the United States that will find their hands forced and attempt some last-minute attacks. So we've got to get all liquids off our flights by tomorrow morning."

Unfazed, Alison fired off her questions—"How could the bomb be made? How long has the UK been aware? When exactly were they moving in?"—for the next forty minutes, until the Toyota passed through NAC security and pulled up at Secretary Chertoff's building.

CHERTOFF, MICHAEL JACKSON, CHARLIE ALLEN, AND A FEW OTHERS were already upstairs when Joe and Alison ran in. I was in Michael's office calling the CEOs of the airlines targeted in the plot, telling them to stand by until we could get let them in on more details. That day, as word of Operation Overt slowly spread outside our tightly controlled group, a steady stream of people appeared, creating traffic between the secretary and deputy secretary's offices and holding impromptu meetings in the reception area. Sometime between seven and eight P.M.—past midnight in the UK—British law enforcement lowered the hammer, quickly moving in and arresting twenty operatives spread out over three cities. After nearly a week of working around the tight controls Op Overt required, we suddenly had the opposite problem: communicating with the entire TSA network and beyond in a matter of hours.

Joe, Alison, and I went down the hall, grabbed a small office with a single phone and initiated an endless series of conference calls to our own folks at the TSA, the FAA, and players within the larger aviation network. In a rare stroke of luck, most of the airport directors in the United States were attending a conference in Reno, putting them on Pacific Standard Time, three hours earlier than DC, and much easier to get a hold of as a group. The three-hour lag also reminded me of Janet out in California; today was our wedding anniversary. I snuck into the secretary's office, whispered "Happy Anniversary" into my BlackBerry, promising I'd call her the next day.

Meanwhile, Joe had crammed his solid frame into a cubicle just large enough for a gunmetal gray desk and a chair. The cube appeared to be unoccupied; the desk was covered with old copies of *USA Today*. While he was keeping Mike Restovich and the TSA's seventh-floor war room up to date, he looked around his surroundings, thinking, *In the movies, I'd be in a spacious, impressive office sitting at a shiny mahogany desk and looking at a bank of monitors.* Instead he was fumbling around with on a phone with sixty unintelligibly labeled buttons, trying to figure out on what number people could return his calls.

Meanwhile, Michael and other senior people at the DHS were personally calling top-ranking members of Congress. Senators and congressional representatives can be briefed at the highest security level, but none of them would be anywhere near secure communications equipment at that hour. There was also a precisely sequenced pecking order in which the legislators had to be informed. Yet another DHS executive was manically dialing around the country to inform our law-enforcement partners at the state and local level.

Amid this barrage of phone calls, Mike Restovich faxed over the operations plans the TSA had devised under false pretenses. Over the past week, we'd spent hours revising these rules, but it was now the eleventh hour, so Alison and I hurriedly pored over the revised Standard Operating Procedure that would ban every cup of coffee, every bottle of water, and every can of shaving cream from every flight at more than 450 airports starting at four the next morning. We scribbled edits and revisions in black ink before passing the documents over to Secretary Chertoff to add his changes. Normally such changes take weeks or months to be approved; we used the expedited emergency process.

"There's been a lot of hands on this thing," murmured Alison as we dictated the final version of the Standard Operating Procedure. "God, I hope no one forgot to put a 'not' in the middle of one of those sentences." In the end, the whole document came down to a person sitting at a computer with three people behind him saying, "Yup. Uh huh. That looks right." There were a lot of possibilities for error. Finally, sometime after midnight, we called everyone back and using the authorities given TSA by law, read them into action.

Mike and his staff had already called up the federal security directors in charge of the nation's airports and told them not to go to sleep that night: "We're going to be sending out some security directives with a big impact for every checkpoint; we need you to teach your staff some new procedures and we need it done by four A.M." The FSDs were told to call in extra staff, with mandatory overtime if needed, and to position the biggest waste barrels they could find at their checkpoints, with explanations to follow.

This was a huge moment for the FSDs. Despite their rank within the agency, very few people outside of the TSA have any idea what a federal security director does, or even what the initials stands for. But that night on the phone, Mike told them that the term "FSD" had been used two or three times during a White House briefing, the sort of recognition and respect the airport directors craved. "This is what we're here for," said Mike. "This is what you've created. This is where the rubber hits the road."

An hour or so later, British Home Secretary John Reid called Chertoff to tell him that the arrests were made and they would be public soon. We immediately called Mike and instructed him to email the finalized SOP out across the country. In addition to major procedural changes, the package included a template for new signs informing passengers they needed to ditch their liquids before passing through the checkpoints. Because most TSA offices don't have printers, employees were dispatched to a Kinko's to print them out. At New York's JFK airport, Bill Hall's team simply made their own signs and posted them around the airport. By two A.M. Eastern Standard Time on August 10, the operation had effectively moved out of our hands. Now it was up to our frontline people.

A LITTLE BEFORE FOUR A.M., JAMEKA MERRIWEATHER, AN AFRICAN American woman in her twenties with a slender build and a huge smile, walked into Memphis International Airport for the early shift. Jameka was a bit of a night owl, but worked as a screener from four until noon to keep the rest of her day free. While getting ready, Jameka noticed a number of people clustered in the airport's TSA office, what she and her coworkers called "our HQ"—the training coordinator, program analyst, and others who didn't normally work in the building. A few minutes later, she took her place at the checkpoint with the other the officers and was informed that, as of that moment, all liquids were banned.

The security gates opened shortly thereafter and the TSOs began explaining and enforcing the brand-new regulations. Naturally cheerful, Jameka repeated the instructions, "You can either dispose of them here, put them in bags to check for the flight, or mail them to yourself" countless times. It wasn't easy telling people to throw away expensive lotions or perfumes—or deal with angry passengers reactions. One woman just missed hitting Jameka's head with her banned perfume bottle, which shattered on the floor. As the morning rush picked up, the garbage cans spilled over with discarded bottles. Luckily, as the story of the terror-cell arrests in the UK broke, the changes got easier to explain.

FURTHER WEST AND AN HOUR EARLIER, JEREMY TRUJILLO WAS ABOUT to begin an early morning shift in Colorado Springs when he was briefed on the new checkpoint policy. By that time, six A.M. on the East Coast, the story was coming out, but since none of Jeremy's colleagues watched national news at four in the morning, they were unsure why they couldn't allow liquids on board. Then, after the checkpoints opened up, it was the passengers who were confused. But soon the story spread: eleven planes were targeted with a liquid bomb indistinguishable from a bottle of sports drink, an attack planned to be at least on the scale of 9/11, but with a death toll easily three or four times the size.

As a member of our National Advisory Council, a group of TSA employees I had created to channel voices and recommendations directly from our frontline staff, Jeremy knew that there were plenty of people unhappy with the national management, but he didn't sense any of this grumbling in the midst of the enormous changes that Wednesday morning. And as the clock rolled over to four A.M. at each of more than 450 airports across the country, the same scenario was repeated as our officers did an amazing job adapting and implementing the new policy. Like many jobs, working a checkpoint can be repetitive, causing the bigger picture to slide out of focus. But over the following week, our officers heard duty call and set an all-time record for attendance. At last confronted by a tangible threat, no one wanted to miss his or her chance to protect the country.

AT ABOUT THE SAME TIME THE BAN WENT INTO EFFECT ON THE ATLANTIC Seaboard, Marjeta Jager, the head of aviation security for the EU, was lounging in a swimsuit on the back of her thirty-foot sailboat. It was about ten in the morning and beautiful, with sunny skies and a gentle breeze blowing across the Adriatic. As she sat drinking coffee with two of her girlfriends, her phone went off, jarring Marjeta. She shrugged and went below deck to pick up my call. For the next five minutes, Marjeta listened in disbelief to the plot's details before I launched into my proposal to immediately ban all liquids for incoming flights.

"Of course, Kip," she replied in her nearly flawless English. "We will act immediately." While I took careful notes, Alison tried to listen in on the conversation so she could report back to our international office. "I believe all our member states will give you total support," continued Marjeta. "This is an emergency, but I just ask one thing. When it comes time to adjust these rules, Kip, please consult with us."

I needed Marjeta's help. All our work implementing the ban in the United States and UK could quickly be undone by one liquid bomb smuggled on board a United States-bound flight from Hamburg, Paris, or Madrid. Promising I would be in touch before any further measures were implemented was a no-brainer.

AN HOUR LATER, I HAD COMPLETED ALL MY INTERNATIONAL CALLS AND went home to shower and change clothes, but there would be no nap. I had to be back at the DHS by six-thirty to prep for a briefing with the president and then stand behind Chertoff at the live breaking-news press conference to follow. I rummaged around my apartment for a lapel pin I had with both the US and UK flags. I knew Niki Tompkinson, my British counterpart who fought to get me briefed on the plot early on, would be watching, and I wanted to show solidarity.

By the time I got back to the rooms where I'd spent the previous evening and early morning rewriting the SOP, they were a madhouse. The secretary's office was jammed. I fought my way over to his public affairs chief and after she had finished up Chertoff's public address, we worked up a serviceable statement for me.

At seven A.M. about ten of us, including Chertoff and Charlie Allen, sat around a rectangular conference table at the DHS ops center looking at a screen before our secure video briefing with the president began. Soon thereafter, Fran Townsend, the Homeland Security adviser, moved through a list of items with her characteristic efficiency. At that point our airport operations were smooth and there had been no flight cancellations due to the security measures. It was a good start but when questioned, I hedged. The UK, five hours ahead of us, was having a very rough day at their airports. The president concluded the meeting by telling Secretary Chertoff that he would be watching, so "good luck," provoking nervous laughter.

Now, a few minutes before 8:00, a gentle rain had just started to fall. I was the first in a line of about six of us who were on our way from the secure spaces of DHS Building 19 to the Department's media center—actually a miniature warehouse with a stage and podium at the far end—to go live on all the networks and announce the details of a major terrorist attack. We all had our places marked on the podium and mine was on the far end so I was the first in line to take the stage. As I stepped into the building, I registered that the floor was slippery. I was aware that to my right was a room packed with reporters and three banks of television cameras, all broadcasting live. Staff people lined the pathway, all helpfully making comments and showing the way. Dead ahead were the stairs, and in a moment of infinite clarity, I could see the twinkle of megawatts of television lighting reflected by the moisture on the steps. Not having slept much for almost a week, I could see myself taking a header.

Fortunately, I safely took my place slightly off the left shoulder of my boss, Secretary of DHS Michael Chertoff, who was dead center at the podium. As Chertoff established himself at the podium and readied his notes, I thought about what I would say when it was my turn. I had jotted down a few notes on a blank sheet of paper back in Building 19 after we had finished the videoconference. The really important material was in Chertoff's remarks and all my effort had been to make sure that his text was comprehensive and accurate. Over the last several hours, I kept putting off writing up what I would say. A few minutes earlier across the street, I realized that since we were walking straight over to go on live TV, I couldn't wait, so I scratched out several bullet points. I carefully put the sheet of paper right on top of the red manila folder I was carrying so that I wouldn't fumble around looking for it when the time came. As the DHS media person was making a final logistical announcement, I glanced down to check my notes. Looking back at me, instead of my key points, was an indecipherable Rorschach-like pattern of pale blue splotches made by the raindrops on my handwritten notes.

But oddly, I wasn't worried about my remarks, I just wanted to get off stage. While we were standing there, a lot of irons were in the fire and I wondered what was going on in the four hundred airports where just four hours earlier we had changed the whole operation, whether there were any signs of terror cells self-initiating attacks, and how the hundred and nineteen foreign airports were doing with the new measures as they launched flights to the United States.

THIRTEEN

DIALING UP 3-1-1

AS THE FIRST DAY OF THE LIQUIDS BAN DREW TO A CLOSE, WE could declare it a success.

From Colorado Springs to Memphis and around the whole country, our frontline people had adapted amazingly well to combat this new threat. While TSOs enforced and explained the new ban, Federal Air Marshal teams covered an unprecedented number of flights, especially to overseas locations. In some situations, FAMs flew the overnight leg from the United States to London and then took the return flight the same day. Adrenaline and sense of purpose were running high throughout TSA.

Sure, some people would hold grudges against us after taking away their champagne or $200 bottles of perfume (although most passengers had the option of putting the liquids in checked bags), but there had been no follow on attacks in the United States or anywhere else. There had been long lines, but no cancelled flights as the UK and other countries experienced. In fact, one of our biggest immediate problems was simply keeping up with the enormous amount of garbage produced as a side effect of the ban.

Within hours, the banning of all liquids had left garbage bins overflowing with discarded coffee, contact lens solution, and water bottles. Many airports simply couldn't find onsite storage for the parade of bulging bags and the empty spaces within massive airport complexes began to fill up with refuse as airport directors scrambled to arrange additional garbage pickups.

Over the next few days we focused on fine-tuning the ban. We had tried to figure out which liquids, if banned, would cause serious problems for passengers and the tricky proposition of defining what constituted a medical exception. One of my own sons is diabetic so I understand the critical, life and death nature of some medications. But, a liquid ban across the entire country left us managing a whole universe of unexpected possibilities. like a visitor from China presenting a brown glass bottle of mystery liquid as medicine. We soon found that there were more bottles that needed to be individually tested than we'd imagined, but after the initial 4 or 5 days, our checkpoints calmed down considerably.

Meanwhile, the disruption to the baggage system continued. Immediately following the ban, passengers started checking everything into their luggage and passing through security with small carry-ons or handbags. All of a sudden, the wait times at checkpoints plunged from the pre-ban levels and planes started loading faster.

The extra weight hadn't disappeared, it had just been pushed over onto our checked baggage operations. Soon the conveyor belts for the explosive detection systems began breaking down. At Love Field, Mike Restovich's former airport, the checked baggage screening process was called 40–40–20, meaning that 40 percent of checked bags had one type of explosives trace done on them, 40 percent had another kind, and 20 percent were hand-searched. This system worked well, but required a bag to be picked up and put on a table. Prior to the ban, the TSA officers had been told not to do that work, that the red caps from the airlines would come and place the bags on the tables for them. But, as travelers began checking everything, the load on these carts ended up tripling and the red caps, counter staff, and our baggage screeners starting getting injured. Soon thereafter, the airlines began complaining to us about all the extra work.

The unexpected chain of events didn't end there. America's aviation system is a huge, complex system and we had suddenly injected a major new regulation into the network. Long after the ban was imposed, the follow-on disturbances continued to echo through the matrix. After the ban, travelers began overstuffing their checked luggage and the extra weight was noticed by the airlines. With more passengers checking the maximum amount of luggage, aircraft hold space was filling up, reducing the amount of lucrative cargo and mail they could carry. Eventually, in large part because of the liquids ban, the airlines decided to recoup on their costs and/or discourage checked luggage by charging a fee for checked bags.

Of course, paying extra to check bags was unattractive to passengers. So, as more airlines began charging luggage fees, travelers began overstuffing their carry-ons *en masse*. There were size restrictions on checked bags, pushing up sales of the wheeled-bags that could squeeze in the maximum amount of clothes. And this growing number of larger, heavier carry-ons threw substantial additional weight—and work—right back at the checkpoint TSOs. Liquids, a very real threat, had been taken off the table, but there was still a cost paid, both financially and physically.

The TSA was also paying a price with the public. Every time small liquid items like mascara and lip gloss were missed by officers, passengers would rightfully ask, "Why do I have to put everything in this little baggie if liquids are still getting through?" Though these items were no threat, the public had only heard the absolutist line: "No Liquids!" If only for the officers' credibility, we needed to reduce the ban to only what we could reliably detect and an amount small enough that it didn't matter if a passenger was carrying insulin *or* concentrated hydrogen peroxide on board.

JUST BEFORE THE AUGUST 10, 2006 LIQUIDS BAN, I CALLED GEORGE Zarur, my trusted science advisor from the TSA, and asked him to come in immediately. As always, he hopped on the Metro to come down. When he got to TSA, he remembers being taken into "a room with a whole bunch of people who didn't look very happy." Of course, I was one of them.

"What do you know about hydrogen peroxide?" I asked

"Not much," said George.

"Can it be exploded?"

"Yes," said George. "The Germans were using it as a rocket propellant for a while."

"If you mix it with something can it exploded?"

"Yes, it's an oxidant. If you add fuel to it like sugar, it will be a pretty solid explosive."

"What about this drink mix?" I said, holding up a bottle of some orange sports drink.

"Well, it's mostly sugar."

"Go and find me a way to detect it." I said.

"I guess we have a problem," thought George as he was being ushered out. It wasn't too long before he figured out what it was.

At that point, science was stacked against what I was trying to do at TSA. Over its first five years, TSA had been fixated on prohibiting items and I had seen the results: TSOs forced into robotic search mode, an increasingly annoyed public, a barrage of criticism every time a banned item made it through a checkpoint, and, in many case, only an incremental security value. I had originally argued against a ban because I wanted TSA to train its officers what to look for and, as quickly as possible, introduce technology that would neutralize the threat. Unfortunately, these bombs were different.

Prior to the liquids plot, the aviation security community had been well aware of homemade explosives, including liquids. In fact, the IED training for TSOs that Lee Kair's team had rolled out earlier in the year included a module on liquids. The most notable liquid explosive, nitroglycerin, was a potent but also very unstable explosive. To avoid losing an arm after jostling the explosive, terrorists would have to stabilize the nitroglycerin, say, by packing the explosive into cotton. And anything that stabilized nitroglycerin would in turn make it very easy to spot with a scanner. But before August 2006, hydrogen peroxide-based bombs were widely considered to be too unstable to carry around in a bag. A Western scientist had been killed in 2002 when a formula believed to contain concentrated hydrogen peroxide spontaneously blew up, essentially pushing future testing of the compound out of bounds.

Al-Qaeda, which had less regard for the safety of their employees—and certainly no insurance worries – had gone way beyond anything scientists in Europe or America had been considering. Working in a laboratory that was not much more than a mud floor in a simple dwelling, a facility nowhere near as advanced as an American high school science lab, explosives technicians had created an extremely clever and opportunistic piece of technology. The experiments were probably also driven by someone pretty bright with a reasonable depth of knowledge in German scientific literature from early in the twentieth century. Whoever had been involved, their willingness to push an envelope of knowledge and personal safety resulted in an extraordinarily powerful and compact liquid bomb formula based on very highly concentrated hydrogen peroxide.

George had to admit it: these bastards were creative. Not only did these novel devices make possible an attack that, like 9/11, no one had predicted, but they were also very easy to make and source. Members of a terror cell could simply go to the local drug store, load up on hydrogen peroxide and other common ingredients, and then cook it down in their kitchen. There weren't simple answers, so George engaged his huge scientific network, calling on the National Labs.

The National Labs are like a series of small cities with buildings in which five to ten thousand scientists worked spread over different campuses in the Southwest. Several of the sites had played critical roles in the development of the first nuclear weapon, including the ones that George got in touch with—Sandia, Livermore, and Los Alamos.

The first question was "Would these bombs work?" There were two ways to answer it. The first was to use modeling software to simulate a liquid bomb explosion in an aircraft. The second was to go out in the middle of the desert, load the explosive onboard, and pop the plane. In both cases the answer was "Yes!" The bomb put a huge hole in the exterior wall of the airplane. The plane and its passengers would be lost.

The next question was trickier and got to the heart of the risk management that needed to guide TSA's security strategy. For me, one lesson of 9/11 was that we will never know nor control everything. Even under ideal conditions, TSA's security network, the aviation system and, ultimately, the world in which we operate, are all far too complex to be predictable. And fending off the best efforts of large, adaptive, and successfully dispersed terror network is not an optimal operating environment.

Nonetheless, American aviation security had been predicated on just such an ability to know and control all threats. Creating a banned items list or installing new technology definitely has some security value. But imagining that you've regulated terror out of existence once the x-ray is installed—or the box cutters are banned—simply creates a perfect opportunity for a novel attack. And, again, our control system will be completely blindsided—just as it was by Lockerbie and 9/11.

For decades, America had accepted these occasional tragedies. But after 9/11 we decided that enough was enough and began throwing immense amounts of money, personnel, and other resources at the threat. Unfortunately, we had largely recreated a flashier, billion-dollar version of the FAA's security. TSA ran the checkpoints, but it was still regulating frontline security from above – business as usual in the federal government. From salmonella to earthquakes to a stock market collapse, our government agencies handled every threat by issuing rules and mandates. And in each case the system was strategically sound—until something unexpected happened. But while tectonic plates will never cease to surprise us and occasionally wreak havoc on the planet, they are a geologic force indifferent to our safety codes. Terrorism was a different threat. Printing up an SOP and announcing that an item was banned just gave the terrorists a blueprint of what *not* to do. We were throwing our control approach up against a threat that was trying to be unpredictable. Every time we'd throw something up, they'd go around it. In the long run, our regulatory approach was bound to be defeated.

After the liquids attack, I saw an opening to change how the TSA dealt with novel threats. After running an enormous number of explosive variables, from three to well over sixteen ounces of explosive with differing concentrations of hydrogen peroxide, and a range of lower to higher sugar content, George gave me some videos of tests. Sandia was able to tell us which formulas would detonate but not critically damage an aircraft, which would do serious damage and which would be complete duds. They also discovered that it wasn't just sugar that could cause hydrogen peroxide to detonate, but that there were 20 different possible compounds. This data was essential, but George wasn't the only one on the case.

A FEW WEEKS AFTER AUGUST 10TH, ED KITTEL, TSA'S TOP EXPLOSIVES expert, was sitting on the other side of an airport checkpoint pondering the ban. It was unpopular and had thrown the aviation system seriously out of whack. Even before it went into effect, he and his team were drilling down on how much potentially explosive liquid could be allowed on a plane. What was an acceptable risk that would allow passengers to carry some liquids onboard? Just then, a woman who had passed through security turned to her companion right in front of Ed. "Look at this," she said, gloating and holding a small bottle. "I got my hand lotion through."

"Wow," thought Ed. "Now the public is gaming the security system because they need some small amount of hand lotion." He went back to his lab and redoubled his efforts.

Prior to 9/11, Ed had stayed tuned into terrorists' preferred explosives in part by reading jihadist literature and bomb-making manuals. Some material could be grabbed off the web, while other information about popular weapons came through intel grabs. The terrorists scrutinized every security measure we introduced and Ed stared back, trying to get inside his adversaries' heads.

One of Ed's main resources was a big closet at the FAA that he'd converted into an explosives lab. He and his team prided themselves on being able to recreate any bomb used in a terror incident, using the weapons to better understand the advantages and disadvantages of the plot before designing a countermeasure. Ed had been at FAA in the 1990s when the al-Qaeda-linked terrorist Ramzi Youssef had been planning his Operation Bojinka plot. Like the liquid bombs a decade later, Bojinka had relied on everyday materials—a Casio wristwatch as timer, a homemade, non-metallic detonator hidden in a shoe, a 9V battery, and an explosive hidden in a contact lens solution bottle—to create a scrappy but effective weapon. On a test run, an operative successfully got on a Philippines Airlines flight, initiated and hid the device under a seat in a life jacket, and disembarked at an intermediate stop. During the continuing flight, the bomb exploded, killing a Japanese businessman.

Because so little was known about the chemistry used to create the hydrogen peroxide bombs—or how safe they were to test—Ed had to start experimenting with very small scale, miniscule amounts of the stuff. As he scaled the bomb up, he'd need to measure the static sensitivity, spark sensitivity, drop sensitivity, friction sensitivity, impact sensitivity and anything else that might accidentally cost Ed a finger—or worse.

After the UK arrests that had disrupted the liquid bombs plot, a complete, operational bomb, one housed in a British sports drink called Lucozade, was never discovered. So, though Ed's team had enough intel to get the raw materials right, they were never sure that they developed a device with the exact concentrations of an assembled bomb. As they began to combine Ed's work with the testing results from the National Labs, Ed's most valuable asset came to the fore. In my search for scientific advice to determine what was an acceptable amount of liquid to allow onto planes, I encountered two roadblocks. The first was that most scientists would go on at length about the facts at hand or answer technical questions, but I seldom heard them finish with, "and therefore we recommend . . ." Likewise, making a firm decision in the midst of a murky situation was contrary to TSA's traditional security strategy. When I had come on board, the organization was very binary: if it was explosive, it was banned. Through the SOP, our frontline workers were trained to stay on one side of this unquestionable line drawn in the sand. The mandate drilled into TSOs was not "mitigate the threat" but "follow the rules." And instead of owning security at your checkpoint, the hierarchical, high-regulated culture would protect you if a novel bomb got through your checkpoint. This risk-adverse inheritance was why I loved Ed's ability to say, "That bright line is an illusion. There are no bright lines." In view of the organization's historic inertia and traditional approach, Ed's willingness to guide us into the world of uncertainty of "acceptable risks" was courageous.

Another critical question that we'd been working on even before the ban, was not so much scientific as ontological: What is a liquid or gel? It wasn't always easy. Were deodorants? Mashed up baby food? Frozen items that might melt? Fresh Mozzarella? Suddenly, all these everyday items—the background noise of life – became the subject of heated discussion as their classification entered into a debate on national security. It was a strange juxtaposition and our efforts to nail down exactly what was a liquid were roundly mocked on *Saturday Night Live:* "What about mustard on a turkey sandwich?" Eventually we settled on a definition: if you dumped a substance out on the kitchen table and it lost its shape, it was a liquid or gel. Outside of his lab, Ed carried out some exhaustive research on other household items. He went to CVS, Rite Aid, Walgreens and bought every small bottle on the shelves—be it shampoo, antiperspirant, or antacid. He needed to know what products were on the market, their different sizes, what allowing each item on board meant giving up in security, and what was the total possible volume if the ingredients were combined. After his field work at local pharmacies, Ed went back to the lab and stuffed as many bottles as possible into a plastic bag.

IN EARLY SEPTEMBER, ED'S TEAM, GEORGE'S UNIT, AND THE TSA'S MAN-agement team wrestled for days with how to finally create a policy. The science had told us that containers above a certain size were required to make a bomb that could destroy an aircraft. The corollary was also true, if the size of the container was x ounces or smaller, no matter what was in it, it could not bring a plane down. Next we debated what size of container would allow most travelers to go an overnight trip. The numbers we arrived at – a calculus weighing convenience, practicality, and safety—hovered between two and four ounces. We split the difference and selected three ounces as the permissible container size.

Then Mike Restovich jumped in with an operations question: "Could we require that all of the three ounce containers be grouped together in a separate bag so that our officers aren't fishin' around for stray bottles?" Mike wanted to avoid a 'lip gloss' situation in which we required TSOs to find things so small they couldn't consistently locate them. Ed added that he would be more comfortable with a quart-sized bag than one that could hold a gallon; putting all the bottles together would limit the total amount of liquids that any one person could bring. We quietly ran this logic past the airlines and asked that they give us feedback on how this would work with their customers.

Surprisingly to me, there was considerable government support for keeping the total liquid ban. In the first place, it was safer. Why get into the question of 'how much is enough?' If we were wrong to allow small bottles through, as history tells us is not out of the question, we could leave terrorists a loophole big enough to kill thousands. After a field test, our own personnel came back and also recommended that we continue the total ban, things were going smoothly at checkpoints. From the public affairs perspective, the clarity of a total ban combined with unprecedented speed of passengers getting through security, argued for the status quo. Why introduce a complex rule that will only make things messier? To me, it was obvious we needed to relax the rule since the total ban was unsustainable, but there weren't many who agreed.

Despite plenty of resistance to a change, we arrived at a conclusion on acceptable risk: three ounce bottles in a quart-size bag. Next we had to get the idea that "there's never no risk" approved by Secretary Chertoff, who first drilled Ed on the details. "Why a zip-top bag, why not something else?" asked Chertoff.

Ed explained that a sealed plastic baggie would concentrate the escaping vapors from the hydrogen peroxide inside a bottle making it easier to detect by sensor or just smell.

Then the Department's Press Secretary weighed in. In her estimation, DHS was coming out well in media coverage of the liquid ban. She turned to me, "I understand what you are saying about the technical merits but this three ounce bottles in a baggie protocol is not intuitive, it's too complex, people aren't going to get it and you are going to get killed over it in the press." Nonetheless, after more discussion about operational issues, Chertoff approved the plan. Then we had to sell the idea to the world; our first stop was Marjeta Jager.

INTERNATIONALLY, THERE WERE PLENTY OF OPEN DIFFERENCES ON HOW to proceed on liquids. Some countries wanted to lift the ban outright, some wanted to keep it permanent. The British post-August 10 measures not only eliminated liquids, but also limited all hand luggage to one small bag that allowed you to carry on your wallet and a paperback book. So while Marjeta and Niki Tompkinson from the UK went around and lobbied individual country heads, I sent Ed to London to meet with scientists on the EU's technical taskforce to make our case for allowing some liquids on board.

The group, Ed and about 20 other technicians and advisors from the UK, France, Germany, Netherlands and a few other countries, met at a conference room in London. There were plenty of difficulties to work through. First of all, every country wanted to do its own individual research. A lab director in Germany or France insisted on doing their own parallel experiments instead of simply reviewing and accepting the results from the US National Labs in Sandia.

Partially because of that approach, and how each country viewed the threat, there were three distinct groups. The first were those who basically dismissed the liquid bombs as a threat. Ed had brought live testing of the quantities that we suspected would be used in the August plot. "For those of you who think that this stuff is all bunk," said Ed facing the group before playing several videos of live explosions, "this is what it does. It blows up. It's in the terrorist manuals and it will go off."

The other extreme were those who didn't want an ounce of the hydrogen peroxide to get onboard. Ed figured that some of this fear was related to hydrogen peroxide's novelty and the historical lack of scientific literature, so he tried to put this new threat in the context of the military and commercial explosives that were well documented.

"Take a look at what he have in the body of knowledge about explosives," he suggested. "We've all tested Semtex, C4, PE 4, TNT—you've all done testing based on the threats of Palestinian bombings in the 1980s. It's well documented. So before we get all crazy here, be very careful that you don't sign us up for new checkpoint standards that are so draconian they will exceed what the more powerful explosives we know about can do."

The group had begun moving towards the center, but weren't anywhere near a consensus. At about 6 A.M. I got a call from Dave Tiedge, the DHS Attache in London and a veteran of international aviation negotiations, who was with Ed in London. "We just broke for lunch. They aren't getting anywhere."

Meanwhile, during the catered lunch of cold cuts and cheeses, Ed was working the room trying to soften up the positions a bit more. After lunch he spoke up again, "OK, let's re-cap. Some of you came in thinking that these bombs wouldn't work at all, I think we've shown that that's not the case. Some of you came in thinking that was way more powerful than it could be based on the chemistry of concentrated hydrogen peroxide and organic materials. We need to drive towards the middle. What else can we do?" By the end of that day, the general concept of what became the baggie rules was in place.

After Ed's meeting, Marjeta continued to work the political channels. Just before the new recommendations came up for a vote, I got an urgent call from her while I was with Bill Hall at JFK. I apologetically broke away from the employees I had been visiting.

"This is very difficult and I need to ask you for some help," Marjeta said tersely. "If you can change from three ounces to 100 ml, I think I can get the votes."

I realized that we needed to give some ground to the Europeans instead of obstinately insisting on getting exactly what we wanted. And I also knew that no one in Europe uses ounces, no one liked ounces, and no one wanted to convert the standard we brought from across the Atlantic to 88.72 milliliters. Fortunately Ed had done testing in milliliters as well—as would most chemists—and had already told me that 100ml was not a big change from a risk perspective.

"Do we have a deal if I say yes?" I asked Marjeta.

"Yes."

"Then, Marjeta, we have a deal," I replied.

This was a groundbreaking achievement. Because the Canadians had already agreed with the 3-1-1 protocol, the work of Marjeta, Ed, George and countless others allowed us to announce that the United States, EU Member States and Canada were all adopting identical security measures for liquids. This was the first time that the United States and EU had agreed in advance on new aviation security measures, a fulfillment of Francois Lamoureux's vision. By year-end, the baggie rules were adopted by the international aviation authority and became the world standard.

ON SEPTEMBER 26, 2006 WE ANNOUNCED THE NEW INITIATIVE. ELLEN Howe, TSA's head of media affairs, had suggested the "3-1-1" logo to communicate three-ounce bottles of liquids and gels in one quart-sized zip-top bag per one person. But, as the press secretary at the DHS had warned, the details of the new measures were a bit of nightmare for Ellen to communicate. It was our biggest risk-based decision to date and the complexity and grey areas implicit in such a solution made the baggie emphatically resistant to sound-bites. So Ellen spent her next month doing interviews and answering questions from, "If it's called 3-1-1, then why can you actually bring 3.4

ounces on a plane?" to "Couldn't you just take everything in your baggie and mix it up and make a bomb?" Even trickier for Ellen was that the answer to the second question was "Maybe."

Theoretically several terrorists could team up and put the entire contents of all their baggies together to make a dangerous, operational bomb. But they would actually have to go somewhere in the secure side of the airport, take their baggies out of their carry-ons, empty multiple three ounces-bottle into a larger container and then hand it off to an accomplice to do the same thing. The hydrogen peroxide formula was extremely sensitive to minute variation, meaning that a spilled drop made a difference in whether or not it would work. Even with a world-class laboratory, the success rate in mixing the formula was around one in three. In addition, the fluid was dangerously corrosive and would cause severe burns if exposed to skin, not to mention that it had a strong pungent odor that would attract attention in airport secure areas, facts known to al-Qaeda engineers. It was a potential risk, but 3-1-1 would force the terrorists to do some bathroom chemistry, which would be very difficult.

A lot of work and logic went into the "zip-top" baggie solution but *accepting* that something dangerous is going to get onboard planes is not what Americans expect from their security. It is confusing, annoying, and unsettling. The day that 3-1-1 went into effect, a Milwaukee man scrawled "Kip Hawley is an Idiot" on his baggie and was launched to internet stardom, inspiring a website with his famous quote printed across coffee cups, teddy bears and t-shirts.

As TSA administrator, I am best known for introducing the baggie; I am well aware that almost no one likes it. But I also know that the baggie took al Qaeda's explosive of choice off the table for aviation attacks, obviating years of their research and development and pushing them to consider less effective bomb formulas. And, with our current technology, we should soon see the baggie disappear. No one will be happier than I.

BY THE TIME 3-1-1 WAS ROLLED OUT, THE FUNDAMENTALS OF THE AVIA-tion security that two million passengers pass through every day, decades in the making, were in place. The first major measures, magnetometers and x-rays, had become standard in the early 1970s to keep knives and guns off of planes as a direct response to the steep rise in hijackings during the politically turbulent 1960s. After Pan Am 103 exploded over Lockerbie, a small amount of international checked baggage was inspected or scanned and passengers had to fly with their luggage.

After 9/11, TSA was created and given a list of mandates, including screening all checked baggage, banning blades and other items from carry-ons, and federalizing airport security. Two months later, around Christmas 2001, UK citizen Richard Reid's attempt to light explosives prompted screeners to ask people to remove their boots and heavy shoes. By the summer of 2006, we also had intel that al-Qaeda could put an effective bomb in just about any type of footwear and we extended the policy by having everyone take off every kind of shoe. Finally, after the liquids ban that lasted most of August and September 2006, I introduced the baggie.

Looking at the checkpoint in late 2006, I could see that each measure had a specific reason and provided some serious security value. But they also told a story of an agency that was still too reactive and too dependent on regulatory prohibitions to parry the very real threat stalking us. We were making progress with better training and the introduction of new proactive security measures like document checking, pop-up patrols of VIPRs, and behavior detection, but we needed to accelerate our pace to keep up with the pipeline of oncoming plots. My first year at TSA had been like a roller coaster, but the ride was just starting to get bumpy.

FOURTEEN

THE NETWORK CHASE

NEU ULM IS A SMALL TOWN TUCKED INTO THE PICTURESQUE Bavarian countryside on the banks of the Danube, 400 miles upriver from Zubair al-Masri's hometown of Vienna. At first glance, Neu Ulm is an unlikely spot to become a hotbed of radical Islam, but its very normalcy carries a message. After the crackdown on Islamic radicals in Egypt following Anwar Sadat's assassination in 1981 let up, a number of the most radical jihadist imams left Egypt and several settled in Germany. In Neu Ulm, two of their leaders founded a study center called the Multi Kultur Haus (Multicultural House) in 1996. In 2001, Zubair, then known as Abdulrahman, had traveled to Neu Ulm as a student sponsored by the Egyptian Islamic Jihad. Abdulrahman spent most of his time in the town's focal point for radical Islam, the Multi Kultur Haus ("MKH"), a two-story brick building on a tree-lined street. The MKH had a grocery, library, and classrooms and served as a base for the supporters of the Egyptian-born al-Qaeda number two, Ayman Zawahiri. The MKH's curriculum was unabashedly militant; one of the center's teaching materials stated, "To triumph does not only mean killing the unbelievers, but also killing oneself in order to strike back at the unbelievers."

Abdulrahman was both popular and respected at the MKH. Older scholars were impressed by his grasp of their interpretation of Koranic teachings, while the teenagers and twenty-somethings related to a young guy who knew their slang and interests. While there, Abdulrahman befriended Omer

Ozdemir, a German citizen of Turkish descent with close-cropped hair and deep-set eyes. Omer had grown up just outside Stuttgart, an hour northwest of Neu Ulm. He was five years older than Abdulrahman, with a strong drive and a quick, tactical mind. Omer was also practiced at traveling under the radar while collecting money from mosques around Germany, which he funneled to al-Qaeda and other radical groups operating abroad. They stayed in touch when Abdulrahman left to resume his studies in Egypt.

Two years later, in 2004, Abdulrahman returned to the MKH and made the acquaintance of a young industrial engineering student named Fritz Gelowicz. Three years older, Fritz was a teenage convert to Islam. He'd grown up comfortably in Munich, where his father sold solar panels and his mother was a doctor. A handsome boy, with light brown hair and fair skin, Fritz was indistinguishable from his peers in many ways. He enjoyed sports, including a ninth-grade stint playing American football for the Bavarian Barracudas. In high school, he listened to hip-hop and began drinking and casually using drugs. At fifteen, around the time his parents divorced, Fritz befriended a Turkish boy named Tolga Durbin. Fritz was drawn to the stability and support of Tolga's Islamic faith. Eight years later, in late 2003, Fritz became fully radicalized, and entered the MKH orbit.

In 2006, two years after they first met, Fritz and Abdulrahman—now Zubair al-Masri—reunited in the mountains of North Waziristan. Their meeting seemed especially fortuitous to Zubair. In July 2006, before the failed liquids plot or the arrest of Rashid Rauf, Zubair had been instructed by his boss, Abu Ubaydah, to search for potential recruits for his next plot. Ubaydah wanted to step up the pace of major attacks on America and Western Europe to about nine months from start to finish. He suggested Zubair exploit his networks in the German-speaking world, so encountering Fritz, a willing and intelligent operative, seemed to him particularly serendipitous.

Zubair's primary role in Fritz's training consisted of explosives instruction. Still interested in using the liquid hydrogen peroxide bombs intended to destroy jumbo jets, Zubair taught Fritz and his partner, Adem Yilmaz, how to manufacture the explosives on a much larger scale. The pervasive restrictions at airports made getting liquids on board a dicey proposal, but taking out a major airport with a gargantuan bomb would be just as effective at killing thousands of people while also paralyzing the international aviation system.

From Zubair, Fritz learned how to refine swimming pool cleaner, available in concentrations of up to 35 percent hydrogen peroxide, versus the 3 percent available at local pharmacies. To avoid tripping the authorities' radar, Fritz and his team were taught to travel to different police districts and multiple suppliers hundreds of kilometers apart while avoiding speeding tickets. Fritz would also have to recruit and train cell members while keeping a low profile. He needed discipline in his budgeting and to limit communications with Pakistan. He wasn't a model operative, but he was well on his way.

"Look," explained Zubair. "Any *Penner* can boil this stuff down. What you have to think about is how are you going to pay for it, where you're buying it, and where you storing it until you're ready to make the devices." In October 2006, as winter came to Waziristan, Fritz and Adem left to launch Ubaydah's next plot.

IN THE AUTUMN OF 2006, THE FEDERAL BUREAU OF INVESTIGATION OB-served a group of al-Qaeda–linked Canadians conducting what looked like preoperational surveillance on Minneapolis-Saint Paul airport, where I had done my TSO training, as well as the Mall of America, a five-story complex with more than 2,500,000 square feet of retail space that sprawled just across the freeway from the airport. We already knew that al-Qaeda sought to establish recruiting networks in the United States similar to the ones that were bringing Europeans to the training camps of Pakistan. We were also aware that the terror group's head of operations, Abu Ubaydah, had made diversity a top priority. But this plot, known as Operation Trident, was the first time we had heard its footsteps in North America.

After witnessing the operational and technological complexity of August's Operation Overt, and then sweating the possibilities represented by this new Toronto-based cell, I realized that the rest of my tenure at TSA would be almost all devoted to move and counter-move against a continuing stream of threats. Although the Canadian plot was defused before any damage was done, my sense that al-Qaeda was hellbent on taking down airplanes was only magnified. Over the past year, our iconoclastic head of intelligence Bill Gaches had managed to bring real reporting to the TSA, but now we were scrambling to figure out what to do with the flood of information.

One morning in June 2007, I walked into our sixth-floor sensitive compartmented information facility for the daily intel briefing and noticed a tall man with dark hair, glasses, and a sharp nose sitting quietly in the corner. The rest of us gathered at the SCIF's conference table. I kept quiet until Bill turned to me and said, "This is Keith Kauffman."

OK, I thought, my mind already overloaded. *Keith. Keith. Keith,* I repeated silently.

Keith Kauffman was an old colleague of Bill's from the National Security Agency. In the 1990s he had been one of the first people at the Fort to jump into the cyber world, learning about the exploitation and defense of information. When he showed up in our briefing, Keith knew almost nothing about the TSA except that it was born out of 9/11 and was supposed to keep planes in the air. During his visit, Keith found our intel office to be more complex than he had imagined. It struck him as a good place to be focused on counterterrorism and a much easier place to be entrepreneurial and experimental than most agencies. He became our deputy head of intel later that month, replacing TSA veteran Joe Salvator, who had been recruited by the FBI to a similar job.

Keith had nearly thirty years in the field under his belt, which brought us some more juicy contacts within the major players like the NSA and the CIA. When these groups release a report to the wider intelligence community, they are primarily looking for the five Ws and H: "Who, what, where, when, why, and how?" But other info—say, details about a person casing the TSA via the Internet—may end up on the cutting-room floor. While a web search as specific as "How does the TSA do its work?" may not set off alarm bells at other agencies, we want to know everything we can about someone snooping in our bushes. Keith brought in some NSA analysts, the people who slogged through the raw bits of intercepted data so our intel and operations people could ask for more detail and suggest how to refine the analysis we got. Although we never learned their real names, it was also a rare chance to thank these people. Most analysts labor in a secure, anonymous space with few opportunities to see their work impact operations in the rest of the world. For us, they are heroes.

Despite his three decades working in intelligence, Keith was not locked into the process-driven bureaucratic mindset that haunts much of the government. He had also been able to drop many of the presumptions about our adversaries still pervasive in many intel agencies. Keith had been thinking continually about networks ever since the cyber wars of the 1990s. Aside from adding another Steelers fan to our Friday custom of NFL jersey days, I could see why Bill had brought Keith onboard. Each had unique approaches to processing the enormous amount of threat reporting that came across our radar. Both were invaluable.

ON NEW YEAR'S EVE 2006, POLICE IN HANAU, GERMANY, STOPPED A CAR driving slowly past the US military barracks there, making a record of the three men inside, including Fritz Gelowicz, a thin man with an easy smile, light brown hair parted in the middle, and wire-framed glasses.

The police thought enough of the incident to begin following his activities and those of his accomplices, another German named Daniel Martin Schneider and a Turkish citizen, Adem Yilmaz. Their surveillance was soon rewarded. After long periods of normal daily activities, Gelowicz would suddenly take off on trips that seemed to be straight out of the espionage playbook. He would hop on a train, get off in the middle of nowhere, and then return on the next train. These trips had no obvious motivation except to lose a tail—and anyway, Gelowicz had been a decoy all along. At the same time, his accomplices were casing storage places for stashing bomb-making material. But Gelowicz's low profile and furtive behavior occasionally lapsed into bizarre displays of publicity seeking: At one point in 2006 he was interviewed by *Stern*, a German news magazine, about whether he was or wasn't preparing a terror plot.

Despite Gelowicz's best (and worst) efforts, the German police soon discovered a cache containing almost 200 gallons of concentrated hydrogen peroxide and military-grade detonators. For comparison, one of the energy-drink liquid bombs capable of blowing a hole in an aircraft was less than a quarter gallon. Even though the cell was under constant surveillance, German authorities also took the precaution of replacing the concentrated hydrogen peroxide with a much weaker formulation. Clearly, August's failed liquids plot hadn't yet convinced al-Qaeda to take hydrogen peroxide bombs off the table.

The TSA had been brought in on the intelligence because the cell's real goal was not aimed only at Germans but, as one of the members later said, "to kill as many Americans as possible." In addition to the military barracks, Gelowicz and crew had also been staking out several nightclubs frequented by US air force personnel and the Frankfurt airport, one of the main entry points for American travelers.

I was very troubled by this reporting. It bore the hallmarks of an al-Qaeda plot with the liquid hydrogen peroxide but we didn't see a clear path back to the group's central leadership. We wondered about whether there was a hidden aspect to this plot, how this sandy-haired, German-born operative with no criminal record had gotten in touch with al-Qaeda, and who his facilitator was. In the case of the August 2006 Operation Glidepath, this role was played by Rashid Rauf, but Rauf had been grabbed by the Pakistani authorities on the eve before Glidepath was set to be carried out—and he managed UK–based plots, anyway. Who, we asked ourselves, was the Rashid Rauf for these German guys? And what else was he working on?

As we continued following the events in Germany, we eventually found a link between Fritz Gelowicz and a man named Omer Ozdemir. From there, the connections spiderwebbed. Ozdemir was known as a transporter of items between Europe and the federally administered tribal areas in the far western portion of Pakistan that had become a haven for al-Qaeda's leadership. Through a southerly route, from Turkey to Iran and then on to Pakistan, Ozdemir transported supplies and tens of thousands of euros collected at European mosques. He also guided recruits to al-Qaeda's training camps. From what we knew about Ozdemir, he was not only a smart operator, but also well connected to many other Europe-based agents and facilitators.

To manage the rapidly expanding social matrix, Keith had his analytical team load incoming data into a program called Analyst's Notebook, a product widely used for war games or financial analysis. The software would not only keep track of Ozdemir's phone number, email address, known physical addresses, roles within al-Qaeda, and nicknames, but would ultimately turn his profile into a kind of living document constantly accruing new connections. When one of these nodes became developed or intriguing enough to deserve a second look, Keith would call me down to the sixth floor, where, with the help of an assistant, he would unfurl a huge paper document across a twelve-foot conference table and start going through it with me.

Eventually, these documents might link Omer Ozdemir to a German-born Bosnian named Nihad Cosic, a battle-hardened veteran of the Balkan wars of the 1990s who was notable for what was described by former trainees as grisly training on how to conduct beheadings. Ozdemir was also connected to a thirty-something Moroccan-born German citizen named Bekkay Harrach, who boasted a long heritage of militant activities that included fighting US forces in Iraq. Harrach was plugged into al-Qaeda's head of operations, Abu Ubaydah. And Harrach, in turn, had a cohort named Eric Breininger, a German-born recent convert to Islam. Breininger was especially worrisome to us; not only because of his European looks and clean record, but also for his proven ability to stay below the radar and an angry attitude that suggested he could be persuaded to be a suicide operative. For some time, Breininger had been roommates with Daniel Martin Schneider in the Gelowicz-led cell. And that was just a slender slice of the links among the growing population of al-Qaeda recruits circulating freely in Europe.

Because we were constantly aware that we were glimpsing only a small portion of the overall picture, pursuing sources that were more obscure was extremely valuable. Keith's social-networking maps would also note looser linkages, like one-time phone calls. For example, a four-minute, thirty-two-second phone conversation starting at 16:38 on Thursday, June 8, 2007, between two numbers associated with minor players might not seem worth fishing out of the flood of data. But when this call illuminates an overlapping link between two previously disparate social networks, it becomes much more interesting.

While trying to wrap my head around this matrix, I also had to wrestle with the tendency of intelligence reporting to track backward as well as forward: New reporting is constantly invalidating what had previously been bedrock assumptions. In this sense, the intel environment resembles archaeology or paleontology, in which the discovery of a new artifact or fossil shatters decades of sophisticated guesswork.

Tom Hoopes shocked me this way one morning in early 2007 after pulling me aside with the ominous words, "Sir, if you could stay just another moment, there is something interesting that has come up in relation to Operation Glidepath." After Hamza Rabia had been hit and the mission called off, we thought all the operatives were dead or in prison. He refreshed my memory about the details we knew. One operative, Mohammed Zillur Rahman, and the cell's leader, known as Imran, had both been killed in fighting on the Afghanistan border. The other member of the cell, Rangzied Ahmed, was captured by Pakistani authorities in August 2006. Tom told me it was now believed that those three plotters had not been intending to attack the UK, but America. What's more, the shadowy Imran was not dead but presumed to be in the Pakistani training camps, going by the names Waqas or Zubair al-Masri. After the near miss of Glidepath, I was consumed by everything related to the plot, but once the leader of this cell aimed at the United States reappeared, my focus shifted to this man known as Waqas.

During 2007 and 2008, I spent as much time as possible in the sixth-floor SCIF, reading the reporting, studying diagrams and lists, and listening to analysts spitballing possible connections and theories about where plotting might be going. But I also had to travel a lot, both because it was part of the job description and because it was the best way to stay in touch with the front lines. Since I wasn't normally near a secure line, Keith kept me up to date on the current ten to twelve threat streams with simple mnemonic cover names. With Bekkay Harrach, for example, we went through a two-step process. First we found something easily relatable to him—his initials, BK. We then thought of something else with a BK, Burger King. When he had info on Harrach, Keith could tell me, "Hey, we got something today on the Big Whopper." We had a passel of pseudonyms like "Rockethead" and others.

Another clue was not code for a specific person but for somebody getting whacked. Because Brian Urlacher, the Chicago Bears' linebacker, was known for his devastating tackles, his surname became synonymous with "a good hit." For instance, if an al-Qaeda operative of note met an untimely end, thus thwarting any plots that might have been underway, Keith could keep me up to date by simply texting "Urlacher Rockethead" to my BlackBerry.

But whenever possible, I liked to dig in myself. On weekends, I parked in a secure briefing room, leaning forward in one of the black ergonomic chairs that surrounded the conference table and getting sucked into a parallel universe comprised of scraps of data and electronic intercepts. When I wasn't traveling, I stopped by the intel shop before the morning SVTC so I could bounce ideas off Bill Gaches and Tom Hoopes. Some mornings there was a bit of extra entertainment.

About ten minutes before every teleconference began, sound techs at each agency came in to check the mics in their respective briefing rooms. I soon became accustomed to this background noise while reading intel about, say, a Belgian terror cell:

"CIA, do you read me?"

"I hear you loud and clear."

"NSA, do you read me?"

"I have you, five by five."

But sometimes the mic at an agency would be left live, and some inadvertent gems were broadcast to the whole intel community: someone at one of the Department of Defense agencies talking about a lousy date experience, or interagency rivalries being aired, like this one: "That freaking CIA guy! He comes rolling in here and he thinks they've got it owned, but I just gave it right back to 'em. I'm so f-ing tired of that bullshit."

There was also some intentional humor. Sometimes, a CIA briefer would drop a plotline from the previous night's episode of *24*, the television show about a fictional counterterrorism task force, into a briefing: "According to uncorroborated sources, German operative Fritz Gelowicz met covertly with CTU officials . . ."

Aside from the occasional Packers game, *24* was one of the few television programs I saw in almost four years at TSA, usually taped, at four A.M. The show portrayed a job and an agency that many of us at the TSA recognized. In fact, with its wall-sized monitors and gleaming computers at open workstations, the fictional counterterrorism unit's control room actually looks quite a bit like the TSA's Freedom Center where operational information comes together and critical incidents are managed. But while we had no Jack Bauer, a hero who singlehandedly defeated terrorists, we did have tens of thousands of resourceful people focused on stopping plots—if we knew where to look.

AFTER THE EIGHT A.M. MULTIAGENCY BRIEFING CAME TO A CLOSE, A group would gather outside the door of our soundproof room, waiting for the intra-TSA brief. Usually around eight-thirty we'd have everyone come in, share what we could that was useful, and then figure out what to do about the various threat streams. Ever since we were caught flatfooted by Hurricane Katrina, I vowed that every threat would result in action of some sort. Now our feverish parsing of intel linking brief phone calls in Pakistan with possible sightings in Germany had to be translated into operations within our large network.

No one was better at this than Mo McGowan, the muscular, white-haired ex-detective from Texas. After I spent forty-five minutes lighting into our operations team with my hair on fire, Mo would speak up in his measured John Wayne way. "Maybe we ought to do this," he'd say, and then very deliberately lay out a plan to add a new person of interest to a selectee list or place air marshals on certain flights between particular city pairs.

Mo's unique ability was to combine specific intelligence with a strategic risk-management approach that actually produced operational steps to secure actual airports in the real world. His work brought together the multiple constituent networks—intel, strategy, our frontline officers, BDOs, FAMs, and the high profile patrol teams called VIPRS—with which I was attempting to replace the TSA's singular, hierarchical, control-based system. Although we were tracking an enormous number of threats in any given week, we didn't want to simply rely on our checkpoints to keep us safe nor did we wish to resort to such draconian measures as turning flights back to Europe or closing terminals.

For example, if we had even vague reporting that somebody was using an airport taxi driver for surveillance or as an attack operative, we could increase the visible presence of K-9 bomb detection teams or uniformed BDOs where taxi drivers would notice them. Or, if we wanted to make a more direct statement, we could ramp up random vehicle inspections of incoming taxis. With our flexible assets, Federal Security Directors, like Bill Hall at New York's JFK, could dial up almost infinite combinations of patrols and other security measures with varying times and locations. By contrast, the classic regulatory model was limited to "on" or "off": You either banned or prevented something absolutely—such as taxis at the airport—or you didn't.

This nimble risk-management model was even more essential once the intelligence spigot was fully turned on. Now the TSA was hearing about not only the proven serious plots, but all the chaff and illusion that makes up the raw stuff of intelligence reporting. We couldn't pursue all of the intelligence leads with clunky regulatory tools, exhausting the agency's human resources and breaking the budget in the process. As we moved through 2007, it took artists like Mo and his predecessor, Mike Restovich, plus a ready supply of customizable security options to maintain intelligent, effective, and sustainable action.

ON APRIL 1, 2007, FOLLOWING A LONG NIGHT SPENT ON AN OVERNIGHT training exercise, Lee Kair was jolted out of a nap by his phone. "Hello?" he answered automatically, without really waking up.

The head of the coordination center at Orlando International Airport, who was normally extremely polite, had an unusual urgency to his voice when he said: "You need to get to the airport right now!"

Lee looked sleepily around his room and saw the Florida sun partially blocked by the blinds. After years working in acquisitions in Washington, plus a couple years cleaning up the TSA's operational side, Lee had decided to get out into the field. He had grown up in Florida and jumped at the chance to take over as federal security director at Orlando International.

After running his hands through his thick brown hair, Lee jumped up and hurried over to the emergency op center in his jeans and a TSA shirt. As he approached the airport, Lee saw news helicopters overhead. A bit closer, he spotted film crews following a man being led out of the airport by police.

Twenty minutes earlier, a plainclothes Behavior Detection Officer had seen a passenger enter the airport, walk around a bit near the windows, then approach the Air Jamaica desk and drop off a bag. Because the passenger was displaying several markers of nervous behavior, the BDO had noticed him as soon as he entered the airport and ordered the bag opened. Inside were all the components of an improvised bomb. The officer spun around and hurried through the airport crowds looking for the passenger, calling over some passing Orlando police once he had spotted the man. They initially thought the BDO was playing an April Fool's joke—"Really? A guy just walked in with a bomb in his bag?" they asked, disbelieving—before surrounding the passenger and dragging him away.

Arriving at the airport, Lee snapped out of the fog of sleep to something more akin to the fog of war. This was the first case of a bomb inside a US airport. Half of Orlando International had been shut down and cleared, and Lee was soon fielding calls from the airport director, local law enforcement, and Secretary Chertoff, plus a local conference call with officials on the inside and a national bridge call with me and others at the TSA. Before he knew it, Lee was even being interviewed by CNN while wearing his rumpled t-shirt and sporting bed head.

That was the least of our worries, although it might have turned out far worse. The Orlando incident was a major catch for our BDOs, highlighting our further deployment of behavior-detection officers, a nationwide expansion of one of the TSA's invaluable security networks.

IN ADDITION TO IMPORTING HIS SIGNATURE BRAND OF NONLINEAR LOGIC to the TSA, Bill Gaches was also good at tapping unconventional sources of information, be they unreleased, top-secret, compartmented data he snagged through inside connections with intel community analysts or completely informal searches that transcended typical government data collection.

Late at night on Friday, July 30, 2007, an alert pedestrian in London noticed an unusually parked Mercedes outside the Tiger Tiger nightclub in the West End. The passerby notified the police, who subsequently discovered a bomb in the trunk. The explosive hadn't detonated because the trunk's seal was too tight to allow enough air to flow inward and ignite the bomb. The police made an eerie discovery when they opened the car. The cell phone meant to remotely trigger the bomb when called showed several missed calls as the plotters tried unsuccessfully to detonate it.

We had had no specific warnings about the attack, but with the heat index rising rapidly, the Tiger Tiger incident was hardly a surprise. I came in early the next day to get the details. Bill and Tom Hoopes were already in the office, looking for threads that might tie the Tiger Tiger crew to any of the other plots on our radar. Secretary Chertoff was up at the DHS with Charlie Allen also on the case. Sensing a lull in the action, I told Bill and Tom that I was going to pop home for lunch. Five minutes later, just as I arrived at my apartment, Bill called me and told me to get back to the TSA immediately.

"What do we know?" I asked, running into Bill's office. He told me that a Land Rover had crashed in front of Glasgow's airport and gotten stuck between the protective bollards just outside the entrance. US intel had ramped up, but first reports were usually wrong. For us, the big question was: Is this a horrible accident, or an attack?

Bill picked up the phone and dialed a contact at Continental Airlines. "Hey, it's Bill. Listen, I've got a funny request. Can you give me the number for your customer support desk in Glasgow?"

He then called up Glasgow and introduced himself. "Are you in a position to see what happened?"

"Yes, yes," said the shaken voice on the other end of the line.

"What happened? Was it an accident?"

"No. That guy aimed right for the barriers."

We immediately called Chertoff's office, where everyone there was still discussing whether or not it was an attack.

"We can confirm that was an attack," I said.

We later learned that, after the failed Tiger Tiger attack, the panicked occupants of the Land Rover had driven overnight from London, finally concocting their desperate backup plan.

JUST AS MO MCGOWAN WAS INVALUABLE FOR INTEGRATING INTELLI-gence and operational networks under the rubric of risk management, George Zarur, the scholarly Palestinian-born technical advisor, brought a huge network of scientists into our security mix. This was essential because, as the Gelowicz case and several other plots showed, hydrogen peroxide remained the al-Qaeda explosive of choice. Despite the 3-1-1 liquid restrictions—less than 3.4 ounces, restricted to one quart-size zip-top plastic baggie—we were aware that operatives within al-Qaeda were online and sniffing for holes in the measure. Initially the only technologies that could detect hydrogen peroxide at the checkpoints required opening containers individually to dip in a test strip. The science was sound, but the procedure was a nightmare from a practical standpoint. Then one day, George called up a friend who was chair of the chemistry department at the Massachusetts Institute of Technology and explained his problem.

"You know," said George's friend, "I have this polymer with very thin capillaries that will emit a light when it smells hydrogen peroxide." The technology—the same used in toy glow sticks—was quite simple: Once the tubes are cracked, chemicals, including hydrogen peroxide, blend with the polymer, emitting light.

George asked his contacts at the National Labs, three of whom had formed a loose consortium, to test the polymer.[1] "You've got to be kidding!" one scientist called back excitedly. "You can detect hydrogen peroxide out of a closed bottle with this thing!" The reason we could detect H_2O_2 in closed containers is that the compound decomposes into highly mobile water and oxygen, making it impossible to hermetically seal the stuff in a container, even one made of glass. The seals always develop microfractures allowing tiny amounts—parts per billion—of the chemical to escape into the surrounding air.

To make this new technology practical for the checkpoint, the national lab evaluated the Fido PaxPoint, a gunlike handheld device manufactured by ICx Technologies that pulled air across a sensor. The Fido was so sensitive it could detect hydrogen peroxide vapors from a closed container sealed in the middle of a plastic bag packed in a carry-on. (One of the advantages of the required baggie was that it concentrated the hydrogen peroxide vapors.)

Additionally, the Fido had a very low false alarm rate, meaning that it would incorrectly flag a substance as hydrogen peroxide very rarely, or in only a few instances out of thousands. After our engineering groups at the TSA reviewed it, the Fido made it out to airports for a field test later that year. We were pleased to finally have a device that directly engaged al-Qaeda's explosive of choice. And we sent what we hoped was a clear message to al-Qaeda planners in a May 2007 news release announcing its deployment to US airports.

THE NEXT TEST CAME ON SEPTEMBER 2, 2007, WHEN DANISH POLICE raided the apartment of a man named Hammad Khurshid, arresting him and prompting the TSA to develop another original, subtle, and flexible response. Khurshid, another Waziristan-trained al-Qaeda operative, had been under close surveillance during the summer since he had returned from Pakistan. In the man's tidy, Spartan apartment, police found one unusual item: a flashy toy remote-control car. With wiring and batteries already built in, the car could be a very effective Trojan horse to get explosives on board a plane.

But the icing on the cake was that Khurshid was also in touch with a seventeen-year-old in Denmark who planned to travel with his family to the United States. Khurshid had asked him to scope out airport security in the United States. Normally we would have put FAMs on the teen's flight without even thinking about it, but Danish authorities have strong gun restrictions that didn't at that time allow our armed FAMs to travel to the country.

Naturally, I was confounded by the FAM restriction, but the whole point of overlapping layers of security is to provide a plan B. We made sure all of our American partners—the FBI; US Customs and Border Protection; and Bill Hall, the FSD at New York's John F. Kennedy, the destination airport—were aware of our concerns. We assumed this was a dry run, so we wanted to be ready, but not too obvious. I also hoped to see what the next-generation explosive device might look like.

The night of the family's departure through JFK, Bill Gaches, Tom Hoopes, and I sat in Bill's sixth-floor office, staring intently at his speaker-phone. The boy's luggage had been pulled for extra screening and now we were getting a readout of their contents: "Looks pretty normal; there's definitely nothing in the way of a live device. In the suitcase there was nothing unusual, just clothes, toiletries, and a remote-control toy car."

Bill, Tom, and I looked up at each other wordlessly.

Good intel sharing with our international partners and the work of our local airports had helped us make a very useful connection. But now we had to figure out how to translate it into action without tipping off the boy—or his handlers—that he was being watched.

Bill turned to Tom. "Why don't you put together a whole bunch of common objects that could hold an explosive charge—and include a picture of a remote-control toy car." We decided to place the list in the intelligence bulletin that went out to our frontline officers to give them a better idea of what we thought might be new threats.

Soon thereafter, Bill and I wanted to take it a step beyond a vague hint in the bulletin. With the holidays approaching, I had no interest in an outright ban of remote-control cars. Instead, knowing that al-Qaeda watched everything the TSA did, we decided to send them a message with a simple press release. Without divulging any sensitive material, we issued a public statement saying that we may be taking an extra look at remote-control vehicles. This was different from our normal approach of announcing new technology deployments as proactive deterrents; this was using sensitive intelligence about what al-Qaeda was planning inside their secret labs and splashing it on the front page. This was a more aggressive approach to using intelligence information and is an example of how far the intelligence community has come in terms of teamwork.

ON SEPTEMBER 4, 2007, TWO DAYS AFTER THE DANISH RAID ON KHUR-shid's apartment, an elite German antiterrorist force raided a rented cottage across the street from a kindergarten in the Black Forest town of Freudenstadt where Fritz Gelowicz and his team had holed up before setting their attack in motion. Gelowicz and his gang turned out to be as inept as they were dangerous. The group made far too many careless mistakes while plotting their bloodbath. They had taken too long to buy the hydrogen peroxide and drawn unnecessary attention to themselves by vandalizing the cars of American soldiers. But the arrest of the "Sauerland Crew," the terror cell led by the "boy next door," was a heart-stopping event for the German public. Worse, the cell's al-Qaeda facilitator, Ozdemir, had slipped away just as the noose was tightening.

Losing track of Omer Ozdemir drove Bill Gaches crazy. Ozdemir was a key connection between Western European operatives like Gelowicz and al-Qaeda's senior plotters who reported to Abu Ubaydah, their number-three man. We had gained some more insight into these connections in August after a traveling gem salesman named Aleem Nassir was captured and delivered by Pakistan to Germany in August. Nassir, in a misguided effort to proclaim his innocence, gave interviews with German media that offered incredible detail of al-Qaeda operations. Other reports placed Nassir in the elite operative camps in Western Pakistan, which suggested a Zubair connection, as well as one with Ubaydah.

As Nassir spilled the beans, Tom Hoopes fed the info into a sprawling network chart. Nassir appeared to be directly associated with Omer Ozdemir and the other German al-Qaeda operatives, Harrach and Breininger, known also to be at the camps. Following the Gelowicz and Khurshid plots, we thought we had exhausted all the social-networking possibilities, but here was another dense node of al-Qaeda operatives and connections. Omer Ozdemir represented an ominous overlap portending network charts to come.

BY THE END OF 2007, I WAS CONVINCED THAT ZUBAIR OR WAQAS WAS related to the Gelowicz plot through Ozdemir. Then Austrian intelligence clued us into evidence that Zubair was also connected to the August 2006 liquids plot. The DHS had tended to downplay Hoopes's claims about Zubair's importance, but he had my full attention. Waqas was a smart, motivated guy who could easily blend into a crowd in Europe. He spoke colloquial German and English (and could imitate both American and British writing styles) and was well-networked throughout Germany and Austria. Waqas hung out in the Pakistani training camps with Abu Ubaydah and other high rollers and had been repeatedly linked to major plots against transportation, including Operation Glidepath, the liquids plot, and Gelowicz's less-threatening plans to blow up Frankfurt airport. By the time we'd plugged all that into his profile, I was flat-out obsessed. In fact, Hoopes started referring to Zubair by yet another nickname, Newman, after the *Seinfeld* character who was Jerry's nemesis.

Then, on December 14, 2007, Rashid Rauf, the young, well-connected, and prolific facilitator of UK-based plots, was transported from the prison in Pakistan where he'd been held since August 9, 2006, to a pro-forma tribunal hearing. Because he was a UK citizen, the British had been furiously working their political channels to push for extradition. During the trip, Rauf asked to stop at McDonald's and then pray at a mosque. The guards agreed, took off his handcuffs, and escorted him into the fast-food restaurant. Once at the mosque, however, Rauf managed to escape, melting back into his terror network without a trace.

This was a devastating blow. Rashid Rauf was the ultimate high-value prisoner. He was hell-bent on taking down planes between Europe and the United States and had proved that he had the methods to do so. Now I had a new worst nightmare: Zubair and Rashid Rauf working together.

FIFTEEN

SHOE SCANNERS, STOLEN BABIES, AND THE END OF THE BAGGIE

BY LATE 2006, JANET HAD LEFT CALIFORNIA TO JOIN ME AND our older son Nick, who had moved up from North Carolina after school, in Washington. With a reassembled family, I moved down the road into something more suitable than the mostly uninhabited man-cave I had been calling home for more than a year. Janet imagined that we might take advantage of Washington's rich cultural life: museums, concerts, maybe shows at the Kennedy Center. But my job pressure was nonstop, and eventually she took her evening clothes back to California and settled into a volunteer job at Doorways, a program for at-risk women.

Nick had a day job, but his real work was to push the latest in technoculture from *Wired*, Ars Technica, and Boing Boing to me. He showed me something called the IdeaStorm from Dell Computer's website that they used to get user feedback and suggested that we use the model for unfiltered employee cross-communication. It had a voting mechanism so that workable suggestions with widespread TSO support floated to the front page. Mo McGowan and I were frequent visitors to what we called the IdeaFactory and it continues today. Nick also brought me bad news. When a passenger wrote, "Kip Hawley is an idiot" on a baggie in Milwaukee and a TSO gave him grief, it got in the news. I called Nick from the road and he said, "I have some bad news. I went online and tried to reserve the URL www.kiphawleyisanidiot .com and it is already registered to somebody. But it's OK, maybe I'll write 'Kip Hawley is my Daddy' on mine." On how we handled criticism, Nick said, "Dad, it's about transparency, not defending yourself," he'd tell me over a late-night dinner. "Nobody believes what you say anyway, so your only chance to get credibility is by being upfront with the bad, the ugly, and the indefensible. People get that. What they don't get is spin."

By the time my son was pushing me to start a blog, we had actually introduced a number of "smarter" security programs at the TSA: the Behavior Detection Officers who provide an additional layer of security independent of the screening inside the checkpoint, professional checking of IDs done by trained personnel with ultraviolet lights and magnifying loupes to prevent someone trying to evade the watch list from getting through with a fake name, better intelligence integration from the SCIF to the frontlines with TSOs and FAMs, better training and employee development, privacy-friendly watch-list matching through TSA's Secure Flight program which eliminated the so-called "Ted Kennedy problem" where people with names similar to watch-listed individuals got inappropriately flagged by airlines who used outdated matching technology, VIPRs which teamed FAMs, Behavior Detection Officers, K-9 teams, and local authorities to pop up patrols any time anywhere in the transportation system (now operating at the rate of 8,000 a year), new technology like advanced imaging at checkpoint screening such as mass deployment of the ATX bag scanner which was faster and more accurate than anything previously deployed. And even if large segments of the American public did not believe in our checkpoints, they at least seemed to recognize that out-of-control wait times were generally a thing of the past. But the TSA had never really gotten the kind of traction we needed with our customers. So much of what I had been focused on over the past few years was building overlapping networks—strategy, intelligence, technology, operational options—that created a more robust security overall. Gaining the willful participation and support of the public would give us access to the largest and most dynamic network out there. But Nick was right, merely defending the TSA was a fruitless task.

Lynn Dean, a member of our media team with dark hair streaked with silver and an ironic sense of humor, was on vacation in Florida visiting her husband's family when the inevitable happened. During her introduction to his aunt and uncle, her husband mentioned, "Lynn works with the TSA."

The aunt frowned. "I have a hip replacement," she declared, "and every time I go to the airport they treat me like a terrorist. I even have a laminated card from my doctor and they won't accept it!"

All of a sudden Lynn was on call, back in media-relations mode in the middle of a family barbeque. "Well," she replied, "if we started accepting laminated cards for anything, we'd see millions of them." Warming up, she continued, "I have stationery from when I was an intern at the White House. I could go print a letter on it and copy the president's signature, saying that I can ride on Air Force One, but they aren't going to let me near the plane. We even have people faking boarding passes, so we can't accept the card."

"But why are they picking on me?" asked the aunt.

"Well, you're going through a metal detector and there's metal on your body. So it sets off alarms. Here's the other problem. We had a man come through and say to the officer, 'I have a pin in my hip. I know the drill. I'm going to set off the metal detector; just wanted to let you know.' He's as friendly as can be. Sure enough, the alarm goes off, and when the officer does the pat down, right where the man said the pin was where the officer found a gun. And he just hoped that by being friendly they wouldn't be that thorough."

"Why would he do that?" asked the aunt, incredulous.

"They do it every day. It might not even be that; it might be someone hiding something in a wheelchair—that's our problem. The officer doesn't know who you are, and he sees people lie all the time."

By the end of conversation Lynn had a convert. "All right," said the aunt. "I'm on board. Thank you." Unfortunately, we can't send Lynn to every family gathering, so with my son Nick whispering in my ear, I began insisting that we start a blog.

When I first raised the idea of a blog during a National Advisory Council meeting with our frontline staff, Bob Burns, the solidly built garage rocker turned TSO, winced in his chair. *Really?* he thought. *I'm not exactly sure how this is going to turn out. But if he can get past everybody who says he's tying himself to a whipping post, I'm kind of excited.* Most everyone else had a different reaction.

Whenever I mentioned the idea to anyone outside of media relations, they would look at me as if I was drunk or had finally cracked. The lawyers, although tech savvy and supportive personally, were skeptical of the idea's impact because it would create an official communications channel that was not reviewed even as it allowed TSA-haters to publish every bad anecdote and conspiracy theory about our operations. It might result in some legitimate criticism as well. But what I saw was a unique opportunity to engage our customer base, the traveling public. In fact, it was the very things lawyers hated about the idea that made it valuable. You can't control a real blog—and that's the beauty of it. It creates an avenue for interaction, and because it differs in style and tone from a press release, its transparency might give us a chance of building credibility among our more fair-minded critics.

But both our legal department and DHS had objections to my suggestion, so I began hopping onto other security-related blogs, some of them with only twenty followers, and posting comments under my own name. I told the lawyers and the DHS that I was going to keep posting, arguing that it would be far better to have a blog process than me going rogue whenever I had free time. Michael Jackson swooped in and anointed the idea from his vantage as deputy secretary, and the TSA Blog was born.

First, I knew I could not be the blog's voice. We didn't want someone from the hierarchy running the show; we didn't want a huge TSA seal over the comment stream; and the writing wasn't going to follow the Associated Press Stylebook. We needed something authentic. So Lynn Dean did a search to find out which current employees already had blogs.

Among them was Bob Burns, who wasn't convinced the blog was a terrible idea for the TSA, and had been posting a collection of his own musings—a record he'd just bought, thoughts on a current event—online for a few years. As a kind of screen test, we invited Bob to respond to public reaction on the liquids ban in his own voice. The jokey but helpful tone of his writing was more like that of a Southwest flight attendant than an official government blog. At one point he mentioned that "contrary to popular belief, Kip doesn't own stock in the manufacturer of Ziploc bags." And he had the job—although it was a volunteer gig at first.

Once Bob and four other employees with field experience were in, we used the free application Blogger to construct our platform. Among other considerations, we made sure that readers could post anonymously, without fear of being placed on the no-fly list. Two days later, the blog launched. We had 2,000 comments on our first post. Suddenly the TSA had a presence in the limitless dimensions of cyberspace, attracting a multitude of different people with different motivations. Some had simple travel questions, others were legitimate security critics, and plenty brought their axes to grind. My son Nick also made sure we posted a "Delete-O-Meter" to be transparent about how many submissions we tossed, usually for profanity or threats of some sort.

In addition to simply interacting with all these new social matrices, we embedded our blog with some unique abilities for handling criticism. A couple years after it was launched, a female blogger claimed on her blog site that TSA officers had taken her baby away during a checkpoint search at Atlanta's Hartsfield-Jackson airport. The posting, which narrated every parent's nightmare, went viral, inflaming innumerable websites. After taking a bit of a beating—plenty of people at the TSA itself were also shaken by the report—we were able to determine the woman's flight number and pull the closed-circuit TV footage at about the time when she would have been passing through the checkpoint. We soon found a woman holding a baby who resembled the person in a picture posted on the blogger's website. With the video rolling, we saw the woman get pulled aside for secondary screening and then wait a while for a female officer to do the search. She becomes agitated, and for many travelers, it's easy to see why. But her most serious allegation, that her baby was physically removed from her, was completely false. She held her baby the whole time—and made her flight. Once we had the footage we tried to contact the woman, but she didn't respond, and since she was being so aggressive with her allegations, we posted the footage on our blog.

Dealing with that damaging situation through the traditional media channels would likely have been not only awkward but also somewhat ridiculous. We could have released the video to television—if we could find a channel willing to play more than ten minutes of raw checkpoint footage. Going to the *New York Times* with the evidence wasn't a much better option. The woman's claims were certainly damaging our credibility, but she was a mom with a laptop, not someone actively interfering with our checkpoint operations. What she did have was access to an endless network of bloggers and texters and tweeters who could link and repost her story ad infinitum. So, instead of trying to bludgeon a single woman with national newspapers or network news, we simply released the footage into the blogosphere.

The Mommy Blogger was not an isolated incident. Very few people *enjoy* going through security, and a decent number are always ready to believe the worst about the TSA. Slamming the agency was an easy way to get huge public exposure, or an easy excuse for missing a flight. A passenger flying out of a Southern California airport claimed a TSO had made him remove his glass eye during screening, causing it to get infected and him to miss his flight back to work. It was an outlandish excuse, but his boss had no trouble believing it until, once again, we pulled the tape that showed he was simply late arriving to the airport.

Once he began blogging full time, Bob also handled an incident in which a passenger with a new Apple MacBook Air laptop got caught up at the checkpoint and missed his flight while screeners examined his newfangled computer. The critics soon came out, mocking the TSA for not knowing what a laptop is. From Bob's experience operating screening equipment, he knew that the ultraslim Air probably did look unusual. He went out to a warehouse near Reagan National where the TSA had set up a mock checkpoint and filmed a video explaining how the laptop looked different from others in the scanner. The post was titled "Blogger Bob Explains the MacBook Air"—the name stuck.

In addition to launching information into the ether, Blogger Bob, Lynn and the blog team also made light of the often-bizarre world of checkpoint security. One morning, I sent Bob a story about an officer at Reagan who spotted what appeared to be a razor blade sitting inside a book. After requesting a bag check, he realized that the passenger was a priest and the razor was in his Bible. Lynn noted the incident in a post called "You Can't Make This Stuff Up," suggesting that if someone really did want to smuggle a razor on board a plane, dressing up as a priest and hiding the blade in a Bible was a pretty good idea. Another day, the TSA found five guns in bags, leading to a post that began, "You haven't even had your morning coffee yet and officers have found . . . ?

In yet another incident, police in Connecticut discovered a chicken stuffed with dynamite near a railroad track, a different TSA asset, and Bob decided to write an entire post of corny poultry puns entitled, "Why Did the Chicken Cross the Road?":

> While this story is not directly related to the TSA, it shows that a bomb can be hidden anywhere by those with *fowl* intent (pun intended). We thought we'd have a little fun, we hope you enjoy it:
>
> We're not sure why the chicken crossed the road, but we do know what happened after it did.
>
> On June 10th in Simsbury, Connecticut, police found a pipe bomb stuffed inside of a raw roasting chicken. The chicken was noticed on the side of the road by a passing motorist with a *bird's eye view* . . .

The Police Chief declined to comment due to the pending investigation, so at this point, we're not sure who *hatched* this *bird-brained* plot or why.

It is possible that some misguided youth were *egged* on to make the poultry projectile. But the real intent is unknown.

The Hartford Police Department's bomb squad took *stock* in the incident and arrived on scene to detonate the chicken. The road was closed during the detonation, preventing anybody from crossing. (Including Chickens) One member of the squad stated it was *poultry* in motion (yes we're kidding).

We hope that nobody takes advantage of this incident by using tired old chicken puns (how lame would that be). Remember to report all suspicious activity.

Bob
EoS Blog Team[1]

Bob got a few chuckles, but one of the innumerable critics, Anonymous Marshall, was first to the comment board: "Well, at least the TSA is good at something: diversionary tactics, i.e., when you're getting blasted in one thread you quickly put up another." But such is the nature of the beast. You can't have a credible blog without criticism and from the beginning, we've only edited for foul language, threats, hate speech, and other fairly fundamental criteria.

The TSA Blog, along with other Web 2.0 innovations like the Idea Factory, an internal website for employee feedback within the organization, have gone on to win awards. Blogger Bob was also recently named one of the DC area's Tech Titans by *Washingtonian* magazine. But the blog was certainly not the only device we relied on to try and gain some foothold of support with the American public.

IN SPRING OF 2006, A WOMAN WITH AUBURN HAIR AND SHARP BLUE eyes began appearing at our eight-thirty staff intel briefings. I had asked Ellen Howe to fly in from Washington state on her own dime to interview for our top PR position. Once she got there, I upped the ante and convinced her to sell her seventeen acres nestled in the Cascades, her horses, and her husband's business to move her family to DC. When she arrived on the eleventh floor of the TSA's east tower, a mess awaited her.

The TSA's public standing was so low it reminded Ellen of her stint in the early 1990s doing media relations for a nuclear weapons site. She was greeted by countless print, TV, and web sources screaming about the TSA's lack of professionalism. Reporters' calls were regularly misrouted or lost, and the organization's process was so young and incomplete, she observed that "If all of the top people in this office got hit by a Mack truck, no one could come in the next day and issue a press release." There were forty-five people working in the office, but no real system in place.

Beyond the lack of structure, the agency was also operating under the same flawed strategy I saw elsewhere in the TSA. When I read through our old press releases, I was struck by the similarity among every one of them. No matter what the question, our official statement was always in 3-D: deflect, defer, defend. In other words, they said nothing aside from bland statements like, "The TSA has a variety of security measures and we believe that the public is well served by our process." When an incident flared at a checkpoint, the usual response was not to explain what had happened but say something along the lines of "proper procedure was followed." The PR people weren't incompetent, but they were defensively following the same top-down control strategy that had hobbled our screeners and intelligence gathering. To have any chance of making headway with the media, you had to be willing to stick your neck out a bit.

Ellen's first moves were basic. On any given day, her office would be dealing with the Big Five networks—CNN, ABC, NBC, CBS, and FOX—as well as the *Wall Street Journal,* the *New York Times,* the *Washington Post,* the Associated Press, and scores of other requests from regional media outlets. She attempted to engage reporters beyond issuing press releases. Her staff spent time with them, fostering personal relationships. The media would always love screw-ups—and in addition to whatever complaints were reported from checkpoint operations there was a virtual industry in generating headlines made up of regularly released reports from the DHS Inspector General and Government Accountability Office. They were legitimate stories, and Ellen couldn't quash them anyway. But if she loosened her grip and offered more access, she might get some good stories thrown into the mix as well.

In an attempt to humanize the 50,000 people working at the airport, Ellen arranged for NBC to follow a Behavior Detection Officer around for a day. Ellen got a mock checkpoint set up to teach *Today* show host Meredith Vieira how to divest properly and move through the line more easily. And she led CNN on a covert test to attempt to get banned items through a checkpoint. The TSO failed and cried when he realized what had happened, but the next step was for our testers to explain what he did wrong. It wasn't the result we wanted, but it was a risk we were willing to take in the name of transparency.

The TSA needed the public's support more than most agencies. But our open approach sometimes put us at loggerheads with the Department of Homeland Security. One of the best ways to lose your job in DC is to go to the media before your boss, in my case Secretary Chertoff. So we ran everything by the DHS first. Later on, as our PR team was building up credibility, we asked to go on *Oprah*. DHS's response was blunt: "Why? There's really no value in that. And you'll probably get a black eye on that one." But we eventually managed to get a wonderful officer on the show to share some stories on the topic of civility based on her varied experiences at the TSA. This sort of message could come across as manipulative if delivered by a PR rep, but hearing directly from a frontline officer helped people to see our workforce from the other side.

Toward the end of Ellen's and my tenure, we were approached by *60 Minutes* for a story about checkpoints, but the DHS nixed that idea as certain to contain only bad news and criticism—until *60 Minutes* called back and said, "We're going to do this story with or without you." We agreed to cooperate.

For the filming, the show's reporter Lesley Stahl showed up at the TSA's Freedom Center with what I thought was an "I'm going to kick your ass" attitude. It seemed like a very bad situation, but to my surprise, she delved into the details and talked to officers directly. She even spent a day at our "Engage!" training out in Reston, Virginia, the cutting edge two-day fully interactive experience that Stephanie Rowe and her team had put together to give TSOs the tools and confidence to use their experience in making better security decisions. Two officers who conducted Engage! sessions, LaDonta Edwards from BWI Airport in Baltimore and Gary Wilkes from Reagan National in Washington, ended up in a sit-down on-camera interview.

During Stahl's visit to Baltimore/Washington International Airport, we showed her an ATX machine, the new, smarter and much more powerful devices at the checkpoint that scan carry-ons. We had placed an order for nine hundred of them across the country because we believed they had the capability to keep ahead of Zubair's bomb innovations. An officer and I showed Lesley how the machine worked. When we finished with our demonstration, she said, "I want to put my purse through."

Uh oh, I thought. *This is the "gotcha" moment. She's got something sewed inside.* After scanning it in several passes through the conveyor and failing to find whatever it was hidden in her purse, I took apart her mascara, completely disassembled a very nicely engineered glasses case, and with the screening officer, examined the interior stitching on her purse, but found no threats. "Honestly," she said after a while. "I'm not trying to trick you." She almost seemed a little hurt that we didn't trust her. But it came out as a very fair piece when it aired on Sunday December 21, 2008.

Finally, to ensure that Ellen wouldn't be just another uninformed automaton at the podium, she was given a security clearance and access to intel about ongoing plots. This was unusual, even for the head of media relations. When the DHS spokesperson issues a statement that "there is no credible, specific, or imminent threat at this time," he or she normally has no idea whether or not it's true. Ellen would be more authentic if she were fully integrated into the TSA rather than a drone we dispatched to shield us from the outside world. And the media was our most important asset in engaging the most valuable network out there: the American people.

Yet there is a conflict at the heart of the TSA's efforts to reach those people that didn't make Ellen's, Blogger Bob's, or Lynn Dean's job any easier. To keep the public safe, we rely on classified intelligence reporting and sometimes unpredictable security techniques that to the average American traveler may appear simply unfounded and capricious. Many people expect their security to be something firm, definable, and straightforward. But the nature of the threat we all face makes such an approach foolish and myopic. Of course, the TSA has made plenty of mistakes—some bigger than others, and many sensationally reported—which didn't help our standing with the passengers who pass through our checkpoints. But while we can certainly do a better job of communicating, we cannot always release the classified intelligence that supports our annoying policies. The most frustrating example is that most people assume that Richard Reid's failed shoe bomb attempt in 2001 is the reason that shoes are still removed, yet there was current intelligence while I was at TSA that made it a no-brainer to continue the policy. When the courier in Fritz Gelowicz's 2007 hydrogen peroxide bomb plot brought Gelowicz the detonators for his bombs inside a shoe, we worked with the NCTC to release photos of the shoes, but that got no traction, so to speak. And even if our operations were perfect, they would still involve seeming inconsistencies—a tough hurdle to building any relationship.

ONE DAY IN 2007 STEPHANIE ROWE, WHO WAS IN CHARGE OF THE IDEN-tity-based programs at TSA, including Registered Traveler, accompanied me to a meeting with Ted Olson, one of the most respected and powerful lawyers in the country. Stephanie, who normally poured her considerable energies into solving TSA's mission challenges rather than political issues, had no idea who he was at the time, but one glance at the marble and dark wood accents in Olson's downtown Washington office told her that she was definitely in one of the preeminent halls of DC power.

We sat down opposite Olson and his client, Steve Brill, the founder of the CourtTV cable channel and *American Lawyer* magazine. The subject of our meeting was Registered Traveler, a proposed public-private partnership that would allow frequent flyers to submit a background check and pay $100 to move more quickly through airport checkpoints. Brill was a major investor in the program, and while I had green-lighted the program in 2005, it had floundered as companies offering the service had done little other than take the money and let "members" cut to the front of security lines.

Before long, Olson became angry with me, believing I was stonewalling innovation and hiding behind the mantle of "security." I'm used to taking some heat, and I knew that Steve had him torqued up in anticipation of what I would say, so out of respect for Olson, I took one for the team and listened unperturbed to Ted's impassioned lambasting.

Stephanie, on the other hand, was outraged. I could feel the steam coming out of her ears as she fidgeted and rattled in the chair next to me. When she got home that night she went on a tirade to her husband, David, about the conversation. After she was done, David said, "You really don't know who he is, do you?" He gently explained that she had just been in a meeting with the former US Solicitor General, the legal counsel to President Bush's 2000 campaign, and, on a personal level, a man who had tragically lost his own wife on the American Airlines flight flown into the Pentagon on 9/11. Olson was also a close friend of Secretary Chertoff though he never used that relationship to put further pressure on us.

The idea that the TSA should segment passengers into higher- and lower-risk populations was not a bad concept—indeed, it was part of our original mandate. With 2 million people a day, the TSA could provide better security and quicker lines for everyone if a number of preapproved people went through an expedited security screening.

But it wasn't until 2003, at the urging of then–secretary of Homeland Security Tom Ridge, that the TSA opened a Registered Traveler program office. Because the TSA leadership was too busy fighting fires, the agency decided to let the private sector figure out the details of Registered Traveler before coming back for approval. By the time I arrived in 2005, RT, as it was known, was concluding a successful technology pilot in DC, Minneapolis, and Orlando. A small population of frequent flyers had been issued biometric RT cards and, after verifying their identity at special card readers, were able to proceed to the front of the security line. Expectations were high. The promise of bypassing long queues and demeaning security treatment fired the imagination of the American frequent flyer.

In October 2005, after a few months on the job, I was invited to a congressional hearing on RT that offered a rare chance for the TSA to score a clear public-relations win and maybe gain a few fans, at least among frequent flyers. Unfortunately, there was a security issue. The so-called vetting for RT members was only an immigration status and terrorist screening database check. Meaning that if you weren't an illegal alien or already on the FBI's radar as a terror suspect, you were good to go. Under these criteria, the July 2005 London Underground bombers would all have been eligible for RT cards. So at the hearing I announced that the private sector had to work out a business model to both fund RT and add security value while not inconveniencing the general public and then come back to us for a security evaluation. Then I went back to work on other, more pressing issues.

By 2007, when Stephanie and I met with Brill and Olson, RT was still moving along, but remained essentially a "cut to the front of the line" benefit without any value added in the background check or changes to the security process at the gate. I had given Stephanie responsibility for RT, but her main priority was fixing issues related Secure Flight, the TSA's own program, which required passengers to register basic personal information before flying. The info was then matched against the no-fly list, a task previously handled by the airlines.

Even after the meeting at Ted Olson's office, RT remained on Stephanie's back burner until she found herself spending more and more time dealing with Steve Brill, who was spending a ton of money to promote Registered

Traveler. Brill, Stephanie soon learned, had reached people higher up the food chain throughout the federal government. His connections sometimes made her work difficult, and the constant pressure from senior staff at the DHS, Capitol Hill, and elsewhere made her life miserable. She took comfort in the fact that if the political heat forced her to leave TSA, she could always go back to the private sector and draw a much larger paycheck.

The program's goal was to get RTs through the checkpoint as easily as possible. The proposal even included a propietary product, called a ClearCard, that would replace a government-issued ID. But RT ultimately offered zero additional security value. The "background checks" were little more than a marketing point. Though Brill and the program's other sponsors wouldn't have known it, virtually all of the serious al-Qaeda operatives involved in major aviation plots would have easily cleared RT-type screening. I wanted the checkpoints to be easier and faster too, but I couldn't possibly allow RT cardholders to keep their shoes on when I knew that al-Qaeda was training operatives with clean backgrounds and shoe bombs. I also wasn't crazy about the idea of giving our imprimatur—and therefore, the government's stamp of approval and public money—for a private-industry "security" venture.

Because Brill was tireless in his lobbying, PR, and media efforts, I suggested ideas to develop the product, like training behavior-detection officers or doing off-airport security screening in midtown Manhattan. He was earnest but uninterested in getting involved in the security process—he saw that as our job. Brill just wanted to get RTs through checkpoints quickly, and preferably wearing their shoes and jackets, with their laptops in their cases. After an excruciating and lengthy process, and tantalizingly close to the holy grail for frequent fliers, Brill finally uncovered a new technology that could have changed the whole picture: a combined biometric card reader and ShoeScanner.

The ShoeScanner was a technology pioneered by GE that would, in theory, allow travelers to walk through a small, floor-based, explosives detection system with their shoes on. It was a great idea. Everybody hated taking their shoes off, and offering this service to travelers would be a huge boon to the ClearCard program. It also encouraged me to get behind RT. But after we had publicly heralded a trial of the device at Orlando International, George Zarur found something in the technology that, in an ironic twist, our much-maligned overly bureaucratic process had missed during the ShoeScanner's expedited review. For the next month, George tested what the device did, and it was not enough to stay in airports. Instead of partnering with private industry to improve and speed up security, we ended up with egg on our face. But pulling the units was our only choice.

The battle finally culminated in Congress, a body that had long been a booster of the RT program. Secretary Chertoff was good enough to accompany me to the closed-door congressional hearing. "Explain to me," Chertoff said, "why a member of the American public should send his information to the government, ask us to issue an ID, and then turn around and pay $100 to an outside businessman to go to the head of our line?" Chertoff hammered home the security points with his relentless logic. We never got the improved, expedited security that could have improved our credibility and in the end, the whole saga was just a distraction from what we knew to be active plotting against aviation. But at least the full-court press on Registered Traveler was over.

THE SHOESCANNER WAS NOT THE ONLY IMPERFECT TECHNOLOGY George sniffed out. Back in 2002, he had been instrumental in helping the TSA meet its mandate to purchase and install those massive CT-based EDS machines that scan checked baggage. Having had a front-row seat to the process, George knew it hadn't been the cleanest operation, but in the years since, he had realized that another device based on older AT technology, widely used standard x-ray machines with more than one pulse generator, provided almost exactly the same security value at less than half the cost of the CT machines.

The main difference between different x-ray scanners is the number of angles they provide. "Regular" checkpoint x-rays, the kind that had been in use since the 1960s, cost about $40,000 and only provide a top-down view of luggage, which can present a serious security limitation. AT scanners run around $150,000 and see three or more angles, providing a good, sharp image of what is inside most suitcases. CT scanners are at the far end of the spectrum in terms of cost—close to $1 million—and imaging, providing a 360-degree view of a bag. But while CTs provided the most complete picture, ATs were not only considerably cheaper, they were faster and much easier to maintain. In 2001, when the decision on which EDS machines to deploy was made, AT technology was known in the United States and used extensively in Europe. But despite all their benefits, the AT devices were a non-starter.

The Federal Aviation Administration's Research Development and Human Factors Laboratory in Atlantic City, staffed by a rock-star group of scientists, had given CTs their sole nod of approval—a decision that meant spending $1 billion on those machines versus $150 million for the ATs. And there was not much debate. The lab's seal of approval decided which vendor would win million-dollar contracts, and the lab had determined that the ATs were unable to detect one particular threat (among hundreds) that could take down a plane. Nobody was going to sign off on an order for a device that the lab claimed left an open door in the nation's security. That is why, for so many years, the enormous EDS checked-bag scanners have sat in the lobbies of airports from Washington Dulles to Portland, Oregon. An unanticipated consequence was that AT manufacturers, seeing the writing on the wall that TSA would only sign off on the MRI-type machines, abandoned efforts to improve AT scanners. This left a virtual monopoly on billions of dollars or orders for two companies, Invision and L3, until TSA, largely through George Zarur, gave the signal in the 2006 timeframe that TSA would consider AT as a viable competitor. More than ten years later, cheaper, more reliable, faster alternatives to MRI-based scanners might finally be a TSA-approved alternative in 2012.

On my first visit to the FAA lab in July 2005, I got a full tour complete with an explosives demonstration. Because the standards used to test equipment could provide terrorists the key to defeat security technology, the lab operated under a James Bond–like aura of secrecy. The engineers spent their days brainstorming about how to make cleverly disguised bombs and then try their hands at executing them. My walk through one of the Lab workshops was like being backstage at a theatrical prop shop. Luscious chocolate cakes, sports equipment, cool gadgets, and designer clothes were on display, each one a deadly bomb. On a later trip I reviewed results from different body scanners and noticed that the test subjects didn't look like everyday passengers. I inquired about where the test subjects had come from and heard, "Ah. Well. Ah, we contracted with an Atlantic City modeling agency."

But once I was sworn in as administrator, I got an earful from airport and airline operations people about the cost and disruption of the CT-only decision. I convened a meeting with a previously-established blue-ribbon panel consisting of airport, airline and TSA executives to revisit the question. But after I left the room, the TSA technology staff dismissed my concerns, saying that I didn't understand the science. Since they viewed any consideration of AT technology as a security sell-out, change was coming over their dead bodies.

In 2006, when I discovered that my request to review the CT/AT issue had been killed as soon as I turned my back, I asked George to reexamine the issue independently. It was simple request, but it chafed some of the people who had done the original testing at the then-FAA labs. They may have seen it as a political infringement on pure science, but to me, it looked like the lab's insulated existence had an unintended dark side. The scientists were judge and jury for all TSA security technology. There was no external peer review; infallibility was assumed. And not only was their network a closed circuit, they didn't incorporate the agency's intelligence resources into their work to understand the true nature of the threat. So, when a decision had to be made about how to replace the machines that screened carry-on baggage at checkpoints, I was a bit wary of the lab's insistence that CT was the only way to go.

The checkpoint x-rays that the TSA inherited had first been deployed in the 1960s. Known as TRXs, they relied on a single x-ray source on the top of the box and produced grainy images. We desperately needed to upgrade them, and a kind of AT technology, based on multiple-view x-rays and known as ATXs, was available. Aside from their complete imaging of bag contents, I liked the flexibility of the ATXs because they were capable of accepting new search algorithms. Any time the terrorists tweaked explosives formulas, we could just swap out the scanning software instead of buying a whole new machine. The FAA lab, however, was pushing for the more sophisticated CT-based solution at our already overcrowded checkpoints. These machines had many of the same problems associated with their larger cousins that scanned checked baggage. They cost much more and could process only about half the 400 bags an hour necessary at our checkpoints. Moreover, their bulk completely blocked the TSOs' view of the passengers they were screening. And they were not ready to be installed.

Seeing a steady stream of aviation plotting, I didn't want to wait for the CTs to be perfected. By this point, I also wanted a second opinion, so I asked George to go back to the larger scientific community and his impressive range of contacts. George called up a guy he knew at the Department of Defense, who suggested doing our testing at an old hangar at Tyndal Air Force Base, just east of Panama City, Florida. Three weeks later, George and some scientists from the Lawrence Livermore national lab and DHS Science & Technology office were set up at a site on the Panhandle, isolated enough that if something went wrong, it wouldn't draw attention. Besides, the Air Force tested bombs there.

A few days later, as they were running different hydrogen-peroxide concoctions through the AT machines, testing for possible differences in their electronic signatures, a researcher yelled out, "Wait! It looks different from water!" The hydrogen peroxide in that machine did look slightly different from water. Eventually the AT was calibrated to differentiate hydrogen peroxide from wine, water, shaving cream, and contact-lens solution—and, as margin for error or if terrorists tried using many small bottles, to detect it even in minuscule quantities. George paused in the muggy Florida air to consider the implications: a readily available and cheap technology that could recognize threat liquids.

We called in the AT vendors, gave them our data on hydrogen peroxide detection and told them to start working on an algorithm that would automatically set off an alarm when hydrogen peroxide was detected. George insisted that the companies share their system performance and image format data so that TSA could open up algorithm development to a much wider audience of image analysis experts. That was strongly resisted by the manufacturers who wanted to retain their software rights and argued that they could move faster on their own. But, by mid-2009, George no longer had the air cover that I had provided, and the decision to let TSA share test data was reversed and each vendor is now free to bundle their proprietary black box scanners on their own time and price schedule.

The rest of the world has not waited. Today, AT systems have been certified for liquid threat detection and are deployed at many European airports.

SIXTEEN

THE PREDATOR

"WHEN YOU GUYS CAME IN HERE LAST SUNDAY, DID YOU FEEL the energy in the room?" exhorted the lanky, African American man in a well-tailored dark suit.

"Yeah!" the crowd of about five hundred Transportation Security Officers responded, with scattered clapping around the Marriott Fair Oaks hotel ballroom in Fairfax, VA.

"Did you feel the energy in the room?" The speaker brought the polish of a news anchor and the panache of a matador. "That's the same energy we want you guys to bring back out there into the field. We are the TSA, right?" said Calvin. "Who are we?" he implored.

"T-S-A!" The rapt audience was casually dressed with nametags at the end of a weeklong training program.

"Who are we?" Calvin's voice rose in volume and intensity as he paced back and forth, holding a microphone in one hand and gesturing with the other.

"T-S-A!"

"Question: Who's better than us?" asked Calvin.

"Nobody!"

"Who's better than us?" yelled Calvin.

"Nobody!" responded the crowd, the officers coming to their feet.

"Hey!" said Calvin. "We've got a couple days left. Let's go out there with some energy and bring it to the field."

As Calvin turned to walk the microphone over to me, he spun around to face the room, asking one more time, "Who are we?"

Hundreds of officers began cheering, some of them climbing on their chairs:

"T-S-A! T-S-A! T-S-A! T-S-A! T-S-A!"

It was the autumn of 2008. Gale Rossides, the Deputy Administrator, and I were standing to the side of a low stage while Calvin Moore, a Transportation Security Manager in his thirties, was inspiring a large crowd of TSOs in a Marriott a half hour southwest of DC. Even to me, the scene was unbelievable—the successful culmination of a yearlong training exercise called Engage!, a program with antecedents in an almost four-year-old failure.

In November 2005, I had announced the creation of the TSA's National Advisory Council as a way to promote more integration and communication between the field officers and HQ. Since then, a select group of our frontline people had come to DC for a week every three months to tackle the toughest issues facing TSOs. In the spring of 2006, I excitedly introduced a proposal for pay raises and bonuses, the first time in the TSA's five years of existence that officers would be eligible for increased compensation based on their individual performance. I had expected a surge of enthusiasm, but after a handful of lukewarm comments, Wayne, a TSO from Alaska and the council's co-chair, broke it to me: "Kip, we all appreciate what you are trying to do. But if you are asking whether this is going to move the needle with our workforce, the answer is no. This proposal just isn't going to cut it." My stomach sank.

An hour later, in the seventh-floor Situation Room, normally used for managing critical incidents like Hurricane Katrina and potential terror incidents, I gathered Wayne and his co-chair, along with Gale, Mike Restovich, Mo McGowan, and our financial and human-capital folks. We laid out the numbers. Our congressionally-approved budget to pay TSOs was essentially flat, any opportunity for pay raises came out of the 2 percent adjustment for inflation—clearly not enough to drive system-wide behavior change.

But after further discussion, we managed to find some more cash by pegging payments to attendance. If a TSO doesn't show up for work, he or she gets paid even while a substitute has to be paid overtime to cover that shift. Spread out over a 45,000-person workforce during a year, that absenteeism adds up to a huge amount of money—and an equally big area to target savings. "How about," I asked Wayne, "if we put $50 million on the table?" My idea was simple: fund pay raises and performance bonuses entirely out of the savings garnered from the officers' improved efficiency.

A year later, in February 2007, the agency paid more than $60 million in increased compensation. The next year, the payout was more than $75 million, with the money awarded solely based on how well the officers handled their security duties, funded entirely by their improved performance. This higher attendance, lower attrition, and fewer injuries (actually cut in half) meant that our checkpoints were better staffed and, as a result, wait times for passengers decreased. By 2008 we'd also increased job mobility, and thousands of TSOs had been promoted into jobs like Behavior Detection Officers or Federal Air Marshals. But it wasn't enough.

Every morning at intel briefings we saw evidence of novel bombs and new operatives. The fact was that our technology still lagged behind the al-Qaeda innovation cycle. Operatives including Zubair and Rashid Rauf would surely be able to design attacks that would evade our checkpoint process unless we equipped and empowered the frontline TSOs to pick up on clues that were outside our Standard Operating Procedure. We needed to engage them on a whole new level.

By the spring of 2008, after months of the tireless dedication that were the norm when Stephanie Rowe was driving an operation, a Stephanie mantra was, "We specialize in being tired," the plan was presented to the NAC for approval. But as I sat in the back of a NAC session I had popped into, it was apparent that something was missing. In the midst of the TSOs' daily work, the immediacy of their mission had worn off. The principal purpose of the Engage! program was to stop near-term attacks aimed at exploiting holes in our security, but that driving narrative was stifled.

After a while, I got frustrated enough that I stood up and walked to the front of the room. "I want to tell you a story," I said, launching into an unclassified version of Zubair's real life story. Ten minutes into the tale I realized that nobody in the room was breathing; they were on the edge of their seats, not making a sound. I described how Zubair, whom I called "Fritz Gelowicz" for the story, looked like he could be my son and played soccer as a kid. He was funny, likeable, and would have been at home on any US college campus. "Fritz" knew our equipment, he understood our SOP, and he had been working on a bomb that we couldn't detect. We had just received intelligence that he and four others had left their training area and were headed our way. The room was rapt the whole time I was describing this threat. I knew I was onto something—my speeches never tested this well—so Stephanie approached our top two intel guys, Keith Kauffman and Tom Hoopes, to write up a screenplay for a realistic video that would explain to the officers in no uncertain terms how valuable their work was and that the threat was not only real but it was coming at *them,* the officers at TSA checkpoints.

Soon thereafter we began training a core group of eight people to be instructors when the Engage! program rolled out. All the instructors needed to be zealots like Calvin Moore and the irrepressible Memphis TSO Jameka Merriweather. They would have to spread a positive but urgent energy as we slowly expanded the class sizes. We needed 1,100 trainers like them to reach 56,000 officers, more than the capacity of sold-out Yankee Stadium. And, starting from scratch, this force had to be ready in less than six months.

By September 2008 we had instituted training sessions across the nation, creating among our employees a palpable enthusiasm that, as Calvin demanded, was brought back to airports across the country. By the end of the year, our officers had fully accepted their critical importance in defending travelers across the country, the TSA was ranked highest among government agencies in a public survey, and I owed a begrudging nod of recognition to a charismatic young man from Austria. The threat he embodied pushed us at HQ to remain focused on the challenges ahead.

BY 2008, TOM HOOPES, THE GOATEED INTEL ANALYST WHO I HAD COME to rely on for his ability to link up disparate dots, had spent much of his previous two years trying to puzzle out that man, Zubair al-Masri.

In early 2006, following the near miss of Operation Glidepath, Charlie Allen initiated a top-secret program called Amalgam which was tasked with following up on Glidepath leads and try to any advance warning on its next iteration. A few months later, one of Amalgam's valuable nuggets was that a Glidepath operative named Imran was still alive and operating in Pakistan, despite initial reports of his death. Although most of the very few people with access to Amalgam—Tom was one of the only ones at the TSA—believed that Imran was merely a disposable foot soldier, Tom took a contrary view. If the guy was selected by the top al-Qaeda leaders as one of three people to deliver a major blow to the United States on the order of a 9/11, he was worth watching on that basis alone.

Amalgam members later received further information about Imran's identity. He was an Austrian twentysomething with native German and near-fluent English whose appearance allowed him to easily fit into a crowd in Europe or America. Hoopes also found out that Imran had taken the name "Zubair" and had been involved in the transatlantic liquid plot. Later in 2007, Amalgam produced intel that al-Qaeda was recruiting white Western-ers and bringing them to special camps where Zubair was a trainer. But de-spite his ubiquitous presence in the major plots during my tenure, Zubair was not attracting mainstream agency attention. Tom still wasn't sure why.

Through his intelligence and quick wit, Tom had developed his own small network of iconoclasts at other agencies, giving him access to intel that wouldn't have made it to the TSA via official reporting. Agencies issue intel-ligence as "products," and although keeping track of all the products can be daunting in itself, Tom also worked the scraps that fell by the wayside. Because lots of "uncorroborated" reporting doesn't meet the credibility stan-dards necessary to be included in official products, Tom had to go dumpster-diving for these morsels. Most of them were complete garbage, fabricated by a source to get paid or a mistranslation of a hard-won scrap of information. But some of them were critical. Sometimes Tom would piece together separate seemingly unrelated nuggets from a CIA report and NSA fragments and see if he could find a way to piece them together into a new insight. His mental-ity that anything *might* be of value, made it easy for others in the intelligence business to call Tom and brainstorm.

One of Tom's equally heretical colleagues, Ellen, called him midweek in February 2008. Actually, her name wasn't Ellen, but Tom knew that was the only name he'd get unless he started working alongside her at the Fort. The woman called Ellen wasn't normally chatty, and she did not disappoint this time.

"Hi Tom, Ellen. Do you have a gray phone?"

"Nope," said Tom wondering what was up.

"Can you get to one?"

"Yeah."

"What's the number? Roger that. I'll call in five minutes."

Tom put down the phone and cocked his head to look at a wing rem-nant bearing a red Soviet star hanging on his wall. "Huh?" Gray phones are hardwired to the most secure telephone system in the government. There are three of them at the TSA HQ, all in the vaulted area where Tom worked. They weren't used much.

Tom got up and walked into the narrow, fluorescent-lit corridor. It was not like Ellen to be melodramatic. His phone was already cleared to a level just a few notches below the gray phones. They had even talked about Amalgam matters over his office line.

Tom swiped his access card outside the Intelligence Watch Area, a vault within a vault, and punched in a code to enter. Inside were about half a dozen analysts looking at banks of computer monitors underneath plasma screens. The overhead speakers emitted a disconcerting but regular beep, a signal that the line connecting the Federal Aviation Administration, the Department of Defense, and the TSA was open. In critical aviation incidents an operator could simply hit "un-mute" and started talking. Tom paged through the notebooks of the latest cables and intel products on the supervisor's thirty-foot curved desk that took up the front of the room.

The gray phone hung unceremoniously on the wall behind a stand of printers. It had a matte steel cable-cover running down to the floor. Tom leaned against the wall and waited for the phone to ring.

"Tom," began Ellen. "I have some undisseminated intel and I'd appreciate it if you could protect me on this." Ellen's call was probably so secret in part because it was bad form to get out ahead of the dissemination process. If the info leaked out, Ellen would be in very deep muck.

"I just got something from our technical people. But you gotta protect me on this!"

"Right," said Tom.

"I think your little buddy is up to something. One of our partner services got information on a guy in Waziristan. He has been lying low, but last week started becoming active. We couldn't figure out who it was or what he was doing. There wasn't anything notable about his activities. We saw that he was interested in the UEFA Euro 2008 soccer tournament in Vienna."

German speakers in Waziristan who were interested in Austria. Tom felt a jolt of adrenaline.

We now think this guy may be in contact with Omer Ozdemir.

Something very interesting: he's also looking at the TSA, at information related to TSA's testing liquid explosive screening technology at US airports.

Waziristan, Austria, Germany, soccer, Ozdemir, liquids, US airports; Tom focused his gaze at the wall straight ahead. After two years of poking

around, Tom knew it had to be one person, albeit someone with innumerable names: Imran, Waqas, Zubair al-Masri, or Abdulrahman Hilal Hussein.
And this formidable and well-networked opponent was looking at the TSA.
It was a feeling a bit like looking down at your chest and seeing a red laser dot
targeting your heart.

For the next five minutes Tom tried to get Ellen to tell him all she knew
while appearing noncommittal. Ellen ended with one last request for Tom to
cover her. It was likely that this information would never be disseminated,
except via the supersecret and limited Amalgam channels.

Tom went back to his office, closing the door and then his eyes. He had
to tell his boss, but keeping a lid on the intel—and preventing Ellen from
getting burned—was going to be tough. With one last look at the Russian
wing stuck on the wall, Tom headed down to see Keith. "You're not going to
believe this," he said.

After half an hour, Tom and Keith had sliced it in every way they could
think. Was this misdirection? Was it a different Zubair? Some other mistake?
Did the information Ellen provided mean anything? When was the last time
they had an Ozdemir sighting? Why Ozdemir? Didn't they use detonators
hidden in shoes in that last Ozdemir plot, the one with Gelowicz? Dare we
say liquids?

After a pause in the conversation, Keith said, "Jeez, we gotta tell the
boss." Keith flipped to the page in his notebook with the executive seventh-
floor schedule to see where I was.

AFTER KEITH AND TOM CAME INTO MY OFFICE TO DROP THE BOMBSHELL
of Zubair's Internet activity, I knew we were in a race against time. We had
to keep Zubair off the scent of our real vulnerabilities while we rolled out
defensive measures as fast as we could. I could never confirm that they were in
touch with Zubair, but we knew that Zubair's contacts in Austria were acting
unusually by meeting furtively and avoiding any electronic communication.

Maybe once a month, an intelligence snippet would blip up on the
radar that could be interpreted as relating to a possible attack on the Euro
2008 soccer championships. The championship's final game was to be held
in the Ernst Happel Stadium just across the Danube from where Zubair
used to live. Several US carriers provided service to Austria and Switzerland,
and while we could not connect the dots of Euro 2008 chatter and Zubair's
home turf, I knew that in retrospect if something happened it would look

like an obvious connection. So, I dropped in on Vienna about a month before the tournament started.

I made a point to take a high-profile security tour of the Vienna airport, complete with K-9 sweeps of US-bound aircraft. When I met with the acting ambassador at the US embassy, we talked about the Zubair threat. Eventually my host asked me whether I took the threat seriously.

I looked at him curiously for a second before responding. "I'm here, aren't I?"

IN THE SUMMER OF 2008 ANDREW COX, THE FORMER STREET MUSICIAN who I'd moved into our strategy team, field-tested a curveball in checkpoint security. For years, retail employees made a habit of approaching people they suspected of being potential shoplifters and asking, "Can I help you with something, sir?" The question was meant to be a pleasant, if unsubtle, way of letting the customer know he was being looked after. More recently, the FBI had initiated a program called SafeCatch that took the same principle and applied it to bank robberies. For decades, bank employees had few options to deal with suspicious people who entered their branch. Unless there was a local security officer on hand, the tellers were instructed to be passive, not to approach the suspect, and comply with the robber if threatened—eerily similar to the terrorism training that flight crews received before 9/11. But under SafeCatch, employees are instructed to utilize a sort of amped-up customer service by warmly greeting any suspicious characters, and making sure they receive lots of personal attention. The approach was piloted in Seattle-area banks in 2007, which saw a significant drop in robberies.

So in the summer of 2008 at LA/Ontario International Airport, a gleaming white building 40 miles east of Los Angeles, Andrew tested out a technique we called Decision Gates, a technique that presents passengers with choices in as many places as possible. To a terrorist, facing these choices adds unwelcome complexity and generates opportunities for them to make a mistake or get noticed by security personnel.

The usefulness of this scenario was premised on two ideas. First, a little bit of personal interaction usually calms innocent passengers who just want to get to the other side, while typically spiking the nervousness felt by terror operatives, smugglers, and other criminals. Secondly, market research has shown that, given a choice between going left and right, an overwhelming percentage of people select the latter. Making the already unpopular left-lane option less appealing with dim lighting, et al., further tipped the odds that people exhibiting normal behavior would go right. Of course, almost nobody who chose left was actually a criminal or a terrorist, but the two options gave passengers a chance to demonstrate behaviors that might raise a flag.

Our Federal Security Director in Salt Lake City, Earl Morris, tried a different approach to self-selection that had more to do with expediting the flow through security, an approach he dubbed "Black Diamond lanes." The idea was that if you had security officers out in front of the security line questioning passengers about how quickly they could get through the checkpoint, the public could then be segregated by speed, with the faster, frequent travelers in the Black Diamond lane—a reference to the steepest slopes at ski resorts, reserved for expert skiers. Likewise, the less-traveled passengers and those with handicaps or small children would be steered toward the slower green lanes.

Passenger feedback was very positive, and here was a chance for travelers to have some control over the security process. The numbers also showed a marked improvement in hourly throughput, an average of more than 20 percent. More significantly, there was a drop of more than 10 percent in alarm rates, the real killer in slowing down security lines. Apparently when people feel less rushed they remember to pull out the laptop or take off the heavy belt, surefire ways to trigger an alarm. As the whole process became more efficient and calmer for everyone, the security environment also improved.

By the end of 2008, the TSA had designated liquid-and-family lanes in every airport. In addition to helping people who need a little more time than others, the option was in preparation for a modification of the liquid restrictions. I intended to offer a trial program that allowed people to bring liquids of any size through the checkpoint provided they went through the liquid-and-family lanes. Since by that time we expected to have the new ATX machines at every airport, and George Zarur's liquid-detection tests showed their virtually flawless performance in finding threat liquids, we could do away with the baggie. Liquids would still have to go separately into the gray bin, but there wouldn't be any size restriction. The TSA could roll this out today at most security lanes in the country if it wanted, and nobody would be happier about bagging the baggie than me. Ironically, with the new algorithm, it is actually preferable to have large bottles. I used to joke about changing the rules so that you could *only* bring containers larger than 3.4 ounces. George was the only person who found me funny. But I was not joking when I wrote a blog post in October 2008 in which I said that the baggie restrictions would likely be lifted in the year ahead because by then I knew that ATX was already capable of detecting liquid explosives.[1]

By Thanksgiving 2008 we had deployed ATXs virtually everywhere, all we needed was to load up the new software and announce the new policy, But I kept hearing from our technology team that the false positives were still too high and needed just a little more refinement. Though the new policy was still unannounced when I left in January 2009, I remained confident that the new head of TSA would be able to get a fast start by bagging the "baggie" 3-1-1 rule and allowing liquids back on board almost without restriction. I later learned that opposition from the vendor community convinced mid-level TSA technology officials to shelve the effort and wait for manufacturers to create a brand new fleet of scanners that could find threat liquids while still inside carry-ons. Meanwhile, the fully capable ATXs operate in airports around the world while the software that would allow the TSA to discard its "baggie" policy sits somewhere in a data vault deep within some government facility.

At the airport in Richmond, Virginia, we also experimented with incorporating explicit randomness into the process with a security lottery. Passengers could either choose to move through the normal checkpoint or walk up to a laptop and press a button that sent virtual ping-pongs ball flying. The different options included the full menu of possible security actions, from an item-by-item exam of carry-on bags to a quick swipe of the hands, a light upper-body pat down, or a full-body MRI. But although passengers would be aware of the various types of screening, they wouldn't know which was theirs until the balls landed. The lottery widened the range of possible security measures for any individual passenger without having to subject everybody to the full gamut every time.

In addition to adding formalized elements of randomness, many of these measures allowed the TSA to liberate our TSOs to use their talents. Checkpoint technology can do a number of extraordinary things very well, but it operates with a sometimes-fatal consistency. The most dangerous incidents are those that only happen once, outside of set search parameters. Unlike inanimate technology, people are very good at discarding assumptions and dealing with ambiguity in real time. Tapping into these abilities was critical; we needed to plug our human element into a network that was more powerful than any computer.

IN JUNE 2008, MARK SULLIVAN, HEAD OF THE SECRET SERVICE, CALLED me to ask for help covering the US presidential primaries and conventions. I agreed to lend him a number of officers, in part because our people were so good at securing areas with large crowds, but also because working with an elite force like the Secret Service has a prestige which could only boost the TSA's morale.

Though different from most TSA work, working with the Secret Service primarily involved the physical screening of people who came to the rallies and speeches. The conventions, however, provided an excellent opportunity for a terrorist strike to eliminate an entire party's leadership and had their own dynamics. We were tasked with providing blanket coverage of Minneapolis-Saint Paul airport for the Republican convention as well as the Democrats' event in Denver.

A few months before the Democratic Party convention, we heard on the National Counterterrorism Center's morning SVTC about a call to a Denver-area number from someone in northwest Pakistan. After some more information came in, the FBI linked the calls to Sheikh Said, then al-Qaeda's number-three man, and Najibullah Zazi, a naturalized US citizen from Afghanistan who worked as a limo driver at Denver International Airport.

As the July convention drew near, Zazi's presence at Denver International loomed large. Here was a man known to be communicating with al-Qaeda already working at the very airport we needed to secure. The FBI was looking for a prosecution and needed to build a case to show that he was actively working in pursuit of a terrorist act, but we couldn't ignore the possibility that Zazi aimed to attack while major political figures were pouring into the airport. This scenario was a constant source of tension between our agency, which favored overt action on Zazi, and the FBI, which didn't yet have enough evidence to detain him.

This inherent conflict was not limited to the FBI. The TSA often approached the same intelligence from a completely different angle than the major intel players. Obviously all the counterterrorism agencies obsess about stopping attacks but there are some nuances at the edges. While the CIA or the NSA are primarily concerned with gathering as many valuable pieces of data as possible, and the FBI is interested in information that can help arrest and prosecute criminals, the TSA is responsible only for *preventing* attacks on transportation, an enormous, specific category that is also a favorite target of al-Qaeda. We don't care as much about gathering information or putting people in jail as we do about making sure that we have done everything possible for a plane to land safely. So throughout my tenure, we often found ourselves clamoring for action while the CIA warned us not to burn their source or the FBI pushed back at us for "interfering" in their criminal investigation.

With obvious options like detainment off the table, we had to figure out how to neutralize Zazi without letting him know we were onto him. We decided to position some of our high-visibility VIPR patrol squads, complete with K-9s and well-armed police, near the limo and taxi stands to send a very loud message that security was on high alert everywhere in the airport.

We can't be sure what impact, if any, our heavy presence had on Zazi, but on the convention's last day, he hopped a flight out of the United States to Pakistan. The FBI continued following him after his return, eventually arresting him in September 2009 after he had driven from Denver to New York for a planned suicide attack on the city's subway system. Instead of killing hundreds of commuters during a Manhattan rush hour, Zazi's lasting legacy was a raised awareness of the number of viable domestic terror networks which, even as our intel looked closer, continued to branch outward, sprouting different links and connections like the matrices we'd been watching in Europe.

UNTIL 2008, ONE OF THE BIG QUESTIONS IN INTEL CIRCLES WAS, "WHERE are the homegrown American terrorists?" We saw them almost everyplace else in the world: British terrorists had exploded themselves on trains in London, while Belgium and Germany had citizens known to have become suicide bombers overseas. Finally, in October 2008, Shirwa Ahmed, an American of Somali descent, became the first American suicide operative when he blew himself up in northern Somalia, killing more than two dozen. But the American who caused the most concern that year was a former Catholic altar boy and Little League player named Bryant Neal Vinas, known as "the American al-Qaeda." Vinas had trained along with western European operatives by Zubair al-Masri in Waziristan. As a native New Yorker coached by a man who was casing TSA security over the Internet, Vinas was near the top of our list of persons of interest. Soon he was grabbed by authorities in Pakistan and brought to the United States for questioning.

One night in November 2008, after leaving TSA for a senior job working intelligence for the FBI, Joe Salvator called me while I was in Keith's office on the sixth floor. "Hey. How ya doing?"

"Fine," I answered. It was eight at night, so I was pretty sure this wasn't a social call.

"Do you know what's going on?" asked Joe.

"No?" I guessed.

"OK," said Joe, half swallowing his words. "Well, there's this info from Vinas . . . about his possible target. He may have been looking at blowing up the Long Island Railroad during the holiday season," Joe mumbled. Then clearer: "You gotta wait 'til you hear it through the system before you do anything, but you might want to start planning."

I later found out that Vinas, who was in FBI custody at the time, had started talking about how he had a map of the LIRR. Joe's TSA-trained ears perked up, a believable terror threat on transit was being disclosed three days before Thanksgiving, among the biggest travel days of the year. Joe knew the source was good and wanted to get the intel to others who could use it. It was coming out in the next few hours anyway but if you had people to move around, there was a big difference in getting a heads-up at eight o'clock or getting the same news after midnight.

"Don't burn me," he insisted. "But you need to know."

Thankful that Joe had stepped outside his professional box, I got in touch with our operations people and we quietly flowed in air marshals, so that if we needed hundreds of FAMs in the morning they would coincidentally already be in New York. The next day the potential threat became public and the TSA was part of a very visible law-enforcement presence.

ALI KHEL IS A SMALL SETTLEMENT SITTING AT A CROSSROADS ON THE fertile plain east of the Indus River and west of the hills separating the plateau from Pakistan's population centers near Lahore. A pay phone on a white pole is the lone marker along the Kalur Kot Road that serves as Ali Khel's main drag. A few dozen narrow storefronts line one side of the anonymous paved road. Ali Khel is host to an open-air fruit-and-vegetable market where varieties of local produce are sold. Donkey carts and tractors do double duty as transportation and display shelves as local men in sandals and traditional loose shirts and billowing pants, known as the shalwar kameez, mingle, bargain, and go about their business. Ali Khel is one of dozens of small, self-sufficient dots on the landscape of northwest Waziristan, part of the Federally Administered Tribal Areas stretching along Pakistan's border with Afghanistan.

The FATA is the geopolitical center of the West's global conflict with Islamic fundamentalist terrorists, and that is why even tiny Ali Khel shows up on maps in rooms as far away as Washington DC, and Langley, Virginia. Ali

Khel, like its neighbors, has tribal connections with other settlements, and under 2008's political lineup, it is within the orbit of senior Taliban commander Hafiz Gul Bahadur, a major player in national politics. Bahadur's deputy is a prominent cleric named Maulvi Sadiq Noor. Although headquartered about a hundred miles to the northwest, Noor had a secure compound nestled in Ali Khel and protected by an eight-foot-high perimeter wall. He sometimes let al-Qaeda officials use his safe house, and after prayers on Friday, November 21, 2008, six men arrived in dusty Toyotas and went inside.

The night was calm with clear, warm skies. Under a waning moon, two hours before sunrise, a pair of thunderous explosions rocked Ali Khel, shaking buildings throughout the area. Noor's safe house was reduced to rubble, hit nearly simultaneously by two twenty-pound warheads brought to their target by American Hellfire AGM114 missiles that in turn were launched by electronic command from an invisible, unmanned Predator drone in the silent skies above.

It didn't take long for Noor's Taliban henchmen to figure out what happened, and they moved immediately to seal off the compound where its central building lay burning amid thick black smoke. One of the guests' pickup trucks lay upended and on fire, but another of their vehicles appeared largely undamaged. The Taliban soldier in charge, Syed, a stocky thirty-six-year-old farmer whose family had lived near Ali Khel for generations, knew that time was short. When an air attack like this occurred, there were usually foreign spotters or Pakistani troops waiting nearby to swoop in and grab the victims' bodies—or whatever was left of them—containing DNA markers.

Syed knew it was a disaster that the Americans had discovered Noor's safe house and followed the al-Qaeda guests to it, but something could be recouped for the Taliban if they prevented the Americans from learning whether or not their targets had been killed. There was also the matter of a quick and proper burial, but that was secondary right now. Syed quickly checked the perimeter defense and grabbed one of the men to go with him into what remained of the building. It was now about a quarter past five; with daybreak was only an hour away, there was less time before someone showed up and took control of the crime scene.

Syed could see that little remained of the main living quarters, which were now a smoking crater. A wall behind the kitchen was still standing, however, and Syed thought he saw movement in the surrounding smoke. A tall, slender, bearded man seemed to be doubled over, coughing and staggering backwards. As Syed got closer he saw that the other man was in fact bent over dragging a wiry, fair-haired man from the debris. Calling for a car, Syed ran over to offer help. *They're going to be OK,* thought Syed as he exchanged words with the taller one and went inside. Syed knew immediately that he'd made a mistake. The fire was hotter than any he'd ever known, and he couldn't see or breathe. Minutes later the remaining wall from Noor's safe house sagged inwards and collapsed, punctuated by a final burst of sparks and smoke.

The Taliban dispersed. A truck pulled up next to the public telephone on Kalur Kot Road and a brief call was made. The old truck then rattled west, heading for the mountains, as the sun came up behind it on November 22, 2008.

BACK IN VIRGINIA AT EIGHT A.M. THAT SAME DAY, I'D BEEN UP FOR A FEW hours checking my email when my BlackBerry buzzed. The message was from Keith Kauffman, with the subject heading: BIG HIT. I followed his link to an article about an explosion that had killed al-Qaeda operative Rashid Rauf. I was shocked. Rauf was one of al-Qaeda's top operational people over the last decade. What's more, despite his high profile, he'd been very success-ful at evading capture and death. Rereading the article, I saw a small detail tucked toward the bottom of the story. It noted that the drone strike had also killed another al-Qaeda operative named Zubair al-Masri.

After a few seconds of disorientation, I took a deep breath, feeling an amazing surge of relief. The al-Qaeda operative who had haunted my living nightmares had been neutralized. Then, just as quickly, I settled back into a familiar sense of foreboding. What did the report really mean? Confirming a Predator strike is very difficult, since it calls for sending in a US or Pakistani reconnaissance team to collect DNA or fingerprints from a mud hut that's just been reduced to dust by a 5,000-pound bomb.

Even if Zubair were dead, one of the most important lessons of the past four years was surely that operatives were replaceable. Al-Qaeda was a resil-ient organization that learned from its successes and blind spots. We knew that they already had other adaptable personnel who spoke English and knew their way around the Internet, those critical skills for employment throughout the globalized world. Zubair, the embodiment of lethal terror planning, was reported dead, but with a steady stream of fresh plots, our security emergency continued. Connections could be rewired, the network reorganized, and plotting and attacks would continue.

SEVENTEEN

ZERO HOUR

JANUARY 20, 2009, HAD LOOMED LARGE ON MY CALENDAR
for months. It was my last day as administrator, but the personal relevance
of leaving the TSA was buried beneath our feverish security preparations for
Barack Obama's inauguration as president of the United States. With more
than a million people on the National Mall and one of the largest live television audiences ever, the event would be a massive spectacle of democracy—
and a dream scenario for terrorists. A simple backpack bomb hidden beneath
a winter jacket would kill hundreds in the tightly packed crowds. Worse, one
of al-Qaeda's trademarks is a coordinated sequence of attacks meant to kill
first responders or serve as a diversion to a bigger catastrophe. Intelligence
reporting had already highlighted threats to mass transit, the primary means
of transportation for most of the crowd, as well as three major airports nearby,
all of which were our territory and our responsibility.

I started the big day early. At 1:04 A.M., I woke up wondering if a rolling
wave of global terrorist attacks culminating with America's inauguration had
already begun in the Middle East. I knew that our preparations were done or
were at least under way. More than 300 TSA officers from all over the country
were camped out at a conference center in Fairfax, Virginia, their wake-up
call was in about three hours. They had been assigned by the Secret Service to
screen guests entering the Capitol grounds. I knew that about two dozen K-9
bomb-detection teams were on their way to Washington overnight, called

in at the last minute to deepen the security coverage on the mall. Hundreds of air marshals would soon be boarding flights headed to Washington. All of these efforts were being tracked at the TSA's massive operations center in Virginia, but they would have little impact on events in the Middle East.

It would have been about 8:04 A.M. in Amman, Jordan, and my imagined scheme wasn't just late-night paranoia, but one reading of the hard-won intelligence gathered over the past year. Once again, there were a multitude of possibilities. But viewed from the right angle, these dots connected and came together in sequence like dominoes tumbling in the Persian Gulf, through the Mediterranean, across the English Channel, and over the Atlantic, culminating in huge attacks right up the Potomac. Late the night before, the Federal Bureau of Investigation had been chasing a lead that some terrorist plotters were already in the DC area. But at that hour I managed to avoid rehashing the whole matrix of threats. If something happened abroad, our watch officers would immediately call me.

I woke up again at two. It was now getting into London's rush hour and my BlackBerry hadn't gone off, a good sign. Also, every morning at that time, the National Counterterrorism Center put out a situation report with the combined analysis of all the intelligence agencies. If the NCTC had any new information on an attack on the inauguration, I'd be getting a call shortly, but not through my classified phone: Another reminder that I would be leaving my job within twelve hours was the dusty outline on my bedside table where my boxy, black secure telephone had been. Without classified calls at home, I'd either have to speak in code on the BlackBerry or just go to the office.

At precisely 4:30 I woke up for the last time that morning. It had been years since I set an alarm clock in my apartment. My phone still hadn't rung with any bad news, but the lack of an early overseas terrorist attack might just mean that the inauguration was the trigger event and the rolling attacks would head to Asia. In any event, it was show time for us. I began checking my email and prepping for meetings.

A little after six, Janet dropped me off down the road at TSA headquarters. It was frigid but clear, decent weather for the event and no need to worry about a bunch of flight cancellations and mobbed airport terminals. Right before Christmas I had long-delayed surgery to fuse my left ankle, they used titanium screws, which, though large, do not alarm airport metal detectors. I made my way into the building with my newly rebuilt ankle propped up on a scooter festooned with its own plastic hula dancer, a parting gift from Bill

Hall. I rolled to the elevators without my customary brown bag containing a peanut butter–and-apricot sandwich. My mandated government retirement began at noon; for the first time I could remember, I would be home for lunch.

On the sixth floor, I made my final approach to the forbidding, bank-vault gray steel door that guarded the intel shop. I swiped my access card and entered the PIN and hauled open the seventy-pound door. Inside, the place was buzzing. I spied Keith Kauffman in the hall and tried to catch his eye. He looked back at me and shook his head with a wry smile that said, "How many times do I have to tell you that we've already briefed you on everything we know?" I dropped in on Tom Hoopes and asked him to speculate on the possibilities for today. He threw up his hands and laughed before going through it all one more time.

One person we were actively tracking had flown the previous summer from Africa through Europe to the United States, landing in Philadelphia. From the City of Brotherly Love, he hopped on a commuter flight to Reagan National. Why? There is simply no normal reason to fly through Europe and then Philadelphia to take a puddle jumper to Washington, DC, a city with lots of direct service from both Europe and Africa. But there is one very abnormal reason to do so: Commuter flights from nearby Philadelphia use runways at Reagan National that sometimes take them almost directly over the Capitol. And the bad smell didn't stop there. After landing at Reagan, this individual drove directly to Dulles, DC's major international airport some forty minutes from the city, spent the night out there, then the next day made the hour-plus drive to BWI, just south of Baltimore, to fly onward.

None of this activity is illegal, or even grounds to get on a watch list. But it is the kind of nightmare itinerary that most travelers would have done anything to avoid. If our peripatetic African visitor was doing surveillance or a test run in preparation for an attack involving aviation on the inauguration, you'd be hard pressed to construct a more efficient schedule.

Throughout 2008, there had been an undercurrent of reporting about al-Qaeda shifting focus and resources from Pakistan and Afghanistan to east Africa and Yemen. One plot reported by FBI sources in Africa suggested that the lead operative for the attack would arrive in the United States about a week before the inauguration, landing in Seattle and working his way east to Washington. While there was a lot of skepticism about the sources, Customs and Border Protection analysts found a guy matching just about all of the descriptors arriving from Africa into Seattle midweek who was now at large in the country.

Then, on Friday, as most of the government was shutting down for the long inaugural weekend, the FBI got access to an African source who gave them a great deal of information, much of it corroborating previous reporting. The next night, the man who arrived into Seattle popped up on the radar in Chicago. The following night, he took the last flight out from O'Hare to London, using somebody else's passport to elude the watch list he was now on. The FBI alerted UK authorities, and after being detained upon landing, he was escorted to baggage claim, where officers discovered what appeared to be his real passport. Suddenly, the suspect managed to bolt into the busy Heathrow airport crowds. He was later spotted on a surveillance video departing the airport and was never seen again. Was his rushed departure related to further FBI interviews conducted the same day in Africa? Did the FBI disrupt an attack right there?

We couldn't be sure. Tom and I focused on what we knew of several active threat streams. None of these plots had enough solid information to add up to the intelligence community's magic formula of "specific, credible, and imminent" that turned a plot into an officially actionable situation, but the inauguration was a dream target. If I had learned one thing about intel in the past three-and-a-half years, it was not to wait for a gift-wrapped plot to drop into my lap.

We agreed that the scariest intel around inauguration plots involved al-Qaeda–affiliated individuals in Somalia. Not only was Somalia's civil war a sort of living laboratory for the group to train and test, but there were plenty of American operatives there. Just three months earlier, Shirwa Ahmed, a twenty-seven-year-old from Minneapolis, became the first American suicide bomber, taking dozens of people in northern Somalia with him. Ahmed was among a number of young Americans, largely of Somali extraction, who had gone to there to fight in that country's long ongoing conflict before coming back home. The idea of native-born Americans returning to the United States with explosives and commando skills was not reassuring. And their numbers at terrorist camps were steadily increasing.

Even more alarming, we knew that Harun Fazul, the al-Qaeda leader behind the US embassy bombings in Dar es Salaam, Nairobi, and Tanzania, not to mention rocket attacks against airliners, was in close proximity to these training camps. A skilled, ruthless al-Qaeda veteran would be very interested in potential Somali-American operatives. (Fazul remained very active in terrorist plotting until he was reported killed at a roadblock skirmish in 2011.

In July 2010, he was linked to the World Cup suicide bombing in Uganda, and in August 2010, he was connected to the indictments announced by US Attorney General Eric Holder relating to Somali al-Shabaab terrorists targeting the United States.)

AT HALF PAST SIX I LEFT TOM HOOPES' OFFICE, HEADED DOWN TO THE garage, and climbed into one of the black Suburbans that would take me out to the Freedom Center, the hub of the TSA's information network. Because the major roads were closed to the public today, we sped along the George Washington Parkway. I looked across the Potomac at buses filled with the school bands that would march in the parade, along with bundled-up families walking resolutely through the freezing cold to the mall. This was a big day in America; it was impossible not to feel the energy. But my mind was still stuck replaying the possible threat streams.

After about thirty minutes, we arrived at an unmarked building sitting among other similarly undistinguished structures near Dulles airport. Inside the Freedom Center's main entrance, twisted steel beams from the World Trade Center stood amid blocks of limestone from the Pentagon and a piece of the aluminum wing from United Flight 93, three jarringly poignant reminders of our mission.

We headed straight for the Watch Floor, the baseball field-size core of the building that is crammed with desks and officers monitoring multiple screens. Still more monitors hang overhead, and at the front is a series of thirty-foot screens that show aircraft in transit all over the globe. Every single security breach over eight modes and nexuses of transportation—from planes and trains to gas pipelines and maritime ports—pours into the Watch Floor in a constant stream. Right below the radar images of airspace, intel feeds crawl across the computer monitor, just like on CNN.

I went into a secure area off the Watch Floor to a SVTC for the eight A.M. morning briefing. In addition to the usual faces from the FBI, the Central Intelligence Agency, and the Department of Homeland Security, John Brennan, the president-elect's designated Homeland Security adviser, was also linked in. The transition was under way.

Of the hundreds of reports Hoopes and I had plowed through earlier that morning, one in particular sticks in my mind. A few days prior, local tribesmen had discovered the corpses of four young men at a small, remote training camp in North Africa. The remains were unmarked and autopsies impractical, but it seemed that the four had died either by poisoning or some sort of biochemical accident. Was it bad meat? Or had they maybe been practicing for today on the mall?

In a way, this was the perfect metaphor for how I had spent nearly the last four years of my life. Twenty miles to the east, a soon-to-be president was putting the finishing touches on an address he hoped would inspire literally hundreds of millions of people in this country and around the globe, and here I was in a windowless cavern debating whether four dead bodies in Africa constituted a small tragedy, a complete anomaly, or an alarm bell so loud that we would soon hear it screaming across the National Mall.

Some people walked into the following TSA intelligence briefing thinking it was a festive or at least historic day, but Keith Kauffman, capturing the mood from the previous SVTC, started the meeting off brusquely, with no good-morning banter and a sense of urgency. He ran through the action items on the Somali threat and confirmed that we had Behavior Detection Officers and intelligence analysts out at area airports. Lee Kair reviewed our TSO deployments in support of the Secret Service and new Federal Air Marshal head Bob Bray gave an update that the two dozen K-9 teams requested by the Secret Service just the day before, were all on station.

Nonetheless, my exit was imminent. At half past ten I walked out on the Watch Floor to say thank you, got my security debrief, turned in my credentials and, most thankfully, my BlackBerry. Our leadership team posed for a picture and then I headed back over to the TSA's brown towers in Arlington. My head was a little scrambled, and not in the way I'd become accustomed to after years of chasing threats. I went up to the sixth floor one last time to say a final thanks, and when the vault door slammed behind me, I walked down the hall, pushed the button on the wall, and stood for twelve seconds in the mechanized whirr of the elevator. Then the doors opened and I walked out into the bitingly cold January air, once again a private citizen.

I had been stripped of everything before leaving the building, including my car and driver. I called Janet for a ride, but she wanted to watch the inauguration. As I clicked off, the haunting phrase from the *9/11 Commission Report* ran through my mind: failure of imagination. But how do you know when your imagination fails? Were we still missing it, looking at the intel dots but blinded by our own biases? How could we slow down the scrambling and unscrambling of these invisible threats? When is the emergency over?

RESOLVE

AFTER SPENDING MORE THAN FOUR YEARS THINKING, LIVING, and breathing the TSA—with the last three and a half as administrator—I left the agency weighed down with as many questions as when I'd arrived. It wasn't that I'd learned nothing, but seen from the inside, my original questions about national security had morphed and multiplied. And, soon after Inauguration Day, I found that these concerns had followed me home, where they continue to prod, poke, and remind me that a resourceful and intelligent someone is currently targeting America's transportation system, and there is no simple way to stop him. But my time at the TSA has also left me with a few ideas on how to move forward.

I do recognize that an account of the TSA narrated by me brings a legitimate scrutiny of my performance during my tenure at the agency. I readily acknowledge my share of failures. An introductory list would include not designing job safety into the TSA's start-up; under-resourcing public communications in general, and specifically in the case of the baggie; letting the Registered Traveler program flounder in limbo for years; and under-engaging with a number of key constituents, including our own Federal Security Directors, outside contractors, and many of our stakeholders. But although I am the narrator, neither this book nor the important issues surrounding TSA are about me.

TSA administrators, myself included, come and go, while many of the same old problems at the agency persist uncorrected. The agency is massive and complex; we can't simply press the reset button every time someone new takes the reins. In 2005 I had some naïve notions about hopping into the saddle and wrangling the organization into shape. But within a few months, it dawned on me that rather than desiring a new direction charted by Chertoff and me, the organization at large was comfortable following the well-defined path in front of them, almost without critical thought about the uneven footing and steep incline. While virtually every individual TSA employee is passionate about the counterterrorism mission, as a group, they stubbornly resist steps outside the beaten path, especially if urged on them by someone at the top who won't be around when they are called to account. Individual leaders may push useful initiatives, but there seems to be a magnetic force that snaps the TSA back to a path of frustration and criticism. That is because the fundamental problems relate to the very structure of the TSA itself.

The TSA was created with a burst of energy and can-do spirit. But despite innovating in the process of building the agency, we did not give corresponding thought to the operation of ongoing security activities themselves. While the term "failure of imagination" was not popularized until 2003, after the 9/11 Commission's report was released, the TSA of 2001–02 had many symptoms of this myopia. While there was a massive investment in new technology and a broadening of the mission, we hadn't built a *new* aviation security network as much as we had built an amped-up version of the previous system, one in which government employees simply replaced private contractors. In fact, we missed the opportunity to engage the best of America's private sector when we created an extremely limited test pilot of privately operated screening checkpoints. The TSA handed private contractors a copy of the Standard Operating Procedure, told them not to deviate, and then paid their expenses plus an 8 percent profit margin. This was not innovation and competition; this was a clone of the TSA process with a markup. In my weekend paperwork inbox during 2007 was a thick packet of documents containing the contract renewal for San Francisco's private-sector screening company. I was astounded to find no performance improvement or cost-reduction provisions in this $90 million annual iteration of the "private sector."

The TSA's original strategies were largely grafted from the Federal Aviation Administration's pre-9/11 aviation security operations. Since the FAA's primary role is ensuring aviation safety, which has unbending parameters based on the laws of physics, its regulatory nature makes sense. But using regulation as the primary tool to stop adaptive terrorists does not. The TSA's inherited foundation of rule-based security—whether dealing with passengers, private industry, other countries, or its own employees—cemented a rigidity in its operations that continues to handicap the agency today. Critiques of the TSA almost always talk about the need for "risk management" in the design of TSA's security measures, but the nature of the risk you are addressing makes a huge difference. For linear risk, like aviation safety, control mechanisms and regulation are well suited. However, for non-linear risk such as we face with adaptive terrorists, complexity theory with its concepts about connected adaptive networks and resilience are more effective. In other words, if we want to effectively use risk management in counterterrorism, we need to move away from a system designed, built and now operating by rules created for the wrong type of risk.

In 2001, Congress and the administration together set up the regulatory structure of TSA in ATSA. I was at the nascent TSA and completely supported implementing ATSA's model and a fast start for the agency. When I returned in 2005, some of the passion I felt about changing our strategy could be attributed to my second thoughts about the initial wisdom of sprinting to the finish line in the early years. After 9/11, upgrading and expanding our airports' technology-based security capacities seemed like a no-brainer. There was certainly plenty of room for improvement. But rather than integrating technology with people and maximizing the unique skill sets of both assets, the TSA's major technology initiatives were aimed at replacing people with technology.

Machines are best at executing instructions flawlessly and uniformly at low cost over extended, uninterrupted periods of time. An advanced imaging scanner will locate 100 percent of the explosives they are built to find. But the billions of dollars it costs to install these systems doesn't mean we can go to sleep each night without worrying about bombs in bags. It is only a matter of time before an al-Muhajir invents a powerful new explosive that our machines won't detect. Operating on autopilot is the answer only if we possess the means to anticipate all threats, a foresight that we will simply never have.

We only compound this limited scope of vision by using our frontline workforce as replaceable versions of our scanners. The screeners' initial role was to operate according to a rigid Standard Operating Procedure that mimicked the operation of a computerized scanner. As Carl Maccario observed, thinking was not an important skill for screeners; it was grounds for discipline. But "thinking"—or more specifically, real-time processing of information and reacting appropriately to situations beyond any set of rules—is a human talent unequalled by any piece of technology. An integrated security system, one that uses technology to network intelligence and other information, machines to scan people and bags for known threats while allowing people to use their abilities to pick up on subtle clues signaling unidentified threats, is our best bet for a checkpoint security solution. The reimagining of the screeners' role as a Transportation Security Officer was a step toward linking the frontline checkpoint operations with everything happening behind it. Rather than have a self-contained screening process that robotically enforced a static prohibited-items list, TSOs were meant to connect to and interact with the scientific and informational capabilities that are such a powerful part of twenty-first-century America. Zubair and others can defeat a rigid, predictable series of obstacles, but they are out of their depth if we mobilize, integrate, and sustain the whole portfolio of tools available in Western society to render them irrelevant.

The other pillar upon which Congress constructed the TSA, rigid regulation, may have served the nation well in the previous century, but found itself to be outmoded when it faced off against al-Qaeda and other contemporary adversaries. Just as with technology, the major problem with the regulatory approach is an inflexibility that leaves gaping blind spots.

The TSA regulates airlines and airports to insure that they provide a baseline array of security activities. Specific measures—making security-awareness public announcements or visually inspecting a set percentage of catered meal trays—are representative of an exhaustive list of security efforts, but ones that also quickly become rote and observable. A rule-based system doesn't stop terrorists who react to our defensive measures by simply changing their method of attack. Banning certain items merely gives them a complete list of what *not* to use in their next attack.

An unintended consequence of recording measures to assure compliance is that the very act also ensures that the rules' minimum requirements become the maximum delivered. Just as the impressive million-dollar scanner will never detect a previously unimagined explosive, strict regulations on airlines, airports, and even on TSA employees discourage these people from ever stepping outside of the prescribed parameters. Acting outside the rulebook leaves that person open to disciplinary action, while coloring inside the lines gives them a shield in case anything bad happens.

In regulatory security, employees are held accountable for their process rather than the end result. Such rule-based approaches tend to bleed our workforce of personal accountability. But the business of stopping terror attacks is binary: either the plane landed safely or it didn't. And if it didn't, saying that all procedures were followed to the letter is not going to satisfy anyone. In the dynamic, high-risk operating environment of the TSA, it is not only the means, but the end that matters.

While some TSOs were terrified to have the SOP's cloak of protection taken away, others, like Jeremy Trujillo and Jameka Merriwether, were excited that HQ was encouraging them to think on the job. Moving forward, TSOs need the freedom to operate within a more flexible framework that recognizes their field experience with millions of passengers as an invaluable security resource. When we talk about advanced technology, let's remember that the most sophisticated computer on the planet is the human brain. TSA employees include tens of thousands of good people who have the skills, tools and experience to take on and defeat al-Qaeda planners like Zubair—if we get behind them and let them do their job.

Such improvements as the pay-for-performance system developed by Gale Rossides and others; Lee Kair's revamped TSA checkpoints in 2005 and 2006; Mike Restovich and Mo McGowan's measures to utilize the experience and judgment of the TSOs; and Stephanie Rowe's efforts on Engage! were designed to drive home, and give incentives for that sense of accountability to TSA's frontline officers. In 2011, the TSA announced the implementation of collective bargaining for TSOs, which could mean that pay incentives for better security performance will be replaced by a system based on seniority. In other words, as long as an employee isn't fired, he or she will receive comfortably predictable raises all the way out to retirement. I fear the implementation of this mindset and do not believe that it builds a culture of high performance, results-based accountability. That should concern us all. Ironically, the fallout from a unionized TSO workforce may bring truly innovative private security options into the market for the first time.

One area where TSA has out-performed the public expectation is the Secure Flight program, rebuilt by Stephanie Rowe and her team, and implemented in early 2009. Secure Flight, after a floundering start, is the biggest step forward in security since 9/11. Built from the ground up with privacy protections, the program allows TSA to use real-time intelligence information, tied to constantly updated passenger travel information and adjust security measures down to the specific flight level. It used to be that security measures were like a massive on/off switch where everybody got the identical security process. Under Secure Flight, and enabled by checkpoint technology that links boarding passes and passenger identification to its information systems, TSA can customize security such as place an Air Marshal behind and next to a specific passenger of concern or allow quicker screening of lower risk passengers. The possibilities are so tantalizing from a security perspective that great care and discipline must be sustained to respect the privacy and civil rights protections, which if breeched, could shut down the program.

By the end of 2005, I realized how essential it was that the TSA connect its actual field operations to the information available from the intelligence community. Charlie Allen taught me that our operations could be intel-driven, but the idea that most relevant intelligence should prompt action struck many in that community as atypical. The Central Intelligence Agency provides policy makers with invaluable insights into terrorist planning, but their reports are almost always couched in politic words that will cover the agency whether an attack actually occurs or the information turns out to be completely bogus. Here again is the issue of accountability. Virtually every terrorist activity reported in a briefing carries a qualifier that suggests that action against a particular plot is not quite ripe, leaving out or dancing around one of the big-three words: "specific," "credible," and "imminent." As a result, intelligence briefings can become thrilling, elaborate story-time breaks for government executives that rarely result in action.

Instead of spinning tales from a distant fantasyland, Bill Gaches, Tom Hoopes, Keith Kauffman, and Joe Salvator spent their briefings with TSA executives evaluating and suggesting implementation of specific security actions—whatever was appropriate—throughout airport operations, technology development, strategic thinking, even media relations. Integrating incoming intelligence and outgoing activity is not as easy as it sounds. We have become accustomed to basing preventive actions on verified data, largely because evasive actions cost money or are inconvenient. A nimble strategy of constantly moving, ever-changing security actions respects budgets and doesn't require intelligence providers to meet an unreasonably high level of precision in order for something to be done to address a particular threat. Focusing our efforts through the prism of intelligence was just one way to connect the TSA to various transportation-related networks, an approach that can increase effectiveness exponentially.

Similarly, George Zarur, Ed Kittel, and others were able to plug the TSA into the security opportunities presented by the scientific community. When

Marjeta Jager reached out to connect the EU and US security strategies, it strengthened us both. Frontline workers like Jameka Merriweather and Jeremy Trujillo were powerful catalysts to connect TSOs with one another for the success of the TSA's mission.

At the specific airport level, the TSA developed a variety of flexible security layers, such as the behavior-detection force championed by Carl Maccario. Andrew Cox's "Playbook" strategy, which sprung from his interest in complexity theory, would provide local law enforcement, airport employees, and the airport-based TSA workers a virtual encyclopedia of possible security actions and let them choose a customized and frequently changing set of counterterror measures. Over the entire network, these specific security actions at individual airports would be different and therefore unpredictable by a terrorist conducting surveillance. What's more, it would allow these semi-autonomous parts to come together as a holistic security network, one with a value greater than the sum of its parts—and one completely alien to the TSA's traditional top-down regulatory regimes. The concept delivered excellent results when tested at airports like Saint Louis, but got watered down in implementation when headquarters tried to dictate the plays and some airports recoiled against the perceived intrusion in local operations.

Connecting networks and engaging people are cheap and effective measures, but ones that run contrary to what America—and much of the TSA bureaucracy—expects from our security operations. Many of us still imagine security as a set of common-sense, airtight rules bolstered by powerful technologies, not a series of connected networks working toward overcoming a terrorist risk that is nonlinear and ever changing. And this dilemma brings us back to Northwest Flight 253, the Detroit-bound aircraft targeted for destruction on Christmas Day 2009.

The incident, in which a twenty-three-year-old Nigerian named Umar Farouk Abdulmutallab successfully smuggled a bomb on board a plane in his underwear, revealed multiple cracks in our system on the part of both our intelligence community and the international aviation security network. But in the subsequent hue and cry and search for someone to blame, something escaped public attention. When Flight 253 began its initial descent, the "Underwear Bomber" ignited his bomb, causing it to do little more than smoke and burn him and some upholstery. This was not simply a lucky escape.

In 2006, based on the intelligence developed by British security services, we realized that liquid hydrogen-peroxide bombs had joined shoe bombs as al-Qaeda's weapons of choice. The liquid bombs were powerful enough to destroy a plane, were undetectable by primary security screening, and relatively easy to source. With this in mind, TSA's aviation security networked partners went to work. Again thanks to Marjeta's leadership at the EU, the international community adopted the 3-1-1 restrictions to protect against liquid-based bombs, and airports including Amsterdam's Schiphol, where Flight 253 originated, began checking for shoe bombs. Once these top weapons were off the table, al-Qaeda's bomb makers were forced toward the fringes of explosives effectiveness. These technicians—including, I believe, Zubair al-Masri—researched and developed a powder-based bomb that could fit into a pair of men's briefs. But the device had one major flaw: to be small enough to pass through the security measures undetected, the explosive could not detonate, let alone destroy, an aircraft.

At the TSA we were aware that the scope of security actions needed to stave off all types of underwear bombs and a myriad other serious but not catastrophic avenues of attack was simply not sustainable. During my tenure, we considered implementating the current very intrusive law-enforcement–style pat down, and rejected it on the risk-management basis that the security benefit was not worth the negative blowback and operational difficulty. While I do not criticize the TSA's holiday-season emergency decision in 2010 to institute the intrusive pat downs, I believe that they do now need to be replaced by a combination of trace detection, random measures, and body scans.

The TSA looks at all bomb types and other methods of attack and brings scientific analysis into the risk-management debate. Based on the results of painstaking work by George Zarur, the National Laboratories, Ed Kittel, as well as scientists at the Federal Bureau of Investigation and the Department of Defense, we were reasonably sure of what would destroy an aircraft and what would not. There are many factors that go into the equation. The type of explosive is important, but so is the exact formula and the techniques necessary to prepare, store, and transport the explosive. Size matters a great deal. A bomb of x size might be catastrophic, but a bomb of x minus 20 percent might not even be incapable of damaging an aircraft. The radical difference in outcomes between these two bombs is critical in determining what kind of scanning equipment should be used for two reasons. First, knowing what x is for each explosive allows TSA to test and know which scanners are able to find quantities that could be dangerous and take measures to mitigate those threats. Second, it may cost a great deal more to require machines that find explosives down to x minus 20 percent than it does to require that they detect x. Because it allows informed, risk-based purchasing decisions, knowing x is vital for security as well as budgeting purposes.

George was able to get credible answers to the x-question as an added benefit of his independent review of whether only MRI-type scanners should be allowed. Three National Labs, Lawrence Livermore, Los Alamos, and Sandia did exhaustive testing in close cooperation with Boeing to calculate accurate x values, using modeling techniques developed in the nuclear weapons program as well as live fire tests, or, more informally, blowing up objects including retired aircraft fuselage. Because the values of x were so sensitive, the whole exercise became a compartmented classified program codenamed Project Newton.

Soon, the National Labs' rigorously peer-reviewed process produced values that dramatically differed from our current working numbers on the mass amount needed for a variety of explosives to yield catastrophic results. These x values had been established in 2001 by the FAA's Atlantic City labs and had informed the government's purchase of hundreds of the bulky, million dollar MRI-type scanners. But Project Newton revealed that the explosives charge that so concerned the FAA after 9/11 turned out not able to knock down the principal aircraft types in use by 2007. The George Zarur-led National Labs study also suggested that our original certification standards might have left open an unexpected vulnerability (which has now been closed). Had we known in 2001 what Project Newton later showed, perhaps the government would have included ATs to compete with the MRI-type scanners and saved billions of dollars in acquisition, installation, and maintenance costs.

For TSA, this was earthshaking data, but the seemingly straightforward, if lengthy, exercise of updating the x value eventually became politicized. Faced with this correction of their earlier work, equipment vendors and scientists sympathetic to the FAA's earlier efforts set off a highly contentious counterattack. Meanwhile, lobbyists appeared on Capitol Hill whispering that a secret project underway called "Project Newton" threatened to undermine national security. I was pushing hard to change the checked baggage scanning certification standard to reflect Project Newton's findings, a move that would have kicked off a world-wide competition for innovative technology solutions. In the midst of the issue's politicization and the obfuscation of peer-reviewed scientific data, my efforts to upend the status quo never came to fruition. As I left TSA, the National Labs and Atlantic City Labs were set to run analysis on smaller regional jets as a coordinated collegial effort. Back in California, however, I learned that the money to move forward had been reallocated to other projects, shutting down Project Newton, TSA's most promising technology effort.

Aside from the explosive-specific x value, placement of a bomb represents another value that can be more important than you think. The belly of the aircraft is hardened for structural safety reasons, and there is a lot of deadening material in the form of cargo and suitcases. A relatively larger bomb is needed there, and that makes it easier for us to find them in air cargo or checked baggage. Upstairs, next to the window, above the fuel tank is a good place for a bomb attack but, as happened with Abdulmutallab, the price of getting to that perfect placement was that he could do so only by smuggling onboard a bomb that would not destroy the aircraft. Without the shoe and liquid restrictions, there is no doubt in my mind that al-Qaeda would have used one of those bomb types on December 25, and we would have lost that flight. A security system that leaves open the real possibility of a non-lethal bomb (or any other dangerous object) making it on board is counterintuitive, but embracing risk management means making these choices. The situation on Christmas Day 2009 was undeniably ugly—neither the bomber nor the bomb should have made it to seat 19A—but the hated shoe policy and the disrespected baggie-based security measure ultimately, in my opinion, saved Flight 253. Al-Qaeda was forced to use a bomb that did not and, I believe, could not work.

One thing is clear about the terror threat: it will continue. In the time since I left the TSA, the focus of al-Qaeda's plotting against the West has expanded to the Arabian Peninsula and east Africa. There is no continent exempt from al-Qaeda activity, and no matter what organizational form it takes, the ranks of radical Islamic terrorists will continue to be a threat to our society. Tom Hoopes told me in a 2007 briefing about the European cells that seemed to proliferate with every passing week. He commented about my Zubair obsession that it didn't matter whether he even existed; the key thing was that it gave me a focal point to visualize a person working to penetrate our defenses. There are, as Charlie Allen once told me, a hundred Zubairs, and I believe him. European investigators have pulled the threads of what may be the best-organized and longest-existing network of recruiters. We would be remiss in believing that al-Qaeda networks do not exist in the United States. Abdullahi Ahmed, Anwar al-Alaki, Adam Yahiye Gadahn, and Bryant Neal

Vinas are all Americans who have taken action on behalf of al-Qaeda, and we know of dozens of second-generation Somali American youths who have had terror training. We need to acknowledge that we are missing the key link in the radicalization process, and that we must work to strengthen our domestic communities as well as our international soft-power efforts.

Over the past ten years, most Americans have had extensive personal experience with the TSA, but this familiarity hasn't necessarily created a harmonious connection. The agency has repeatedly come under criticism—some of it quite valid—from Congress, the media, bloggers, and travelers. One of the oft-repeated suggestions is that we should adopt the "Israeli method." The Israelis do provide impressive security, but one of the pillars of their security system is strong public support. Israeli citizens accept the continued existence of a common enemy that requires them to tolerate the necessary inconveniences required by their government's security policies. In order to sustain a similarly broad national security policy here, it needs to be understood and actively supported by a large majority of the American people.

Resilience is a key attribute of complexity-based networks, and when this is combined with a stalwart public, it becomes an additional security layer of enormous power. The British call this stoic but vital approach "Keeping calm and carrying on." Likewise, with a mortal threat hanging over them, the Israelis do not clamor for ironclad security solutions. They know that terror plots are ongoing and that some will be successful, but they remain relatively unfazed. In America any attack, no matter how small, is much more likely to lead to a series of public recriminations and a witch hunt. Demanding accountability is important, but expecting 100-percent bulletproof security is simply setting up a system for failure.

Security is a series of trade-offs with plenty of room for public debate. Allow everyone to leave his or her shoes on and the line moves faster, but maybe a shoe bomb gets through. Compel every passenger to go through a full-body scan, pat down, and questioning and the plane will be safer, but the wait times exponentially longer. Hire enough TSOs to move every passenger through within two minutes but you add hundreds of millions to the taxpayer's bill. I hope to encourage more Americans to engage TSA's policies constructively, neither in awe of the agency nor the threat we face, but with the clear realization that we are debating nothing less than our own survival. When we achieve a national consensus on our security strategy, we then have a chance to sustain the effort with steady support. Even the best security measures, unless resolutely sustained, like the Air Marshals pre-9/11, wither away to our peril.

It has been ten years since 9/11. In that same time, the TSA has spun into overdrive, careening through misadventure and occasional, often-unsung moments of heroism. America sprang into action on September 11, responding to the largest national emergency in a generation, but we cannot continue to draw on that energy permanently. And because the terror threat is not diminishing, we must find a sustainable balance between public support and TSA security measures that reliably get the job done.

A system where travelers hold their breath in silent dismay when tiptoeing past beleaguered TSOs doesn't provide the security we need. Smart security does not happen inside a pressure cooker among unhappy participants. We made it ten years without another terror catastrophe, and that was not a given—so in the binary judgment of counterterrorism, the Transportation Security Administration has been a success. We can, however, do better. In 2001, faced with unprecedented attacks, we reacted swiftly and decisively. It is now time to take the initiative, stretch our imagination, and accelerate innovation in order to move toward a lasting security system of which we can all be proud.

GLOSSARY OF NAMES

GOVERNMENT PERSONNEL AND ASSOCIATES

Allen, Charlie	DHS head of Intelligence, CIA legend
Basham, Ralph	TSA start-up, Secret Service Director
Brill, Stephen	Registered Traveler entrepreneur
Brown, Dana	Head of Federal Air Marshals Service, TSA
Burns, Bob	TSO, Blogger Bob
Cannatti, Ashley	TSA start-up, Counselor
Chertoff, Michael	DHS Secretary
Clyde, Alison	TSA policy, assistant to Administrator
Cox, Andrew	Complexity Theory expert and TSA strategist
Dorn, Jenna	Mass transit Administrator, DOT
Ekman, Paul	Behavior scientist
Gaches, Bill	former NSA, TSA Intelligence head
Garvey, Jane	former FAA head, DOT
Hall, Bill	former Port Authority, TSA FSD at JFK
Hawley, Kip	TSA start-up advisor, fourth TSA Administrator
Hoopes, Tom	TSA Intelligence top analyst
Houlihan, Kevin	TSA start-up head of Operations
Howe, Ellen	TSA head of Public Affairs
Jackson, Michael	Deputy Secretary DOT, DHS
Jager, Marjeta	European Union security executive
Jamison, Robert	TSA Deputy Administrator
Kair, Lee	TSA Acquisitions, Operations head
Kauffman, Keith	TSA intelligence head
Kittel, Ed	TSA explosives expert
Lamoreux, Francois	European Union Director General
Loy, Jim	second TSA Administrator
Magaw, John	first TSA Administrator
McGowan, Mo	TSA Operations executive
Merriweather, Jameka	TSO, "Engage!" training leader
Maccario, Carl	Behavior detection security expert, TSO
Miller, Hans	TSA start-up, BWI project
Mineta, Norm	DOT Secretary

Moore, Calvin	TSA manager, "Engage!" leader
Oberman, Justin	TSA start-up, Identity programs head
Pankow, Walter*	former DoD, FAM start-up exec
Quinn, Tom	TSA start-up, FAM head
Resing, Dave	TSA explosives expert
Restovich, Mike	TSA start-up and Operations head
Robinson, Mike	TSA FSD in New Orleans
Rowe, Stephanie	TSA Consultant, Head of identity programs
Rossides, Gale	TSA start-up, Culture champion
Ryan, Ronald*	UK Security Services official
Salvator, Joe	TSA Intelligence deputy, FBI
Smith, Ben	AT Kearney consultant, TSA start-up
Stahl, Lesley	*60 Minutes* Correspondent, CBS News
Stone, David	third TSA Administrator
Sullivan, Mark	Secret Service Director, DHS
Tompkinson, Niki	UK transportation security head, Dft
Townsend, Frances	Homeland Security Advisor to President
Trujillo, Jeremy	TSO, Advisory Council member, TSA
Williams, Rebekah	DHS Advance, TSA Chief of Staff
Zarur, George	Scientist, TSA technology advisor

ALLEGED TERRORIST CHARACTERS

Abdulrahman Hilal Hussein,	the Austrian-born alleged al-Qaeda operative who is a major character, used multiple names listed immediately below. All of those names refer to the same individual.

Abdulrahman Hilal Hussein
Abu Zubair al Masri
Imran
Waqas

Abdel Basset al-Megrahi	head of security for Libya Arab Airlines
Abdullah Ahmed Ali (AAA)	UK liquid bomb plotter
Abdullah Youssef Hussein*	father of Abdulrahman Hilal Hussein
Abdullahi Ahmed	alleged 2011 American Somali suicide bomber
Abdulrahman Hilal Hussein	Austrian-born alleged AQ operative
Abu Abdulrahman al-Muhajir	AQ explosives expert
Abu Hamza Rabia	AQ head of external operations
Abu Ubaydah al-Masri	liquids plot, AQ head of External Operations
Adam Yahiye Gadahn	American born, alleged AQ spokesperson
Adem Yilmaz	Gelowicz friend, co-plotter "Sauerland cell"
Ahmad Shah Masud	chief of Northern Alliance
Aleem Nassir	German citizen, alleged AQ operative
Ayman Zawahiri	AQ leader
Bekkay Harrach	German AQ operative 2008–2011
Bryant Neal Vinas	American-born convert, AQ operative

---

* pseudonym

Eric Breininger	Harrach colleague, German AQ operative
Fritz Gelowicz	German "Sauerland cell" leader
Hammad Khurshid	Danish AQ plotter
Harun Fazul	long-time AQ figure, especially Africa
Mohammed al-Masri*	al-Qaeda's head of external operations
Mohammed Zillur Rahman	Glidepath* Operative
Naji al-Libi*	AQ explosives expert
Najibullah Zazi	Denver-based alleged AQ operative
Nihad Cosic	Bosnian AQ operative
Omer Ozdemir	German colleague of Aleem Nassir
Ramzi Yousef	1993 World Trade Center bomb maker
Rangzieb Ahmed	Glidepath* operative
Rashid Rauf	UK citizen, liquids plot leader for AQ
Sheikh Said	very senior AQ official
Shirwa Ahmed	first American suicide bomber
Sonja Blinzler	alleged wife of Abdulrahman Hilal Hussein
Umar Farouk Abdulmatullab	Underwear Bomber

---

* pseudonym

GLOSSARY OF TERMS

AFSD FOR SCREENING
The overall TSA manager for passenger screening operations at an airport is called the Assistant Federal Security Director—Screening.

AMALGAM (INTELLIGENCE PROGRAM)
Special Classified program run by DHS to track terrorist leads. "Amalgam" is a pseudonym.

AMERICAN AIRLINES FLIGHT 77
Hijacked and crashed into the Pentagon on 9/11. 184 victims. The TSA Administrator's office looks directly onto the crash site.

ATX MACHINE
Scanning technology that gets its name from "advanced technology" x-ray and uses more than one source of radiation to assist in two and three-dimensional images of items in bags. The software is as important as the equipment parts in generating usable information from the scans.

ATSA   AVIATION AND TRANSPORTATION SECURITY ACT
Signed into law on November 19, 2001, ATSA created TSA and gave it most of TSA's authorities and responsibilities. Its legal cite is: 49 USC 40101.

BASS   BEHAVIOR ANALYSIS SCREENING SYSTEM
A behavioral-based screening system introduced in Boston.

BDOS   BEHAVIOR DETECTION OFFICERS
TSA behavioral analysis specialists are called BDOs. The program started in Boston and became a national program in 2006. BDOs can be in uniform or undercover.

BUILDING 19 AT THE NAC
The Department of Homeland Security's headquarters is known as the "Nebraska Avenue Complex" and sits in upper northwest Washington, DC near the National Cathedral. Building 19 is one of the main locations for senior level meetings and offices.

CBP CUSTOMS AND BORDER PROTECTION (DHS)

Dating back to 1789, the CBP now is a core CT agency within DHS charged with protecting the United States and its borders from dangerous people and objects. TSA works closely with CBP and they frequently conduct programs together at international airports.

C4

A type of military grade high explosive containing RDX and known as a "plastic explosive." TSA's screening equipment is highly effective at identifying its characteristics.

CASIO F91W–1

A digital watch with timer accessories reported to be a favorite of terrorist training programs.

USCG US COAST GUARD (DHS)

The Coast Guard is the only military organization in DHS and since 1790 has had the mission to safeguard maritime interests. The Coast Guard was a frequent partner with TSA on counterterrorism operations.

CODE WORD

A special Classified program of the highest sensitivity can be given a "code word" such as "Amalgam" and only people specifically cleared are allowed access to its information. The common context would be, "You better check with the Office of Intelligence, that topic is part of a Code Word program."

CT COMPUTED TOMOGRAPHY

Usually referred to as a "CAT Scan" in the medical field, computed tomography uses x-ray images taken by rotating the x-ray source 360 degrees (like a donut) around the object scanned. The software that interprets all that data is a critical component of a CT system's effectiveness.

CT COUNTER-TERRORISM

There are many organizations and sub-organizations in the US government, including TSA, who have counter-terrorism responsibility. Taken together, although housed in different institutions (like the FBI, Department of Defense, etc.), they are called the CT community.

DCAA DEFENSE CONTRACT AUDIT AGENCY

The Defense Department contracts out more business than anyone else in the federal government and has developed an expertise in managing government contracts. The DCAA is a component of the DoD. TSA called on the DCAA for help in evaluating its program and many of the TSA acquisition staff came from the DCAA.

DELETE-O-METER (TSA BLOG)

A core principle of the TSA blog is to be credible and transparent. There are submissions to the blog that are threats or spam or otherwise inappropriate to post and therefore are deleted. The Delete-O-Meter reports on the blog the number of submissions that are deleted, giving the reader an idea of the TSA blog's post/delete ratio and therefore a reference point on whether the TSA is being draconian in their editorial process.

DEN   DOMESTIC EVENTS NETWORK

On 9/11/01, the FAA Ops Center started a conference call with the other principal players involved with CT activities in the wake of the attacks of that day. That line is still active today and connects players like the FAA with its air traffic operations, NORTH-COM, the FBI, and TSA to each other real-time. If one visits the Freedom Center or other operational facility involved in aviation security, an intermittent tone is heard on the public address system to indicate that the DEN is live. In case of an incident, any party can "unmute" in an instant and be talking with everybody with the capacity to act.

DFT (UK)   DEPARTMENT FOR TRANSPORT

The British Department for transport, headed by the Minister for Transport, has responsibility for aviation security issues. It is a primarily regulatory role and works closely with the European Union aviation security authorities and is a close partner with TSA.

DOD   US DEPARTMENT OF DEFENSE

The largest agency of the US government, DoD's mission is to assure the national security of the United States and receives more than $500 billion annually from the Congress for that responsibility. DoD is a major player in all aspects of CT, including its overseas operations as well as a formidable Homeland Security Command called NORTHCOM.

DHS   US DEPARTMENT OF HOMELAND SECURITY

Created in 2003 to coordinate the many government efforts working on the domestic counterterrorism mission, DHS combined twenty-two component agencies and now has over 200,000 employees and a budget of over $50 billion. TSA is one component. Other major components are CBP, FEMA, ICE, USCIS, USSS, and USCG.

DOT   DEPARTMENT OF TRANSPORTATION

DOT is responsible for the nation's transportation system and one of its major components is the Federal Aviation System (FAA). Aviation security, including counter-terrorism aspects, was the responsibility of the FAA and DOT on 9/11. Under ATSA, the Secretary of Transportation was charged with starting up the new TSA, the largest new government organization since World War II, in under one year. DOT accomplished that task in 2002 and handed TSA over to the new Department of Homeland Security in 2003. They remain integrally involved in the CT community and TSA.

DNI   DIRECTOR OF NATIONAL INTELLIGENCE

Created in 2004 to oversee and direct the US Intelligence Community, the Director of National Intelligence is the President's chief advisor on intelligence matters. The NCTC is within the DNI's organization.

DHS OPERATIONS CENTER

Located in the Nebraska Avenue Complex at DHS headquarters, the National Operations Center (NOC), is the central point where active operational information is consolidated and delivered to senior DHS officials like the Secretary and Deputy Secretary. The NOC works closely with DHS components' individual operations centers like the TSA's Freedom Center.

EGYPTIAN ISLAMIC JIHAD

An Egyptian radical Islamist group headed by Ayman Zawahiri, the Egyptian Islamic Jihad merged with al-Qaeda in 2001.

EA   EMERGENCY AMENDMENT
A TSA directive to compel airlines operating flights toward the United States to adopt certain security measures. See SD.

ENGAGE! (TSA TRAINING EXERCISE)
Engage! was a breakthrough training-based effort introduced in 2008 to equip TSOs with the skills and confidence needed to effectively apply risk management principles in their daily jobs. Unlike other principally teacher-student training Engage! relied on non-traditional techniques and required interactive participation and dealt with smuggling techniques, explosives' characteristics, behavioral cues, the use of teamwork, and attempts by terrorists to evade the standard operating procedures. All TSA passenger-screening personnel received the training.

EU   EUROPEAN UNION
Comprising twenty-seven European Member States, the EU has primary legal authority over a variety of issues. The European Commission, located in Brussels, has executive responsibility. There is a Directorate within the Commission with responsibility for aviation security. TSA works very closely with EU-wide security officials as well as those of the Member States, although the EU is the primary regulatory body for all Members.

EDS   EXPLOSIVE DETECTION SYSTEM
ATSA required the use of "explosives detection systems" at US airports and gave TSA the responsibility to install them. The term does not refer to a particular technology and relies on TSA to use its judgment on what machines and/or techniques meets the "EDS" standard.

FAA   FEDERAL AVIATION ADMINISTRATION (DOT)
A component of the Department of Transportation, the FAA is the nation's aviation authority and is responsible for aviation safety and the air traffic control system among other things. Prior to 9/11, its responsibilities included aviation security. ATSA assigned those responsibilities to TSA.

FATA   FEDERALLY ADMINISTERED TRIBAL AREAS
Part of Pakistan in the northwest of the country bordering Afghanistan, the FATA is believed to be the location of al-Qaeda elements.

FAMS   FEDERAL AIR MARSHALS SERVICE (TSA)(DHS)
Federal Air Marshals are often known as FAMs and their organization was significantly upgraded in quality and number after 9/11. FAMs are believed to number in the thousands and cover flights on a worldwide basis. They are among the most highly trained CT personnel in the US government. FAMs also support the CT mission in a variety of ways outside their flying duties.

FBI   FEDERAL BUREAU OF INVESTIGATION
The FBI is the most visible federal law enforcement agency and has responsibility for investigations into potential terrorist activities. The FBI has task forces in most metropolitan areas that include the other federal, state, local, and tribal law enforcement agencies in the area. They are called Joint Terrorism Task Forces (JTTFs). TSA, through the Federal Air Marshals, has a member in virtually all of them.

FEMA FEDERAL EMERGENCY MANAGEMENT ADMINISTRATION (DHS)

Operating out of DHS, FEMA is charged with the national response to disasters occurring in the United States. FEMA is integrally connected with state, local and tribal officials and coordinates among other federal agencies (like TSA) in providing support when needed.

FLETC FEDERAL LAW ENFORCEMENT TRAINING CENTER (DHS) HEADQUARTERED IN GLYNCO, GEORGIA

FLETC is the interagency law enforcement training organization for 90 federal agencies.

FSD FEDERAL SECURITY DIRECTOR (TSA) (DHS)

Federal Security Directors are the senior TSA officials in a locality, usually a major airport. FSDs have extraordinary authority to coordinate CT activities in the transportation domain.

FIDO PAXPOINT

A gun-like handheld device manufactured by ICx Technologies that can detect threat liquids, even inside sealed containers. They were first deployed by TSA in 2007.

FK AUSTRIA WIEN (SOCCER)

A professional soccer team located in Vienna, FK Austria Wien is one of the most successful teams in that country. The team is used as a proxy for a good professional team that a soccer fan from Vienna might reasonably have followed.

FREEDOM CENTER (TSA)

The Freedom Center, formerly known as the "TSOC" (for Transportation Security Operations Center), is TSA's high tech operational information hub located in a large non-descript building near Dulles Airport in the Washington, DC area. It has instant worldwide reach and frequently houses interagency efforts to coordinate events of national significance. The Freedom Center is the hub of actions related to on-going security incidents and operates 24 hours a day, 7 days a week, and 365 days a year.

FREIGHT ASSESSMENT SYSTEM ("FAS")

An effort to use risk management in the airfreight security context, the Freight Assessment was a large software effort to track freight information.

GSA GENERAL SERVICES ADMINISTRATION

The GSA manages government workplaces, including those of TSA. GSA also provides assistance in sharing best management practices among government agencies.

GAO GOVERNMENT ACCOUNTABILITY OFFICE

The investigative arm of Congress, frequently asked to do studies on the effectiveness of TSA programs.

HELLFIRE AGM-114 MISSILES

A Hellfire is a precision air-to-ground missile, sometimes fired from drone aircraft.

HMTD HEXAMETHYLENE TRIPEROXIDE DIAMINE (EXPLOSIVE)

HMTD is a common peroxide-based home-made explosive with a white powdery appearance.

HUMINT   HUMAN INTELLIGENCE

Intelligence people refer to agents as "human intelligence" (Humint) in contrast to electronic intercepts that are called "signal intelligence" (Sigint).

"I AM TSA"

A TSA effort launched in 2005 to make the point that TSOs were the people who most determined TSA's overall effectiveness and that rather than looking up the chain of command for instructions (and accountability), TSO's could step up and use their training and experience to provide TSA's most effective security.

IDEA FACTORY, THE (TSA)

Modeled after Dell Computer's *IdeaStorm,* the Idea Factory, introduced in 2007, was instrumental in opening up communications laterally across all of TSA. It was the first all-agency, non-hierarchical communications tool to discuss and vet ideas and suggestions. There is a voting component to the Idea Factory so that the most popular suggestions rise to the top.

ICE   US IMMIGRATION AND CUSTOMS ENFORCEMENT (DHS)

ICE came to DHS in 2003, bringing with it the investigative functions of the Immigration and Naturalization Service (INS). ICE investigates and enforces immigrations and customs laws. ICE also has extensive responsibility in cyber crime and child predator cases. The FAM Service was a component of ICE from 2003 to 2005.

INFO CENTER, THE (TSA)

An information hub like the Freedom Center, except for non-operational information, the Information Center provided a central place to get definitive accurate information about internal TSA data.

INSPECTOR   TSA

In addition to FAMs and TSOs, TSA has a force of Inspectors who perform regulatory and security duties away from airport checkpoints. Air Cargo, perimeter security, rail, mass transit, and anywhere in the world with an airport serving the United States are all venues where a TSA Inspector might be seen. In 2008, several Inspector teams with advanced technology were invited to European airports and provided support to local authorities.

INTELLIGENCE WATCH   TSA

Located in a vaulted room inside the vaulted TSA Office of Intelligence spaces in TSA's headquarters, the Watch is responsible for tracking incoming intelligence information and alerting appropriate officials. The Watch has a live audio and video feed to the Freedom Center operating 24 hours a day, 7 days a week, and 365 days a year.

K-9 (OR CANINE) BOMB DETECTION TEAMS

TSA has an extensive K-9 program and trains explosives detection teams for TSA, but also Amtrak, local police and transit systems. TSA has over four hundred teams itself and they are used in airports, air cargo operations, rail and transit environments.

KNOWN SHIPPER PROGRAM

The Known Shipper Program is an air cargo security effort to ensure that air cargo companies know who is giving them packages. It is only a small part of the overall air cargo program that includes all packages being physically screened before getting on a US flight.

MI5 (UK)

MI5, otherwise known as the "Security Service," has responsibility for protecting the UK against terrorism and other threats. MI5 has been a close and effective partner for US partners, including the TSA.

NAC   NEBRASKA AVENUE COMPLEX, PRONOUNCED "KNACK."

DHS headquarters campus in northwest Washington, DC near the National Cathedral.

NATIONAL ADVISORY COUNCIL TSA

Created in November 2005, TSOs and AFSDs-Screening from around the country were appointed as an advisory group to the TSA Administrator. Meeting quarterly the TSA's top leadership, they led the implementation of workforce initiatives like pay for performance, new uniforms, career progression, and benefits improvements.

NCR   NATIONAL CAPITAL REGION

A term used to refer to the greater Washington DC metroplex. An example would be, "The Freedom Center houses the NCR airspace protection effort."

NCTC   NATIONAL COUNTERTERRORISM CENTER

Created in 2004 to be the place where all terrorism-related threat information comes together, the NCTC is located in a new secure complex at Liberty Crossing in suburban Virginia. It is staffed with more than 500 personnel with a substantial number detailed from many CT agencies, including TSA. The Director of the NCTC reports to the DNI and also the President on CT planning. The NCTC chairs the morning CT SVTC profiled in *Permanent Emergency.*

NATIONAL GUARD

The National Guard has been a part of America's defense for more than 350 years and is a reserve force made up of individual state units. The Guard is made up of citizen-soldiers who hold civilian jobs in addition to their Guard duty. After 9/11, about 50,000 Guard service members added security to the nation's airports for about six months. The Air National Guard provides fighter aircraft support to aviation security incidents as coordinated with NORTHCOM.

NATIONAL LABS

Under the US Department of Energy, there are sixteen loosely affiliated National Laboratories who undertake scientific research under the program. Lawrence Livermore, Los Alamos, and Sandia National Labs worked with TSA to provide world class and independent research and analysis to a variety of explosives issues and detection technology.

NSA   NATIONAL SECURITY AGENCY

To say the NSA is enigmatic is literally true since a major part of their mission involves code making and code breaking. The NSA is under the larger DoD and operates out of Ft. Meade, Maryland. NSA's signals intelligence mission is a vital part of the overall CT effort and TSA derived inestimable benefit from timely reporting of even fragmentary intelligence nuggets. The NSA also has a major role in cyber security issues.

NO-FLY LIST

A very small sub-set of the government's large TSDB, no-flys are named individuals who represent a serious danger to attack US aviation activities. In 2009, there were roughly two thousand people on the list, although, because of aliases and name variations, the actual list of names was much larger. Over ninety percent of the individuals were foreign nationals located abroad. Until TSA's Secure Flight program came online in 2009, airlines all over the world received the no-fly list and performed unevenly in that task. Accordingly, many thousands of people a day were flagged by the airlines as possible matches to a watch list. Although their only connection to the watch list was that some part of their name matched somebody's who really was on a watch list, many thought that TSA had them watch listed. The No-fly list and other aviation watch lists (like the Selectee list, used for suspected terror facilitators who were not themselves likely to be an attacker) are managed by the Terrorist Screening Center, which is under the auspices of the FBI.

NORTHWEST FLIGHT 253

On Christmas Day 2009, Umar Farouk Abdulmutallab had a concealed explosive device in his underwear and boarded Northwest Flight 253 in Amsterdam, headed for Detroit. The device went off but the only person injured was Abdulmutallab. The incident started a renewed focus on concealed body bombs.

OPERATION GLIDEPATH

An intelligence code word to describe a 2005 al-Qaeda plot believed to have been directed against the United States and the UK. "Glidepath" is a pseudonym. The plot was disrupted after its senior al Qaeda sponsor was killed in a drone attack.

OPERATION OVERT

Op Overt is what the UK Security Services called the al-Qaeda plot to use liquid hydrogen peroxide bombs to bring down commercial airliners bound from the UK to the United States and Canada. The plot was disrupted on August 9, 2006.

OPERATION PLAYBOOK

Playbook was a TSA program to give more flexibility to airport officials including TSA and local law enforcement based in a given airport. The idea was for them to select a series of security measures for a day or week in advance that would vary according to their resources and security needs. Playbook was not for the passenger checkpoint but was meant to cover the rest of the airport environment.

OPERATION TRIDENT

Trident was an FBI-run operation to monitor potential al-Qaeda threats originating in North America. Trident is a pseudonym.

PORT AUTHORITY OF NEW YORK AND NEW JERSEY

The Port Authority, as it is called, is a joint New York-New Jersey effort to manage the extensive transportation infrastructure in the New York City metroplex. The Port Authority operated security for the World Trade Center complex and has law enforcement jurisdiction in La Guardia, JFK, and Newark airports, as well as area bridges and tunnels.

PREDATOR DRONE

A Predator is one type of unmanned aerial vehicle used by the US government for remote surveillance and/or missile attack. The aircraft typically feeds information back to a control center (that can be thousands of miles away) and might carry several precision guided missiles. The Reaper is another, newer drone model.

Q-FERS QUESTIONS FOR THE RECORD

After a Congressional hearing, the Committee Staff usually sends its witness a series of questions that must be answered in writing. TSA, with a full schedule of Congressional oversight committees, maintained a pace of about two hearings a month in 2008. TSA staff would have to prepare the written responses to the questions for the record submitted after each hearing.

RT   REGISTERED TRAVELER PROGRAM

ATSA, in creating the agency in 2001, called for TSA to test a "trusted traveler" program whereby lower risk passengers received expedited screening and TSA spend more time and money on those with higher risk. An initial program in 2004 at five airports tested the use of biometric IDs and was largely successful although nothing changed in the screening process. Subsequently, TSA's role was to review the security aspects of the program while private sector companies determined what to offer in the market. The RT program ended in 2009.

SAC   SPECIAL AGENT IN CHARGE (LAW ENFORCEMENT TERM)

Law enforcement agencies like the FBI and Secret Service have offices in major cities and the person in charge is called the SAC. TSA's Federal Air Marshal organization uses the same structure and has SACs for major hubs around the United States.

SAUERLAND CREW   GERMAN AL-QAEDA TERRORIST PLOTTERS

After a group of al-Qaeda-affiliated plotters, led by Fritz Gelowicz, were arrested in September, 2007, the German media referred to the group as the Sauerland crew, based on where they were from. The arrests were a major news item in Germany since this was the first time that homegrown Germans were involved in such a large-scale attack believed to be targeting Germany.

SOP   STANDARD OPERATING PROCEDURE

The SOP is actually many different sets of detailed instructions aimed at making sure that TSA's large distributed workforce has common guidelines on how to deliver effective security. There are separate SOPs for checked baggage screening as well as passenger screening and they typically specify in great detail exactly what must be done. An SOP could be "mitigate risk" or it could be a several hundred-page document requiring exact hand motions and foot placement. SOPs are necessary for quality control and consistency but sometimes are criticized for inhibiting individual discretion based on training and experience.

SD   SECURITY DIRECTIVE

TSA has authority (granted in ATSA) to issue SDs to airlines, which require certain security actions by airlines. An example would be that before boarding passengers, a member of the flight crew must check in different areas of the aircraft to check for hidden items. SDs are supposed to be used only in urgent situations because there is no room for give and take between the airline and TSA. SDs are an extraordinary tool to compel needed action immediately to all flights operating in the United States. The international version of SDs are called Emergency Amendments (EAs).

SECRET SERVICE   UNITED STATES SECRET SERVICE (USSS) (DHS)

The Secret Service provides security for the President and Vice President of the United States and a very limited number of other officials and dignitaries. The Secret Service also has other law enforcement investigative duties in cyber security and regarding counterfeiting. The Secret Service has a highly developed risk management system that they operationalize in their protection assignments in all kinds of places and hours, all over the world. TSA drew on people with Secret Service expertise in forming the agency. TSA's first head, John Magaw, was a former Director of the Secret Service. TSA provides TSOs, technology, and K-9 units to assist the Secret Service on an ongoing basis.

SECURE FLIGHT (TSA)
See "no-fly."

SVTC   SECURE VIDEO TELECONFERENCE, PRONOUNCED "CIVITS"
Classified information cannot be sent over standard telephone lines so a secured telephone, cleared for Secret and above, is called a STE and the videoconference is called a SVTC. A common context might be, "I'll have to call you back on a STE." "Are you ready for the 8:00 SVTC?"

STE   SECURE TERMINAL EQUIPMENT
See SVTC, above.

SSI   SECURITY-SENSITIVE INFORMATION
TSA uses a unique category of sensitive information called SSI that was developed out of the requirement to share security information confidentially but not subject to the same logistical burdens as required with Classified information. For instance, TSA has to communicate with thousands of airline and airport facilities around the world to keep everybody on the same page about current security requirements. It would be impractical in that situation to apply the procedures for Secret information, like storing documents in a vault. TSA designates material as SSI that it believes would be harmful to the national security if it were made public, but not so secret that it has to be Classified. A made-up example might be that TSA tells its TSOs to examine X percent of cameras at random.

SCIF   SENSITIVE COMPARTMENTED INFORMATION FACILITY
A SCIF can be a cramped room in the cellar or, in TSA's case, an entire floor of an office building. The key requirement is that the SCIF have strong access control and be free from any kind of eavesdropping. There are set standards and very highly classified information may only be discussed or read in a SCIF.

SHOESCANNER
The most unpopular TSA security measure has been taking off shoes. A device that could reliably detect threat material, like explosives, while passengers walk comfortably through, has been elusive. The ShoeScanner was one such promising, but ultimately unreliable, device. When shoes are looked at through an X-ray machine, it becomes easy to detect if there has been tampering with the shoe. Requiring everybody to take their shoes off makes it highly unlikely that terrorists will attempt such an attack. In 2006, and after, TSA believed that there was strong intelligence that terrorists intended to use shoe bombs to destroy aircraft. TSA also believed that terrorists could hide enough explosive material in a regular street shoe. Without a reliable way to select "100% safe" passengers who could leave shoes on, or a viable scanner to check shoes while still being worn, TSA chose to take the public ire but eliminate that category of terrorist weapons.

SIT ROOM   SITUATION ROOM
A Sit Room is where operational information is tracked and discussed. It is typically in a SCIF, or at least a secured space. Typical of a Sit Room would be video screens, SVTC and STE capability, workstations for staff, computer access, and conference tables. There are many Sit Rooms around government agencies, but the most notable is the Sit Room at the White House, located underground in the West Wing. TSA has a Sit Room near the Administrator's office and also one inside the TSA Intelligence SCIF.

SPOT   SCREENING PASSENGERS BY OBSERVATION TECHNIQUE

TSA's initial version of behavioral security screening was called SPOT. The technique was started in Boston and developed differently from a parallel program used by the Massachusetts State Police called, BASS. Because many people assume that behavioral screening is ethnic or other "profiling," TSA uses an objective behavioral rating system meant to safeguard passengers and BDOs from impermissible profiling. SPOT is much more sophisticated that looking for nervous people or other commonly encountered "tip-offs." The TSA program was expanded to include analysis of microfacial expressions in addition to the other more obvious actions. The combination of objective indicators and deep experience in what "normal" is in the airport context, enables an effective additional layer of security in airports or wherever screening takes place.

TSC   TERRORIST SCREENING CENTER (FBI)

Under the auspices of the FBI, the TSC is the information hub where terrorism-related lists are kept and shared. The TSC was created after 9/11 so people known by one arm of the US government to be suspected of terrorism, would not come up blank if law enforcement encountered that individual, as, for example, in a traffic stop. The no-fly and Selectee lists are two examples from the aviation context of lists kept at the TSC.

TSDB   TERRORISM SCREENING DATABASE

The TSDB is the central government terrorist watch list maintained by the Terrorist Screening Center (TSC). There are many special-use subsets of the TSDB, including the no-fly list. The list is believed to have hundreds of thousands of names.

TS/SCI   TOP SECRET/SECRET COMPARTMENTED INFORMATION

The US government uses a structured process for keeping secret information away from enemies, but accessible to those who have a legitimate need for it. There is a hierarchy to information that is not public. Familiar to newsreaders are categories like For Official Use Only and Law Enforcement Sensitive that are types of information that is not Classified, but not public either. Confidential, Secret and Top Secret are familiar designations, in rising sensitivity, for Classified materials. Above Top Secret are code word restricted and compartmented information, sometimes called TS/SCI.

TSM   TRANSPORTATION SECURITY MANAGER

The TSM is TSA's first level of line management at airport screening checkpoints. The TSM will typically be in a suit with identifying credentials hung around the neck. The TSO is the officer who screens your bag. Lead TSOs coordinate groups of TSOs. A Supervisory TSO is still a TSO but handles management and administrative tasks such as scheduling and overall unite effectiveness. The TSM manages groups of checkpoints and reports to the AFSD-Screening.

TSNM   TRANSPORTATION SECTOR NETWORK MANAGEMENT

Created in 2005 to put a structure to TSA's work with network partners like airlines, airports and mass transit. Until then, the relationship was more arms' length as a government regulator would be to a private sector regulated party. Given the dynamic nature of the transportation business and of security in today's world, TSNM undertook to become engaged and interactive with its security partners. TSNM has since been reorganized.

TRXS   SCANNING TECHNOLOGY

TRXs are the familiar older-style x-ray scanner at TSA passenger checkpoints. They give a single view and have limited processing ability. The more sophisticated AT X-rays have replaced most TRXs at US airports.

TSA   TRANSPORTATION SECURITY ADMINISTRATION (DHS)

TSO   TRANSPORTATION SECURITY OFFICER (TSA)

TSA started in 2002 by taking over the contracts for private security at airports while it hired the permanent TSA "screener" workforce. ATSA did not give the "screeners" career paths and the rush to hire a national workforce combined with a need to standardize security screening left the workforce with very little incentive to improve. "Screener" was a job classification for safety workers in the federal system. In 2005 TSA upgraded the job to TSO, giving it a federal job classification in the security area. TSOs soon began exercising career path options to become FAMs, BDOs, and eventually managers such as an FSD. TSOs also participated in a lucrative incentive pay program that rewarded top performers.

VIPR TEAM   VISIBLE INTERMODAL PROACTIVE RESPONSE TEAM (TSA)

While Operation Glidepath unfolded at the end of 2005, TSA began a program to introduce security teams into unexpected places in the transportation system. Glidepath's intelligence suggested that we expect an attack on transportation but TSA didn't know when, why, or how. VIPRs came together as a way to combine different force packages of TSA assets and deploy them unpredictably. A VIPR team consists of local law enforcement, FAMs, K-9 teams, TSA Inspectors, BDOs and other skillsets. They deploy anywhere at anytime in the transportation system, sometimes partnering with the Coast Guard or other DHS resources. There were over 8,000 VIPR deployments in 2011.

USCIS   US CITIZENSHIP AND IMMIGRATION SERVICES (DHS)

Formerly the Immigration & Naturalization Service (INS), USCIS got its current name when it moved from the Justice Department to the new DHS in 2003. The law enforcement duties of INS went to ICE, another DHS component. USCIS manages visa, asylum, and refugee petitions from those seeking to enter the United States, including those wishing citizenship or resident alien status. TSA works with USCIS on identity programs and biometrics.

TIMELINE

9/11 Attacks	Sep 11, 2001
National airspace reopened by DOT Sec. Norman Mineta	Sep 13, 2001
Kip Hawley arrives at DOT for TSA start-up effort	Oct 18, 2001
A.T.S.A., legislation creating TSA signed into law	Nov 19, 2001
John Magaw becomes first TSA Administrator	January 2002
Adm. Jim Loy becomes TSA Administrator	May 2002
TSA meets daunting start-up Congressional deadlines	Nov 18, 2002
Tom Ridge becomes first Secretary of Homeland Security	Jan 24, 2003
Department of Homeland Security opens	Mar 1, 2003
TSA becomes part of DHS	March 25, 2003
Federal Air Marshals leave TSA for ICE	Nov 25, 2003
Adm. David Stone becomes TSA Administrator	July 2004
Female suicide bombers destroy two Russian flights	Aug 18, 2004
Michael Chertoff becomes Secretary of DHS	Mar 1, 2005
Michael Jackson sworn in as Deputy Secretary DHS	Mar 11, 2005
London Underground attack	Jul 7, 2005
London Underground attack #2	Jul 21, 2005
Kip Hawley becomes TSA Administrator	Jul 27, 2005
Hurricane Katrina	Sep 1, 2005
Federal Air Marshals return to TSA from ICE	Oct 1, 2005
NYC Subway Baby Carriage threat	Oct 8, 2005
"I Am TSA" campaign begins	Oct 10, 2005
Operation Glidepath	Nov 17, 2005
First VIPR Team	Nov 27, 2005
Focus on IEDs, Scissors allowed	Dec 12, 2005
"Screener" upgraded to Security Officers	Jan 31, 2006
National Advisory Committee first meeting	Mar 16, 2006
Behavior detection goes nation-wide	Apr 2, 2006
New TSA.gov debuts	Jun 18, 2006
Expanded TSA patrols in all areas of airports	Jul 2, 2006

Evacuation of Lebanon supported	Jul 14, 2006
Liquid Bomb Plot broken up	Aug 10, 2006
Bomb Tech program expanded	Sep 3, 2006
3-1-1 Liquid Restrictions announced	Sep 26, 2006
Performance Pay for TSOs introduced	Oct 11, 2006
TSO injuries cut in half (2004–6)	Oct 17, 2006
JFK plot disrupted	Nov 16, 2006
EU adopts 3-1-1	Nov 19, 2006
Advanced Bomb test kits deployed every checkpoint	Jan 6, 2007
$68 million paid out in Performance Incentive awards	Feb 2, 2007
Body Scanner pilot started	Feb 19, 2007
Idea Factory goes live	Apr 17, 2007
Advanced Liquid Expolsives Detectors deployed	May 12, 2007
TSA assumes document checking	Jun 2, 2007
Glasgow bombing	Jun 29, 2007
Lighter ban ends	Jul 31, 2007
Remote control toy alert made public	Sep 6, 2007
Germany, Denmark plots disrupted	Sep 17, 2007
Barcelona plot disrupted	Jan 19, 2008
TSA Blog goes live	Jan 30, 2008
$77 million paid out in Performance Incentive Awards	Feb 17, 2008
Euro 2008 threat	Jun 17, 2008
900 new AT X-rays bought	July 4, 2008
Checkpoint-friendly laptop bags allowed	Aug 4, 2008
New blue TSO uniform with badge	Sep 11, 2008
American youths fly to Somalia for AQ training	Sep 17, 2008
Islamabad Marriott truck bomb attack	Sep 20, 2008
Engage! training goes national	Sep 28, 2008
Secure Flight final Rule announced	Oct 21, 2008
First American suicide bomber, East Africa	Oct 29, 2008
Bryant Neal Vinas arrested in Pakistan	Nov 14, 2008
Ali Khel explosions	Nov 22, 2008
New York City Holiday threat	Nov 24, 2008
Mumbai attacks	Nov 26, 2008
Belgian plot	Dec 2, 2008
Somali threat to Presidential inauguration	Jan 17, 2009
Gale Rossides becomes Acting TSA Administrator	Jan 20, 2009
Janet Napolitano sworn in as DHS Secretary	Jan 21, 2009
Underwear Bomber attack	Dec 25, 2009
John Pistole becomes TSA Administrator	July 1, 2010

NOTES

CHAPTER NINE: SEARCHING FOR A POCKETKNIFE IN A HAYSTACK

1. "When weapons are allowed back on board an aircraft, the pilots will be able to land the plane safely but the aisles will be running with blood," said Corey Caldwell, a spokeswoman for the Association of Flight Attendants. "US to Relax Airline Scissor Ban," BBC News, December 2, 2005, http://news.bbc.co.uk/2/hi/4487162.stm.

CHAPTER FOURTEEN: THE NETWORK CHASE

1. Lawrence Livermore, Los Alamos, and Sandia National Laboratories

CHAPTER FIFTEEN: SHOE SCANNERS, STOLEN BABIES, AND THE END OF THE BAGGIE

1. Bob Burns, "Why Did the Chicken Cross the Road," The TSA Blog, June 13, 2008, http://blog.tsa.gov/2008/06/why-did-chicken-cross-road.html.

CHAPTER SIXTEEN: THE PREDATOR

1. Kip Hawley, "The Path Forward on Liquids," The TSA Blog, October 24, 2008, http://blog.tsa.gov/2008/10/path-forward-on-liquids.html.

INDEX